Suburban Crossroads

Suburban Crossroads

The Fight for Local
Control of Immigration Policy

Thomas J. Vicino

LEXINGTON BOOKS
Lanham • Boulder • New York • Toronto • Plymouth, UK

Published by Lexington Books
A wholly owned subsidiary of The Rowman & Littlefield Publishing Group, Inc.
4501 Forbes Boulevard, Suite 200, Lanham, Maryland 20706
www.rowman.com

10 Thornbury Road, Plymouth PL6 7PP, United Kingdom

British Library Cataloguing in Publication Information Available

Library of Congress Cataloging-in-Publication Data

Vicino, Thomas J.
 Suburban crossroads : the fight for local control of immigration policy / Thomas J.
Vicino.
    p. cm.
 Includes bibliographical references and index.
 ISBN 978-0-7391-7018-2 (cloth : alk. paper) — ISBN 978-0-7391-7019-9 (ebook)
 1. United States—Emigration and immigration—Government policy. 2. Local
government—United States. I. Title.
 JV6483.V53 2013
 325.73—dc23

                                                              2012039068

∞™ The paper used in this publication meets the minimum requirements of American
National Standard for Information Sciences—Permanence of Paper for Printed Library
Materials, ANSI/NISO Z39.48-1992.

Printed in the United States of America

For My Family

Contents

List of Figures

List of Tables

Preface

President John F. Kennedy's final book was titled *A Nation of Immigrants*. In the book, he honors the history of the millions of immigrants who arrived and called the United States their new home. As the grandson of Irish immigrants who settled in Boston during the 1840s, Kennedy had a history that was a common American story—indeed, a familiar legacy that many Americans share, including mine. My upbringing and perspectives have been shaped by the many stories about my great-grandparents' journeys from Italy to the United States. At the dawn of the twentieth century, they left small villages in central Sicily for the two-week voyage to New York. My great-grandfather, Antonio, settled in Washington, DC, and earned a living as a barber for nearly six decades. His son Dominic would go on to fight in the Second World War and return home to the District of Columbia to find a shortage of housing in the city. As the suburbs opened, he looked to the bedroom community of Beltsville, Maryland, to purchase a small house and settle.

Difficult living conditions and the dreams of economic prosperity prompted many Italians to follow suit. Nearly four million other Italians followed the same journey from the late 1800s until the Great Depression.[1] Immigrants arrived in big cities and made them places to work and play, and above all, call home. Subsequent generations of immigrants moved to outer urban neighborhoods and later, the suburbs. The road to suburbia was paved, and the children and grandchildren of immigrants poured into the suburbs without looking back. Of course, this reflection is just a cursory look at a century filled with dramatic changes. *Suburban Crossroads* is the story of those changes and the dimensions of social and political conflict that followed.

In August 2006, I moved to Texas to begin my academic career at the School of Urban and Public Affairs at the University of Texas at Arlington. The Dallas-Fort Worth Metroplex is like a modern day Ellis Island. Nearly half of the region's six million residents are New Americans that speak over 200 languages.[2] Much of the recent population growth can be attributed to immigrants. The impacts on the region's cities and suburbs cannot be understated, particularly in a suburb named Farmers Branch. A firestorm was about to explode in this bedroom community of Dallas, which had been brewing for a long time. Social and economic tensions grew into hot political conflict as the city grappled with suburban decline and significant demographic change. In a backlash to this swift transformation, the reaction of policymakers and residents was to adopt a law called the Illegal Immigration Relief Ordinance, an attempt to push out new immigrants. As I observed this debate unfold, it seemed eerily familiar to the same stories that I grew up hearing about immigrants a century ago. But, I asked myself, why is this happening now? Why is this debate in the suburbs?

This book is titled *Suburban Crossroads* because it picks up where my previous book ended. In *Transforming Race and Class in Suburbia*, I examined how and why the process of suburban decline evolved and evaluated policy responses.[3] I found that suburban decline was a structural process like urban decline. The book ended with a discussion on "Suburban Crossroads." Older, inner-ring suburbs faced an uncertain future: confront decline with policies to renew communities and embrace new diverse populations, or face the potential of more socioeconomic decline.

My research interests focus on the social, economic, and political impacts of urban decentralization and the resulting policy implications. While the notion of a distinction between the city and the suburb is increasingly blurred, it is still nonetheless important to think about the dimensions of social transition of population, economic transformation, and political change. The concept of spatiality links these ideas together. Place matters. People matter. And, more important, the places where people reside matter. The spatial relationships between cities and suburbs matter for the very reason that they determine the social, economic, and political dimensions of the metropolis. So, it is from this contextual understanding that I approach this book. This is not merely a book about immigration. It is about the consequences of the growing divisions within and among cities and suburbs along these spatial dimensions of socioeconomic and political change. This is the result, in part, of the fragmented nature of local government and the policy responses in cities and suburbs.

This project matured and came to fruition as I moved to Northeastern University. The University's administration, including President Joseph E. Aoun, Provost Stephen Director, Founding Dean of the College of Social Sciences and Humanities Georges Van Den Abbeele, and Interim Dean of the College of Arts and Sciences Bruce Ronkin, provided me with valuable institutional resources that led to the completion of this book. Similarly, I am indebted to the Department of Political Science Chairs John Portz, Suzanne Ogden, and Mitchell Orenstein for their unwavering support of junior faculty. I owe special thanks to Amílcar Barreto, Christopher Bosso, Ronald Hedlund, and Bruce Wallin for their personal mentoring. Amílcar, Chris, Ron, and Bruce have mentored me not only over the final stages of this project but also over the course of my own growth as a scholar, teacher, and citizen of the university. Their own experiences have given me a compass for success.

My other colleagues have provided a collegial environment that makes it a joy to call the department a home. Gerald Bursey, William Crotty, Robert Gilbert, William Kay, David Lazer, William Mayer, Eileen McDonagh, William F. S. Miles, Richard O'Bryant, David Rochefort, David Schmitt, Denis Sullivan, and Michael Tolley took a keen interest in my work and shared sage advice over the course of this project. Governor Michael Dukakis continually pushed me to think deeper (and bigger) about the politics of, well, everything! My fellow junior colleagues, Denise Garcia, Denise Horn, Kirsten Rodine Hardy, and Amy Sliva provided me with much-needed breaks and motivation. Barbara Chin, Janet-Louise Joseph, and Lyle Ring provided valuable administrative support. Finally, it is a rare privilege and honor to work along side faculty whose work has shaped my own perspectives and scholarly insights. I especially benefitted from the previous works of Christopher Bosso, John Portz, and David Rochefort on the many facets of the policymaking process.

Additionally, my colleagues in the School of Public Policy and Urban Affairs and the Kitty and Michael Dukakis Center for Urban and Regional Policy at Northeastern University offered various opportunities for valuable feedback. Barry Bluestone, Laurie Dopkins, Joan Fitzgerald, Stephanie Pollack, John Sarvey, and Russell Williams deserve special thanks.

I am also grateful for two very special colleagues. Liza Weinstein, on the faculty in the Department of Sociology at Northeastern University, is a fellow urbanist that regularly motivates me over tasty lunches and discussions on the city. Bernadette Hanlon, on the faculty in the City and Regional Planning Program in the Knowlton School of Architecture at The Ohio State University, and I have explored our mutual interests in the changing nature of cities and suburbs for over a decade. During these years, her support, critical feedback, and ideas have helped me grow as a scholar and as a person. I am honored to call her a colleague and a friend. Synergies like these make it all worthwhile.

My colleagues in the School of Urban and Public Affairs at the University of Texas at Arlington also played a supportive role during the early stages of the book. I am especially grateful for the support of Enid Arvidson, Edith Barrett, Richard Cole, Maria Martinez-Cosio, Paul Geisel, and Jeff Howard.

I am also appreciative for Robert Whelan's support of my work. He is a consummate scholar in every sense, and our many discussions on the great books that we read helped me immensely. Also, Lisa Benton-Short, Royce Hanson, Donald F. Norris, and John Rennie Short continue to support my growth and development.

Of course, it does not go without saying that I have benefitted and also learned from my students over the years. Their curiosity and inquisitiveness never ceases to amaze me. In particular, students in my courses *Growth and Decline of Cities and Suburbs* and *The 21st Century City* at Northeastern University challenged me and helped to hone my arguments. Michael Hennig, of the University of Texas at Arlington, and Northeastern University graduate students Veronica M. Czastkiewicz, Jarvis Chen, Michael Gaumont, and Jill Kennedy, as well as Claire Shea, provided valuable research assistance during the course of this project.

Earlier versions of various parts of this book were presented and discussed at the annual meetings of the Urban Affairs Association (UAA) and the Association of Collegiate Schools of Planning (ACSP). The UAA served as a valuable outlet for the dissemination of my early ideas for this project. My affiliation with the UAA was particularly beneficial as it provided a welcoming environment and special collegiality for multidisciplinary work in the social sciences. Similarly, the members of the ACSP provided critical feedback. Numerous individuals gave me constructive feedback at various stages in the development of my ideas, including Katrin Anacker, Edith Barrett, Colleen Casey, Maria Martinez-Cosio, George Galster, Juliet Gainsborough, Marie Howland, Dennis Keating, Sugie Lee, Peter Muller, Chris Niedt, Todd Swanstrom, Kyle Walker, Robert Whelan, and Elvin Wyly. Similarly, it was a pleasure to work with the editors and staff of the Rowman & Littlefield Publishing Group, including editors Joseph C. Parry, Melissa Wilks, Elaine McGarraugh and Lenore Lautigar as well as Alison Northridge and Erin Walpole. The reviewers provided valuable critiques and improved the manuscript. The statements in this book are based on my own research and conclusions. I have made every effort to the greatest extent possible to ensure the accuracy of facts, data, and findings. Any and all errors rest with me.

As always, a close group of family and friends provided support at all the right times while I conducted research and prepared this book. Tom Armstrong, my partner and steadfast advocate, deserves a special acknowledgment for always being by my side. Morgan Vicino Ross and Corinne Shea Kieffer were born during this project and give me new inspiration. Plus, an extended family has supported me, including the Armstrongs, the Butlers, the Catalanos, the Halberstats, the Kaunes, the Kieffers, the Nocerinos, the Rosses, the Tippetts, the Strickers, and the Vicinos. Hours of stimulating conversations with Serene Khader, Larry Pacific, and Jay Tifone pushed me to think creatively.

And finally, to the residents and friends of Carpentersville, Illinois; Farmers Branch, Texas; and Hazleton, Pennsylvania: thank you for sharing your stories and for the opportunity to learn.

Thomas J. Vicino
July 2012
Boston

NOTES

1. There is a rich literature on the history of the immigration of Italians to the United States. See generally John W. Briggs, *An Italian Passage: Immigrants to Three American Cities, 1890-1930* (New Haven, CT: Yale University Press, 1978); Donna R. Gabaccia, *From Sicily to Elizabeth Street: Housing and Social Change Among Italian Immigrants, 1880-1930* (Albany: State University of New York Press, 1984); Jerre Mangione, *La Storia: Five Centuries of the Italian American Experience* (New York: Harper Perennial, 1993).

2. See the DFW International Community Alliance, Dallas, Texas. Available at: www.dfwinternational.org, last accessed January 25, 2012.

3. See Thomas J. Vicino, *Transforming Race and Class in Suburbia: Decline in Metropolitan Baltimore* (New York: Palgrave Macmillan, 2008).

We are a nation of immigrants.
President John F. Kennedy
Testimony to the US Congress
June 23, 1963

Chapter One

Introduction

Suburban Crossroads?

Illinois is estimated to be fourth highest in the nation with the number of illegal aliens. Many illegal aliens are hiding in Carpentersville. . . . If we are not able to pass this law, I fear our Village President Bill Sarto and Trustee Linda Ramirez-Sliwinski will move to make Carpentersville a sanctuary city. . . . Illegal aliens will flood our town . . . [If the law passes], the welcome mat for illegal aliens is removed from Carpentersville. Carpentersville will be a better, safer place to live and work when this ordinance passes.[1]

—Trustee Paul Humpfer, Carpentersville, Illinois, October 27, 2006

Farmers Branch is a town of law and order . . . a patriotic, American-loving town. I think it's important to show other cities and towns that you can make a difference, you can stand up for what's right.[2]

—Mayor Tim O'Hare, Farmers Branch, Texas, April 25, 2010

As mayor of Hazleton, I have had enough! Hazleton is a small city, an All-American city. . . . In the City of Hazleton, I proposed, and City Council tentatively passed, the Illegal Immigration Relief Act, a measure that confronts the illegal immigration problem in my town. . . . Let me be clear—this ordinance is intended to make Hazleton one of the most difficult places in the U.S. for illegal immigrants.[3]

—Mayor Louis J. Barletta, Testimony to the United States Senate
Committee on the Judiciary, June 30, 2006

America has changed. Or more to the point, the American suburb has changed. The mythical middle class, lily-white land of free enterprise and backyard barbecues no longer exists. A city has arisen in its place, a city with browner flesh tones, a crumbling infrastructure, and a political system that faces unprecedented challenges. In many ways, in fact, the American suburb has become a twin to its older brother, the American metropolis. This is the story of three suburban communities that have been affected by this change and how the political actors responded—perhaps to the wrong problems, in the wrong ways.

On August 19, 2006, the owner of the Round Lake Beach Restaurant and his family of six, along with an employee and customer, were kidnapped in the afternoon. They were held at gunpoint for ransom by six members of the Latin Kings gang in an older suburban house on the east side of Carpentersville, Illinois. Ultimately, the local police found the victims on the same day and arrested the members of the gang.[4]

On May 25, 2006, 18-month-old Eva Gallegos was at home with her father in Farmers Branch, a suburb located just outside of Dallas, Texas. Two men drove by the house at 11:45 p.m. and fired 13 shots into the house, killing Eva. Farmers Branch Police arrested the two men three weeks later. The men are illegal immigrants and will be deported upon completion of their sentences.[5]

On May 10, 2006, two men shot and killed 29-year-old Derek Kichline on a suburban street in Hazleton, Pennsylvania. He was shot at point-blank range outside of his house for no apparent reason. The defendants, illegal immigrants from the Dominican Republic, had all charges dropped about a year later.[6]

The summer of 2006 was a sad but memorable season for the communities of Carpentersville, Farmers Branch, and Hazleton. Several high-profile crimes committed by illegal immigrants divided residents along dimensions of race, ethnicity, and country of origin. The growth of the immigrant population coupled with these crimes prompted local politicians to seek to adopt immigration policies in their own communities. Over the following years, a fierce political debate erupted over the proposals to enact Illegal Immigration Relief Ordinances (IIROs) to address what was defined as the problem of illegal immigration at the *local* level of government. These crimes served as focal points in the debate because illegal immigrants were charged with them. Sadly, these stories are noteworthy since they honed public attention to the issues of immigration and set off a larger debate over the local control for immigration policy in cities and suburbs.

While these vignettes paint distinct portraits of Carpentersville, Farmers Branch, and Hazleton, it is worth emphasizing that these crimes do not necessarily reflect a larger trend of violence. Carpentersville is a bedroom suburb of Chicago that flourished in the 1950s and 1960s. Farmers Branch is an inner-ring suburb of Dallas that witnessed much growth during the 1970s.

Hazleton is an old mining town located to the northwest of Philadelphia. The link between these communities is that they are small places that until recently had a historically white native population. In the past two decades, they experienced a tremendous growth of their immigrant population. The consequences of that growth were social, economic, and political tensions that grew slowly over time and ultimately provoked a national uproar over illegal immigration. The extent to which these crimes were indicative of a larger problem became a source of debate. Nonetheless, these events ignited the debate over local immigration policy.

Let us frame the larger, national immigration debate to provide context for the local immigration debate. A brief consideration of some background on the evolution of why local governments confront immigration policy is in order. The rapid growth of legal and illegal immigration in the United States shapes these debates. For example, the US General Accounting Office holds that "the population of undocumented foreign-born persons is large and has increased rapidly."[7] The office estimates that the number of "undocumented immigrants" in the US is approximately 12 million. Similarly, the Pew Hispanic Center estimates that the undocumented immigrant population is approximately 11.9 million.[8] In the midst of such a population transformation, public debates have emerged over the best way to confront this new demographic reality.[9]

In 2006, the political debate over comprehensive immigration reform in the United States reached a pinnacle. On May 15, 2006, President George W. Bush addressed the nation about the immigration system. He said:

> Once here, illegal immigrants live in the shadows of our society. Many use forged documents to get jobs, and that makes it difficult for employers to verify that the workers they hire are legal. Illegal immigration puts pressure on public schools and hospitals; it strains state and local budgets, and brings crime to our communities. These are real problems. Yet we must remember that the vast majority of illegal immigrants are decent people who work hard, support their families, practice their faith, and lead responsible lives. They are a part of American life, but they are beyond the reach and protection of American law.[10]

Indeed, these are real problems that impact communities nationwide, particularly the suburbs where a majority of Americans now call home. The president responded to these problems and sought to build support for comprehensive immigration reform. He laid out a five-point agenda, which included: (1) secure the nation's borders; (2) create a temporary worker program; (3) hold employers to account for the workers they hire; (4) face the reality that millions of illegal immigrants are here already; and (5) honor the great American tradition of the melting pot. The president's pledge to

confront and reform the nation's immigration system proved to be too po-
lemical for Congress and their constituents. A lack of consensus divided
politicians and constituents alike, in Washington, DC, and city halls across
the nation.

The US Congress failed to implement federal immigration reform. So the
prospects for reform faded by 2007.[11] In consequence, this spurred numerous local and state governments to confront immigration policy in their own
jurisdictions. In fear of becoming sanctuaries for immigrants, numerous cities
and suburbs (and also states) confronted and implemented their own policies
to limit immigration. The country had not had any federal reform of the immigration system since 1996, when Congress passed the Illegal Immigration
Reform and Immigrant Responsibility Act of 1996. The result was that states
and localities took the law into their own hands.[12]

Suburban Crossroads is about whether communities come to embrace
immigrants or seek to push out immigrants. I am concerned about the implications of the growth of immigrants into suburbs and the local government
responses to demographic and neighborhood transformation. This book
chronicles and critically examines three of the first communities in the nation
to confront the problem of immigration legislatively at the local level of government. Residents of these cities and suburbs feared an influx of immigrants
from their nearby sanctuary cities of Chicago, Dallas, and Philadelphia.
These local jurisdictions developed their own immigration policies, such as
English-only ordinances, local police enforcement of federal immigration
laws, anti-immigrant ordinances related to local employers and landlords, and
elimination of social services like education and public health. Specifically,
I analyze the larger social and economic conditions that shape the definition
of public problems in three communities. This book seeks to explain the political debates that arise from policy proposals to limit illegal immigration,
and then analyzes how and why local governments attempt to take control of
immigration policy in their jurisdictions. In the following sections, I lay out
the primary questions, central theories, and approaches to the research in this
book.

QUESTIONS, THEORIES, AND APPROACHES

There is a vast and multidisciplinary literature in the social sciences on the
topic of immigration. Moreover, there has been a long scholarly interest in the
spatial nature of immigration. The population shift from urban to suburban
areas is less explored in terms of its impacts on immigration, and more specifically, how questions of immigration policy are defined in local communities.

In fact, few works have examined the local policy responses to immigration in the context of the growth, change, and decline of neighborhoods in these communities. While there is a nascent, emerging literature on the study of immigration politics and local policy responses, previous works have not yet considered the spatial divisions within cities and suburbs and the process of neighborhood change in relationship to local immigration policy.[13] However, while there is little work on local immigration policy responses, there is indeed a larger national and international scale literature.[14]

Overall, the book has three primary goals: (1) to demonstrate how and why changing demographic patterns impact communities, with specific attention paid to issues related to race, ethnicity, and immigrant status; (2) to assess how and why the role of suburban decline impacts the social structure, the economic status, and the political power of communities; and (3) to illustrate how and why the impacts of public policy and planning decisions affect different populations with regard to local control of immigration policy. Throughout the book, I draw on and take advantage of numerous bodies of literature to delve into the study of local immigration policy and neighborhood change. To frame my inquiry, I rely on three primary bodies of theory: (1) suburban growth, change, and decline; (2) immigrant assimilation and incorporation; and (3) political definitions of public problems.

Suburban Growth, Change, and Decline

I draw on the literature on suburban growth, change, and decline to frame the understanding of how communities grow, evolve, and change. Specifically, three areas of community change stand out: the growth of suburbs; the socioeconomic change of suburban neighborhoods; and the decline of suburbs. I review each of these themes in turn.

First, the growth of suburbs in the US is well documented. This is a familiar story in the fabric of postwar US history.[15] The rich body of literature on why suburbs grew (and continue to grow) can generally be synthesized into four key areas: public policy, economic restructuring, transportation development, and social and political culture. In Kenneth Jackson's treatise on suburbia, *Crabgrass Frontier*, he chronicles how the role of federal public policies permitted the large-scale growth of suburbs. Jackson shows that the political economy of development benefited from public investments in areas like urban renewal, transportation, and housing, which aided the phenomenal growth of the suburbs.[16] In contrast, Robert Fishman's *Bourgeois Utopias* argues from an economic structural viewpoint that the suburbs are the result of the growth of a middle class, which caused the working class population to shrink. He holds that the loss of manufacturing jobs, transportation advances, and technology improvements allowed for the growth of a suburban middle class.[17] Yet another viewpoint on suburbanization is the work of Sam Bass Warner. In *Streetcar Suburbs*, he demonstrates that suburban growth can be attributed to a complex network of transportation infrastructure of street-cars.[18] One last perspective is Dolores Hayden's argument about the social and political culture of suburban development. She shows that suburbanites often seek green space and refuge in suburbs, while suburban developers aim to create economies of scale for dense development and public subsidies.[19] These key works capture the various perspectives of suburban growth, and they provide insight about how the communities of Carpentersville, Farmers Branch, and Hazleton grew.

Regarding these communities, an understanding of the patterns of suburban growth helps to trace the historical roots. These roots are first about growth. The communities share some similarities and differences in this history. Principally, they share histories of location and transportation. Each of the communities is located near an important river or waterway, and railways service these communities. These factors facilitate growth. They also share a similar economic and population history. For example, Carpentersville's early economy was based on iron foundries, blacksmithing, and the manufacturing of agricultural machinery. Farmers Branch's early economy was based on blacksmithing, grist milling, and farming. Hazleton has a long economic history of coal mining and manufacturing. These communities were formerly places of settlement for immigrants. German, Irish, and Polish immigrants arrived in Carpentersville in the 1870s; European immigrants arrived in Farmers Branch in the 1850s; and Germans arrived in Hazleton in the 1880s. However, these communities differ in their growth periods. Hazleton was the earliest community to grow, and its population peaked in the 1940s. Carpentersville's population peaked in the 1970s, and Farmers Branch's population peaked in the 1990s. Each place experienced a resurgence of population during the 2000s as new immigrants settled in these communities again.

Second, studies on neighborhood change in cities and suburbs offer keen insight that informs us about the distinguishing characteristics of changing and declining neighborhoods in metropolitan areas.[20] Suburbanization can be theorized as a process of invasion and succession. In simple terms, this occurs when the urban population decentralizes from the urban core. Neighborhoods change when high socioeconomic status residents leave one neighborhood for an adjacent neighborhood as lower socioeconomic status residents enter. Then, higher socioeconomic status residents move out to neighborhoods beyond the city, and it results in a self-reinforcing cycle of change.[21] In consequence, the socioeconomic characteristics of neighborhoods change, and then finally, they decline. Scholars have identified these characteristics to include: a decrease in real household income, a decrease in the number of households, the obsolescence of housing stock, and the physical deterioration of neighborhoods.[22]

Third, a growing body of work has identified and linked the process of suburban decline to neighborhood change. Lucy and Phillips, among the first scholars to identify and measure patterns of suburban decline, argue that the next urban crisis will occur in these places—and more specifically, in postwar bedroom suburbs.[23] In her recent book *Once the American Dream*, Hanlon identifies over 1,600 suburbs as places in crisis.[24] Similarly, Short's book *Liquid City* shows that nearly one-fifth of residents of the megalopolis region live in "suburban places of poverty."[25] Building on that work, Hanlon and Vicino analyze patterns of socioeconomic change in the suburbs of metropolitan Baltimore and find that numerous inner-ring suburbs declined since 1980.[26] In particular, they theorize that the decline is related to labor market restructuring, the nature of housing market, and income and racial segregation. They develop a classification of suburbs that move from the "growth stage," to "stability stage," to the "declining state," and finally, to the "crisis stage." Last, in his book *Halfway to Everywhere*, Hudnut offers some hope for declining suburbs as they are well positioned in the metropolis to offer many amenities and resources that residents may look for in the future.[27]

So, what do these works on growth, change, and decline mean for places like Carpentersville, Farmers Branch, and Hazleton? In the context of these communities, we can apply this theoretical understanding of neighborhood change to the history of the growth and decline of these places. This body of work offers an important framework for linking the concepts of demographic transformation and neighborhood change to new policy issues of immigration.

The Assimilation and Incorporation of Immigrants

Immigration to the United States has profoundly reshaped the nation's racial and ethnic composition repeatedly. Consider the Second Wave of immigration. Approximately 28 million immigrants arrived to the United States between 1880 and 1930. These immigrants arrived from countries primarily in Eastern, Central, and Western Europe. Similarly, since 1965, in a subsequent "Fourth Wave" of immigration, some 40 million immigrants settled in the United States. In contrast, these immigrants arrived from Latin America and Asia. This recent and dramatic demographic change has again transformed the social landscape of the nation.[28]

To provide some context on the impacts of these waves of immigration, it is important to consider some theories about how immigrants become part of communities and society. Traditionally, one of the central questions that scholars of immigration confront is: do immigrants assimilate into American society and incorporate their children into a broader society? The assimilation of immigrants into society is a long and multifaceted process that involves the immigrant integrating one's life—socially, economically, politically, and culturally—into a new country.[29] Various theoretical perspectives have guided our understanding about how immigrants become a part of society. Let us consider them.

Four models provide particular insight into the process of becoming part of a society: the assimilation or acculturation model, the racial and ethnic disadvantage model, the segmented assimilation model, and the racialization model. Alba and Nee hold that assimilation "is the process that occurs spontaneously and often unintended in the course of interaction between majority and minority groups."[30] After settling with their primary group ties, immigrants attain values and norms of the new country through the increase of socioeconomic status, intermarriage and ethnic identification, language attainment, and a decrease of discrimination. The racial and ethnic disadvantage model contends that assimilation does not usually occur due to long-standing discriminatory beliefs, which then decreases access to wealth and power.[31] The segmented assimilation model asserts that some individuals have an easier experience assimilating into the country than others as a result of uneven opportunities among immigrants.[32] Last, the racialization model argues that immigrants are "racialized" in the American context just as other minority groups, and as a result, experience similar forms of social and economic discrimination.[33]

The consideration of immigrant assimilation and incorporation reminds us about what is at stake in the fight for local control of immigration policy. How does the recent wave of immigration differ from previous waves? Does the degree of the assimilation and incorporation of immigrants into communities necessarily determine the context of problem definition, especially in relation to the conflict for local control of immigration policy? In other words, do these differences, if any, shape the political debate and agenda? The answers can be found in how immigrants become part of a neighborhood and shape the characteristics of a city or suburb.

Political Definitions of Public Problems

Finally, I draw on the literature on the politics of problem definition to apply to the context of the debate on local immigration policy. The social and political construction of what is and what is not a public problem for society is often a subjective construct. These definitions are the result of a political process that is shaped by actors inside and outside of government. The ways in which problems are defined influence and ultimately determine the approaches to and solutions for a political conflict. Interpretations of a problem vary immensely, and there are generally disagreements on the causation, nature, population, and potential solutions to a public problem. The attributes of the various problem definitions of local immigration issues are reviewed using this framework.

The work of Rochefort and Cobb, Stone, and Kingdon provides a useful framework for an analysis of how public problems are defined. Attributes of a problem such as the causation, nature, affected population, potential solutions, and symbolic nature determine the definitions. The source of the problem, or its causes, is an integral part of the definitions. The following question links the immigrant population to the problem's cause: Are all immigrants causing the decline of neighborhoods? The nature of the problem also shapes the definitions. Characteristics of the problem's nature include severity, incidence, proximity, and crisis. The following questions suggest the nature of the problems: Are there too many immigrants? Are all immigrants illegal? Is there too much? Is violence a problem? Are too many neighborhoods falling apart? Are jobs disappearing? Are language barriers too frequent? The target population of the problem is also an attribute. There are questions about whom to blame for the problem, including immigrants, illegal immigrants, and racial and ethnic minorities. The potential solutions to the problems shape how the problem is defined. For example, is the solution an ordinance to limit illegal immigration? The role of causal stories and symbolic politics further shapes the definitions, and in the end, influences public opinion about the problem.[34]

In sum, these bodies of literature—the growth, change, and decline of suburbs; the assimilation and incorporation of immigrants; and the political definitions of public problems— allow us to frame the conceptual thinking about how and why immigrants settle and transform neighborhoods. Ultimately, they show how and why native residents and immigrants alike participate and shape the debate for local control of immigration policy in their communities.

CONTRIBUTIONS

Suburban Crossroads is a work of several disciplinary perspectives, including political science, sociology, and geography. Varsanyi aptly notes that the study of local immigration policy is "unique and challenging . . . and blur[s] the conventional boundary between, for instance, political scientists' focus on a politics of control—a focus on immi*gration*, which is generally approached from the perspective of nation-state and federal politics—and sociologists' or anthropologists' focus on (a politics of) integration, with a focus on immi-*grants*, more often from the local or urban perspective."[35] Given the breadth of these disciplines, I want to clearly identify the interdisciplinary framework, questions, theories, and approaches of this book. Then, my goal is to situate what this book is about and what it is not. This will help to contextualize my own background and perspectives as well as guide the reader through the following chapters.

This book is grounded in the interdisciplinary field of urban studies. The common thread that links these disciplinary perspectives together is "the urban." The field spans across these disciplines. It emerged in the 1960s as social and economic problems reached a pinnacle in cities.[36] In subsequent decades, scholars continued to ask questions about the nature and structure of cities—and increasingly metropolitan regions—in the social, economic, political, and spatial realms. While approaches vary, urbanists of these disciplines are generally concerned with the processes, products, and problems of human settlements.[37] What links these perspectives together is a keen focus and sharp lens on "the spatial"—the geographies of the city and the suburbs, and the related socioeconomic dimensions that form the concept of place.[38]

I offer three key findings in this book. Situated in the field of urban studies, it contributes to the burgeoning subfield of suburban studies.[39] How and why do suburbanites define the need for IIROs in their communities? What explains the backlash against the local public policies that deal with immigration? The answers to such questions lend to our understanding about the source of political conflict in suburbs and the driving factors of demographic change in suburbs. So, this study moves forward the discussion on local control of immigration policy by adding a spatial lens; that is—a focus on the politics of the suburbs. These jurisdictions responded to the changing and declining nature of the demographic, social and economic events around their suburban neighborhoods. A "Latino threat" prompted many residents of these communities to take the law into their own hands to push out the population that threatened their way of life.[40] The IIRO was the answer.

First, I demonstrate that metropolitan areas experienced a marked increase in social diversity in recent decades. What is most noteworthy is the rise of a new immigrant population in the suburbs. This demographic transformation is the heart of the political conflict in metropolitan communities, and in particular, the places under study in this book.

Second, I argue that suburban policies against illegal immigrants, like IIROs, fueled a backlash against the larger process of suburban decline. In all three cases, native residents grew increasingly frustrated with the decline of the socioeconomic status of other residents, the arrival of immigrants, the flight of employment opportunities, and the decay of public and private infrastructure. This broadens our understanding about the consequences of the decline of suburban communities. I show that older suburban areas are often faced with the socioeconomic decline of their population, the inability to provide decent social services, and the physical decay of public infrastructure. A consequence of the arrival of immigrants to declining communities is a heighted tension between native residents and immigrants. The political fight emerges as groups seek to adopt policies against a new population. The policy rationale is to slow—or stop—the process of neighborhood change and preserve the many aspects of neighborhood stability.

Third, the case studies add to our understanding about the process of public policymaking in the domain of immigration. I examine the process of how public policies are created and what factors lead to adoption, implementation, or failure. I demonstrate that the politics of how the "immigration problem" is defined serves as a factor in determining local policy responses.[41] This furthers our understanding about the role that local governance plays in the policy process in a new domain at the local level—immigration. Finally, this book raises important questions related to planning, administration, and policy for local governments.

The approach in this book draws on several rich traditions in urban studies. I employ a mixed-methodological approach that considers a multiplicity of data from both qualitative and quantitative sources. Building upon my prior work on cities and suburbs, I analyze the demographic composition, the socioeconomic structure, and the politics of immigration policies to study three communities. I collect and analyze US Census data for a host of socioeconomic characteristics for each place. Then, I present a history of each city and consider patterns of development by drawing on secondary literature, governmental archives, and historical records. Next, I analyze the political debate of the immigration ordinances in two ways. I synthesize and interpret the findings from interviews of key actors in the political debate in each locality. Then, I develop an understanding of the politics through a review of public records in each locality and numerous site visits to city council meetings. This triangulated approach allows me to develop key themes about the debates. This serves as a mechanism to compare and contrast the policy outcomes with a matrix of themes. I interpret these findings with supplements such as maps, figures, tables, and various photos. The appendices provide an overview of the specific methodologies as well as a guide to the local legislation in Carpentersville, Farmers Branch, and Hazleton.

This book is not about the politics of national immigration policy, nor is it an in-depth exploration about the legality or constitutionality of local, state, or federal policy responses to immigration.[42] Additionally, the book does not provide a comprehensive survey of the localities that have responded to immigration issues in their own communities. This book analyzes the political conflict over the local control of immigration policy in three declining places. I investigate how and why the people of three communities responded to a quick demographic transformation of residents in their communities—and set a precedent for cities and suburbs nationally. The book analyzes the demographic changes, patterns of growth and decline, and then explores the evolution of the local policies to confront issues of illegal immigration.

In closing, I want to provide some thoughts about the use of terminology in the book, specifically around definitions of cities, races, and immigrants. Regarding cities, the terms *suburbs* and *cities* are often used interchangeably in this book. The places in this analysis are incorporated cities with home rule charters granted from the state, thus making them cities *per se*. However, the historical legacies of these places can be characterized as suburban in nature, both in form and function.[43] Regarding races, I use the US Census Bureau's definitions to identify the race and ethnicity of individuals. For example, white non-Hispanic identifies both the race and ethnicity of an individual.[44] While the terminology to identify the foreign-born population in the US is quite varied, the definitions provide a useful baseline for comparative purposes. Regarding immigrants, I use the terms *illegal immigrant, unofficial immigrant,* or *unauthorized immigrant* throughout the book. These terms shape the debate for local policy issues on immigration. More important, such terms also influence who is perceived as an immigrant, legal or illegal. Such perceptions fuel the political definition of these problem definitions over immigration policy more generally. I generally avoid the use of the term *undocumented immigrant* since the term is often politicized for setting a political agenda. Plus, most unauthorized immigrants do indeed have some sort of documentation.[45]

PLAN OF THE BOOK

In the remaining chapters of this book, I first explore the marked increase in the social diversity of cities and suburbs in metropolitan America, and then I analyze the historical, social, economic, and political dimensions of the local policy responses to immigration in three case studies. Next, I consider the implications for planning, administration, and policy of such local responses, and I conclude by reflecting on the future prospects and challenges for these cases and others.

Chapter 2 explores the rise of the multiethnic metropolis and the noteworthy socio-spatial diversity of people in metropolitan America. Previous work has focused on the identification of immigrant gateway cities, and subsequent work has begun to examine the growth of suburban gateways. According to Anrig and Wang, nearly three-quarters of immigrants prior to 1995 settled in only six states: California, Texas, Illinois, Florida, New York, and New Jersey.[46] But, during the 2000s, various scholars observed that immigrants increasingly bypassed traditional gateway states—instead settling in other states and in suburbs.[47] The transformation of these spatial patterns has important implications for the debate over local immigration policy.

As residents of central cities moved to the suburbs, so did the policy debate over immigration. I identify the historic and contemporary trends in the growth of immigration in metropolitan areas. In particular, two trends stand out. First, the growth of the US immigrant population continues to increase. Second, the spatial decentralization of immigrants from the urban core to the suburban fringe is remarkable. I frame these demographic transformations by linking them to a larger process of public policy change. A conceptual model of this process is presented and guides our understanding about the evolution of immigration in metropolitan America. These demographic changes in metropolitan areas ultimately become a necessary factor for public debate over immigration policy.

Chapter 3 examines the history and demographics of the three suburban communities. Chapter 4 analyzes the three case studies and compares the evolution of the issue, the policy responses, and the policies designed to confront illegal immigration. Chapter 5 focuses on the politics of relief and the various ways that politicians, community leaders, advocates, and residents framed and responded to these issues.

Chapter 6 evaluates the policy and planning implications of this work. I compare and interpret the findings across the three case studies to develop a larger understanding in theoretical terms and practical terms. In theoretical terms, I argue that the line between city and suburb is increasingly blurred. The historic geographic boundaries of immigrant gateways no longer determine settlement patterns. In today's metropolis, immigrants and native residents, move freely between city and suburb. There has been a transfer of immigration policy from the national scale to the local scale. Therefore, localities are free to welcome and embrace the movement of immigrants to their communities. These are sanctuaries of diversity. Alternatively, localities are free to avoid and shun the arrival of immigrants to their communities. This shows that the localization of this policy movement made it possible for communities to chart their own path—even if it meant challenging the law.

In practical terms, it is necessary to plan and think about local policies differently in communities. Specifically, the demographics, economics, and policies of localities create imperatives that mandate this new way of planning and thinking. The demographic imperative suggests that diversity and immigration will continue. The economic imperative suggests that growth and decline are realities, and this process is spatially uneven. The policy imperative suggests that immigrant residents and native residents alike need a political voice and representation. Finally, options for a national and local policy agenda that addresses concerns about both immigration and neighborhood stability are presented.

Chapter 7 considers the following question: Where does the debate go from here? The legal debate is at a crossroads. Farmers Branch, Texas, and Hazleton, Pennsylvania, continue to fight the legal challenges. These cities have each spent over $3 million in pursuit of these legal challenges. I consider questions such as: How should localities use their limited resources? Is the legal challenge worth it? How are democratic values defined in local communities?

Supporters and protesters hold opposing viewpoints. I consider questions about the constitutionality of local policies. Do such local laws preempt federal immigration laws? What role, if any, does the Fourteenth Amendment of the US Constitution play in the debate? Will the US Supreme Court weigh in on this issue? Last, I reflect on the case *Lozano v. Hazleton*. Chief Judge Theodore McKee on the US Court of Appeals for the Third Circuit ruled that such local ordinances are "preempted by federal immigration law and unconstitutional . . . We are required to intervene when states and localities directly undermine the federal objectives embodied in statutes enacted by Congress."[48] Hazleton Mayor Lou Barletta countered, "The city of Hazleton will continue to pursue this case, not only because we are right, but also because other communities are counting on us."[49] Either way, this legal battle—and the fight for local control—continues in these communities and in many others. This debate is increasingly a reality that more Americans will confront.

Whatever the ultimate fate of Carpentersville, Farmers Branch, and Hazleton, along with hundreds of other communities, the debate over the local control of immigration policy in cities and suburbs is far from over. This book tells us about some of the first examples of how communities—vis-à-vis their local governments—dealt with the complexities of population change, socioeconomic change, and larger questions of immigration policy.

NOTES

1. Kristi Jac, "10 Questions for Paul Humpfer," *The Free Republic*, October 27, 2007.

2. Anna M. Tinsley, "Farmers Branch Keeps Up Illegal-Immigration Fight," *Fort Worth Star Telegram*, April 25, 2010.

3. Hearing on Illegal Immigration, Before the United States Senate Committee on the Judiciary, 109th Cong. (2006) (statement of Lou Barletta, Mayor of the City of Hazleton, Pennsylvania), June 30, 2006.

4. George Houde, "$1 Million Bail is Set For Kidnap Suspects," *The Chicago Tribune*, August 23, 2006.

5. Holly Yan, "2 Arrested in Toddler's Drive-By Shooting Death," *The Dallas Morning News*, June 15, 2006.

6. Milan Simonich, "Hazleton Ordinance Aimed at Illegal Immigrants Puts Mayor At Center Stage," *Pittsburgh Post-Gazette*, August 27, 2006.

7. United States General Accounting Office, "Estimating the Undocumented Population a 'Grouped Answers' Approach to Surveying Foreign-Born Respondents," GAO-06-775, September (2006): 17.

8. Jeffrey S. Passel and D'Vera Cohn, "Trends in Unauthorized Immigration: Undocumented Inflow Now Trails Legal Inflow," (October 2008). Washington, DC: Pew Hispanic Center.

9. Legal status refers to whether an alien has legal documents or does not have legal documents. Sec. 101. [8 U.S.C. 1101] (a) As used in this Act (3) states that "The term 'alien' means any person not a citizen or national of the United States." According to the US Internal Revenue Service, "an 'Illegal Alien,' also known as an 'Undocumented Alien,' is an alien who has entered the United States illegally and is deportable if apprehended, or an alien who entered the United States legally but who has fallen 'out of status' and is deportable." US Internal Revenue Service, "Immigration Terms and Definitions Involving Aliens," Washington, DC. See also Michel Martin, "Which Is Acceptable: 'Undocumented' vs. 'Illegal' Immigrant?" *National Public Radio*, January 7, 2010.

10. The White House Office of the Press Secretary, "President Bush Addresses the Nation on Immigration Reform," May 15, 2006.

11. Several congressional legislative attempts failed during George W. Bush's presidency, including: *Secure America and Orderly Immigration Act* of 2005 (S. 1033); *Comprehensive Enforcement and Immigration Reform Act* of 2005 (S. 1438); *Comprehensive Immigration Reform Act* of 2006 (S. 2611); and *Secure Borders, Economic Opportunity and Immigration Reform Act* of 2007 (S. 1348).

12. Increasingly, similar state laws have also passed. For example, Arizona S.B. 1070 was signed into law on April 23, 2010, by Governor Jan Brewer. Known as the *Support Our Law Enforcement and Safe Neighborhoods Act*, the law aims to identify, prosecute, and deport undocumented immigrants in Arizona. See Randal C. Archibold, "Arizona Enacts Stringent Law on Immigration," *The New York Times*, April 23, 2010.

13. Monica Varsanyi, ed., *Taking Local Control: Immigration Policy Activism in U.S. Cities and States* (Stanford, CA: Stanford University Press, 2010).

14. Elżbieta M. Goździak and Micah N. Bump, *New Immigrants, Changing Communities: Best Practices for a Better America* (Lanham, MD: Lexington Books, 2009). See also Wayne Cornelius, Takeyuki Tsuda, Philip Martin, and James Hollifield, eds. *Controlling Immigration: A Global Perspective 2nd ed.* (Stanford, CA: Stanford University Press, 2004).

15. There is a vast literature on the growth and development of the suburbs. For a contemporary synthesis, see Dolores Hayden, *Building Suburbia: Green Fields and Urban Growth, 1820-2000* (New York: Vintage, 2004); Jon C. Teaford, *The Metropolitan Revolution: The Rise of Post-Urban America* (New York: Columbia University Press, 2006).

16. Kenneth T. Jackson, *Crabgrass Frontier: The Suburbanization of the United States* (New York: Oxford University Press, 1987): 190-218.

17. Robert A. Fishman, *Bourgeois Utopias: The Rise and Fall of Suburbia* (New York: Basic Books, 1987): 73-180.

18. Sam Bass Warner, *Streetcar Suburbs: The Process of Growth in Boston, 1870-1900, 2nd ed.* (Cambridge, MA: Harvard University Press, 1978): 153-168.

19. Hayden, *Building Suburbia*, 3-20.

20. Geographers and sociologists based early studies of neighborhood change on the development of spatial models: scholars of the Chicago School developed concentric rings of social and economic development in the 1920s; Homer Hoyt developed the concept of a sector model; and Harris and Ullman developed the idea about a regional multiple nuclei model. Subsequently, these models of development influenced numerous generations of scholars on how neighborhoods in cities and suburbs change over time based on their socioeconomic characteristics. See Ernest Watson Burgess, "The Growth of the City: An Introduction to a Research Project," in *The City*, edited by Robert E. Park, Ernest Watson Burgess, and Roderick Duncan McKenzie (Chicago: University of Chicago Press, 1925): 47-62; Homer Hoyt, "The Structure and Growth of Residential Neighborhoods in American Cities" (Washington, DC: Federal Housing Administration, 1939); Chauncy Harris and Edward Ullman, "The Nature of Cities," *Annals of the American Academy of Political and Social Science* 242, no.1 (1945): 7-17.

21. Mark Abrahamson, *Urban Enclaves: Identity and Place in America* (New York: St. Martin's Press, 1996): 1-32.

22. William G. Grigsby et al., *The Dynamics of Neighborhood Change and Decline* (London: Pergamon, 1987): 1-72.

23. William H. Lucy and David L. Phillips, *Confronting Suburban Decline: Strategic Planning for Metropolitan Renewal* (Washington, DC: Island Press, 2000): 1-20.

24. Bernadette Hanlon, *Once the American Dream: Inner-Ring Suburbs of the Metropolitan United States* (Philadelphia: Temple University Press, 2009): 110-131.

25. John Rennie Short, *Liquid City: Megalopolis and the Contemporary Northeast* (Washington, DC: Resources for the Future Press, 2007): 113-130.

26. Bernadette Hanlon and Thomas J. Vicino, "The Fate of Inner Suburbs: Evidence from Metropolitan Baltimore," *Urban Geography* 28, no. 3 (2007): 254-263.

27. William H. Hudnut, *Halfway to Everywhere: A Portrait of America's First-Tier Suburbs* (Washington, DC: Urban Land Institute, 2004): 400-430.

28. Reed Ueda, *Postwar Immigrant America: A Social History* (New York: St. Martin's Press, 1994).

29. The theory and concept of assimilation is a source of debate. See William A. V. Clark, *Immigrants and the American Dream: Remaking the Middle Class* (New York: The Guilford Press, 2003): 1-28.

30. Richard Alba and Victor Nee, "Rethinking Assimilation Theory for a New Era of Immigration," *International Migration Review* 31, no. 4 (1997): 827.

31. Frank D. Bean and Gillian Stevens, *America's Newcomers and the Dynamics of Diversity* (New York: Russell Sage, 2003): 97-99.

32. Alejandro Portes and Ruben G. Rumbaut, *Legacies: The Story of the Immigrant Second Generation* (New York: Russell Sage, 2001): 44-69.

33. Paul A. Silverstein, "Immigrant Racialization and the New Savage Slot: Race, Migration, and Immigration in the New Europe," *Annual Review of Anthropology* 34 (2005): 363-384.

34. David A. Rochefort and Roger W. Cobb, eds., *The Politics of Problem Definition: Shaping the Policy Agenda* (Lawrence: University Press of Kansas, 1994), 1-30; Deborah Stone, *Policy Paradox: The Art of Political Decision Making* (New York: W.W. Norton, 2001): 1-15.

35. Monica W. Varsanyi, "Immigration Policy Activism in U.S. States and Cities: Interdisciplinary Perspectives," *Taking Local Control: Immigration Policy Activism in U.S. Cities and States*, ed. Monica W. Varsanyi (Stanford, CA: Stanford University Press, 2010): 5.

36. Philip Morris Hauser and Leo Francis Schnore, eds., *The Study of Urbanization* (New York: John Wiley and Sons, Inc., 1965), 1-30; Jane Jacobs, *The Death and Life of Great American Cities* (New York: Random House, 1961), 5-37.

37. See the following definition: "Our characterization of the context is briefly given in terms of the complex realities—the broad domain of intersecting activities, processes, products, and problems—associated with the evolution of human settlement systems. In turn, this context has given rise to an internally organized structure of subfields that now forms the content and recognizable corpus of knowledge in the field," William M. Bowen, Ronnie A. Dunn, and David O. Kasdan, "What is Urban Studies? Context, Internal Structure, and Content," *Journal of Urban Affairs* 32, no. 2 (2010): 200; competing definitions include: Dennis Judd, "Everything Is Always Going to Hell: Urban Scholars as End-Times Prophets," *Urban Affairs Review* 41, no. 2 (2005): 119-131; Joshua Sapotichne, Bryan D. Jones, and Michelle Wolfe, "Is Urban Politics a Black Hole? Analyzing the Boundary Between Political Science and Urban Politics," *Urban Affairs Review* 43, no. 1 (2007): 76-106.

38. Peter Dreier, John Mollenkopf, and Todd Swanstrom, *Place Matters: Metropolitics for the Twenty-first Century*, 2nd ed. rev. (Lawrence: University Press of Kansas, 2004).

39. This is situated in an emerging subfield of suburban studies. See Kevin M. Kruse and Thomas J. Sugrue, eds., *The New Suburban History* (Chicago: University of Chicago Press, 2006).

40. Leo R. Chavez, *The Latino Threat: Constructing Immigrants, Citizens, and the Nation* (Stanford, CA: Stanford University Press, 2008): 1-20.

41. Rochefort and Cobb, *The Politics of Problem Definition*, 1-30.

42. There is a rich body of literature on the many facets of immigration. See generally, Aristide D. Zolberg, *A Nation by Design: Immigration Policy in the Fashioning of America* (Cambridge, MA: Harvard University Press, 2006); Alejandro Ports and Rubén G. Rumbaut, *Immigrant America: A Portrait, 3rd ed.* (Berkeley: University of California Press, 2006); Daniel J. Tichenor, *Dividing Lines: The Politics of*

Immigration Control in America (Princeton, NJ: Princeton University Press, 2002); Gary Gerstle and John Mollenkopf, eds., *E Pluribus Unum? Contemporary and Historical Perspectives on Immigrant Political Incorporation* (New York: Russell Sage Foundation, 2001).

43. Bernadette Hanlon, John Rennie Short, and Thomas J. Vicino, *Cities and Suburbs: New Metropolitan Realities in the US* (New York: Routledge, 2010): 3-111.

44. It is noteworthy to underscore that definitions are based on the self-identification of respondents to the US Census questionnaire. A respondent can self-identify as both a race and ethnicity. Hispanic or Latino may be of any race. See Elizabeth M. Grieco and Rachel C. Cassidy, "Overview of Race and Hispanic Origin: Census 2000 Brief," C2KBR/01-1 (Washington, DC: Census Bureau, 2001): 1-11.

45. Lina Newton, *Illegal, Alien, or Immigrant: The Politics of Immigration Reform* (New York: NYU Press, 2008): ix.

46. Greg Anrig, Jr. and Tova Andrea Wang, eds., *Immigration's New Frontiers: Experiences from the Emerging Gateway States* (New York: Century Foundation Press, 2007): 1-6.

47. Marie Price and Lisa Benton-Short, eds., *Migrants to the Metropolis: The Rise of Immigrant Gateway Cities* (Syracuse, NY: Syracuse University Press, 2008): 1-22; Audrey Singer et al., eds., *Twenty-First Century Gateways: Immigrant Incorporation in Suburban America* (Washington, DC: Brookings Institution Press, 2008): 3-38; Kristi Anderson, *New Immigrant Communities: Finding a Place in Local Politics* (Boulder, CO: Lynne Rienner, 2010): 5-20.

48. Michael W. Savage, "Immigration Law Unconstitutional, Court Rules," *The Washington Post*, September 10, 2010.

49. Terrie Morgan-Besecker, "Barletta: Hazleton Will Appeal Immigration Ordinance Ruling," *The Times Leader*, September 10, 2010.

Chapter Two

The Multiethnic Metropolis
and Its Discontents

Manicured lawns, minivans, and modest-homes-turned-McMansions: They're the sorts of symbols that might come to mind when we think modern suburbia. But peer inside the windows at the people living there and the American suburbs are increasingly complex. We've come a long way since "Leave It to Beaver." The suburbs—or rather suburbanites—represent an evolving America. And what exists today would leave June Cleaver's perfectly coifed head, and even her strand of pearls, spinning.[1]

—*Jessica Ravitz, CNN*

At the beginning of the twentieth century, the United States was a nation of big cities. But at the dawn of the twenty-first century, the United States had morphed into a nation of many suburbs. In 1900, of the nation's metropolitan population, 78 percent lived in central cities, and 22 percent lived in suburbs. Six decades later, the population distribution in metropolitan America had converged so that half of residents lived in suburbs and the other half in central cities. By 2000, the majority of residents then lived in suburbs; in fact, two-thirds called the suburbs home. If big cities were the engine of the economy and centers of population activity during the 1900s, then suburbia drove the economy and was a magnet for population activity as the 2000s began. This spatial shift had dramatic implications—nationally and locally.

This transformation did not occur overnight. The decentralization of people and jobs was a slow shift from the urban core to the metropolitan fringe. The suburbs opened up to the masses in the 1950s, as portrayed by the popular television show *Leave It to Beaver*. But as Jessica Ravitz notes, the notion of the prototypical suburbanite as a white, middle-class resident had long faded.[2] The article is noteworthy because it calls attention to the changing state of suburbia, emphasizing five observations.[3] Urban flight is no longer white flight. White, black, and Latino residents continue to flee big cities for suburbs. Suburbs are as diverse as their central city counterparts, as a multiplicity of racial, ethnic, and immigrant groups settle. Pockets of poverty spread out from the city to the suburb. The aging of the baby boom population is suburban in nature.[4] But, it is important to note that in a cultural context, the popularity of city-suburban dichotomy is as ever-present today as it was in the 1950s.

The increasing complexity of suburbia is noteworthy for several reasons. Suburban governments have generally been ill equipped to respond to these changes.[5] They also lack the resources to confront these larger social and economic issues. Carpentersville, Farmers Branch, and Hazleton experienced these changes. In some neighborhoods, residents grew unsettled as they witnessed these transformations daily, while in other neighborhoods, residents were accustomed to and even expected this new reality. A backlash developed to these problems, and policy responses were crafted. These trends were accordingly the precursors to the political fight for local control of immigration policy.

In this chapter, I synthesize the background issues and set the theoretical context for this study. The growth and decline of suburbia is situated in a historical setting, and then the geography of immigration is examined. Then, I consider the nature of public policy responses to look at how issues are framed.

THE RISE AND FALL OF THE SUBURBS

The growth of suburbia was not an accident, nor was its decline. A brief review of the history of this process demonstrates the role that public policy played in building the suburbs.[6]

What is a suburb? The answers are multifarious. In simple terms, suburbs occupy the space in a metropolitan area outside of the central city. Of course, definitions are more complex. According to Kenneth Jackson, suburbs historically can be described by four characteristics: function, class, separation, and density. Suburbs are residential locations with middle-to-upper income residents. There is generally a spatial mismatch between the location of jobs and the residential location of the labor force. Low-density development characterizes suburban living.[7] However, as many urban historians have shown, suburbs have long been places where pockets of diversity existed among a variety of social and economic dimensions.[8]

Mass suburbanization began after the Second World War. Between the 1930s and 1960s, a set of public policies was implemented to stimulate the market to grow suburbs. In 1934, the National Federal Housing Act provided insurance to private mortgage loan companies to protect lenders from risk and to encourage long-term housing loans. The goal was to strengthen the demand for new housing and encourage developers to build a larger supply of housing units to relieve central cities of a housing crunch. From 1944 onward, the Serviceman's Readjustment Act (also known as the G.I. Bill) provided war veterans with numerous benefits, including tuition support for higher education and low-interest, zero-down-payment loans for new housing in the suburbs.[9] In 1949 and 1954, the National Federal Housing Acts funded the slum clearance and urban renewal of central cities.[10] Then, even more urbanites became suburbanites. Last, in 1954, the Federal-Aid Highway Act funded the construction of over 41,000 miles of roads and highways to connect cities and suburbs. The policies fueled—and even subsidized—the move to the suburbs and the development of new suburbs for generations to come.[11]

The American Dream has been part of the nation's psyche since the nation's founding. In 1931, Historian James Truslow Adams wrote in his book *The Epic of America* that all Americans dreamed of "a better, richer, and happier life for all our citizens of every rank which is the greatest contribution we have as yet made to the thought and welfare of the world."[12] The postwar American Dream was achieved by moving to the suburbs. But this move had many consequences on society.[13] As residents fled central cities for the suburbs, they witnessed dramatic socioeconomic decline.[14] Neighborhoods decayed as the city's tax base shrunk and public services declined.[15] Racial and ethnic segregation grew, and poverty increased. Housing developments sprawled further away from the urban core, exacerbating highway traffic. In the end, uneven patterns of development grew along the jurisdictional boundaries and racial, ethnic, and class lines.[16] The metropolis grew more fractured.[17] The "enduring tensions" of the urban crisis persisted as the suburban dream flourished.[18]

Perhaps ironic, some decades later, the crisis of the city spread to the suburbs like a self-fulfilling prophecy. The fall of the suburbs, particularly older, inner-ring suburbs, began in the 1970s and grew increasingly worse in subsequent decades.[19] By the end of the twentieth century, between one-fifth and one-quarter of the nation's metropolitan population lived in a declining suburb. These suburbs experienced a crisis of diminishing house prices, declining population, and rising fiscal stress—well before the arrival of the Great Recession.[20] Similarly, the poverty rate, in absolute and relative terms, outpaced that of central cities. Household income declined dramatically as well. In summary, Hanlon, Short, and Vicino aptly describe the process of suburban decline:

> The socioeconomic status of suburbs in crisis is severely below most other suburbs. They are nearly as poor as their neighboring inner cities. Suburbs in crisis

are typically minority suburbs close to the border of the traditional urban core. They are suburban neighborhoods with high-poverty rates and low household income. If the population is growing, it is only the result of an influx of Hispanics, immigrants, and Blacks. The existence of these suburbs in crisis exposes the dark side of US suburbanization, what we have identified as the suburban gothic. These suburbs are the new metropolitan calamities of the US. The suburban dream has been replaced by the suburban gothic.[21]

THE GEOGRAPHY OF IMMIGRATION

Through the lens of a spatial scale, the study of local immigration provides a useful opportunity to examine the patterns of differentiation between cities and suburbs. A scalar approach also allows the policy responses to be examined according to the type of local jurisdiction.

Immigrants and the City and Suburbs

Whereas immigrants historically settled in central cities, the majority of immigrants now bypass them to settle in the suburbs. By the arrival of the twenty-first century, approximately half of Latinos and Asians lived in suburbs.[22] The early theories of the Chicago School inform this process. The process of neighborhood invasion and succession, where economically mobile residents relocate to outer neighborhoods and suburbs, illustrates that immigrants also share a similar mobility.[23] However, these frameworks are limited by old theories of social spatial organization in the city. These theories viewed the city as the settlement place for immigrants and minorities.[24] Michael Katz and his colleagues show the limitations of this framework in an analysis of suburban immigration in metropolitan Philadelphia. They argue that urban immigrant enclaves "have been supplemented, even supplanted, by new patterns. Immigrants now usually go directly to suburbs. But their choice of suburb is not random. It rests on both their own economic circumstances and the opportunities for affordable housing and work in different kinds of municipalities as well as, undoubtedly, on family ties."[25] Like Americans, new immigrants have followed the American Dream to the suburbs, too. Indeed, immigrants no longer find vacated housing from whites who once inhabited the central city. Today, settlement patterns are much more variegated in a regional housing market.

Audrey Singer, perhaps the leading expert on suburban immigration, and her colleagues have documented the socio-spatial patterns of immigrant settlements.[26] Building on the concept of cities as gateways for immigrants, they extend it to include suburbs. In a typology of gateways, they identify the suburbs of Dallas as an "emerging gateway"; the suburbs of Washington, DC, as an "edge gateway"; the suburbs of Sacramento, Minneapolis-St. Paul, and Portland as "re-emerging gateways"; and the suburbs of Austin and Charlotte as "pre-emerging gateways." The wide range of gateways demonstrates the social diversity of suburbs today. Likewise, the variation of suburban gateways shows that immigrants settle in many different types of suburbs. There is no one type of suburb that attracts immigrants. In sum, cities are still home to many immigrants. Yet, when new immigrants arrive to the United States, the majority of them settle in the suburbs of big cities. It is clear that immigrants are no different than native residents in their location decisions. They vary widely, but the variation of suburbs attracts many residents in many distinct locations.

The concept of Wei Li's "ethnoburb" similarly offers insights on immigrant settlement patterns in suburbia.[27] While traditional enclaves were located in central cities, ethnoburbs are located in suburbs and span a large territory. As a result, the population density is lower than urban enclaves and more ethnic residents live in suburbs. Li shows that immigrants are more likely to settle in the suburbs of major metropolitan areas. For example, Li demonstrates that more Asian immigrants settle in places like Monterey Park over traditional enclaves like Chinatown. Moreover, immigrants are generally not isolated their own communities; rather, they are integrated into the suburbs' larger economy and civic life. Similarly, Emily Skop has also examined the immigrant experience in her work on "saffron suburbs."[28] In an ethnography of Asian Indians in suburban Phoenix, she illustrates how they develop a sense of community based on their socioeconomic characteristics. The nature of upper-income status and high levels of educational attainment drew immigrants to the suburbs. Whether Asian, Indian, or Latino, maintaining identity while also integrating in the community is a common feature among suburban immigrants.

The immigrant experience is rapidly changing. It is increasingly suburban in nature, and numerous metropolitan areas are settlement homes for immigrants. The geographic dispersion of immigrants is shaped by forces such as the nation's dependence on immigrant labor, the decline of manufacturing, and the need to compete in the global economy. Hirschman and Massey refer to this trend as the "new American mosaic."[29] The shift from city to the suburb is an evolving trend and one that will undoubtedly have social and cultural impacts on residents.

The Devolution of Immigration Policy

There is a nascent but growing body of literature on the devolution and descaling of immigration policy.[30] The concept of devolution refers to the idea of shifting decision making and policy making from federal to state and local levels of government. From a geographic perspective, the scale of governance is, in essence, localized to a smaller unit. In the case of immigration policy, the shift from federal to local is not necessarily an active policy choice or decision but rather a local reaction to the lack of federal policy action. The new wave of immigration has renewed interest in immigration policy at all scales. While numerous push-and-pull factors can be attributed to this interest, Monica Varsanyi has identified two key factors. First, the North American Free Trade Agreement (NAFTA) has pushed economic activity and the Latino labor force toward the United States. Second, the pull factor of a steady private sector demand for a low-wage and low-skilled labor force has pulled Latinos to work in industries such as construction and hospitality.[31] In consequence, the Latino population has surged in many suburbs where these goods and services are in high demand. This social and economic transition did not occur without political conflict.[32]

Monica Varsanyi has pioneered the central theme of this body of work. She argues that three processes shape IIROs: (1) neoliberalism, (2) a closed militarized national border, and (3) new immigrant settlement patterns. For example, in the case of Hazleton, Varsanyi claims, "City governments and residents often bear the brunt of neoliberalizing policies but are simultaneously disempowered by the emerging governance nexus of international agreements, nation states and private corporations to adequately contest the policies that are shaping their destinies."[33] Accordingly, she holds that adopting an IIRO is an act of contestation against these larger forces. Similarly, in the case of Farmers Branch, Texas, Brettell and Nibbs argue that the IIRO debate erupted as a threat to middle-class living. They argue that the IIRO was used as "an exclusionary tool . . . and a platform for legislating a certain quality of life."[34]

This body of work is relatively young, which is a function of the issue's salience and the unchartered territory of this policy domain.[35] What is clear is that a backlash to neoliberal state policy and marked demographic restructuring has influenced the propensity to adopt IIROs at the local levels of government. What is generally lacking is an analysis of the *evolution* of the problems in policy terms. The politics of how local immigration problems come to be defined is not well understood. The politics of the IIRO policy design is not well understood. The political backlash to suburban decline is not well understood. Using a suburban policy lens, I aim to examine these questions through an in-depth analysis of public discourse on the problems, policies, and politics.

PUBLIC POLICY RESPONSES

What is a public problem, and what is the rationale for public intervention? The answers to such questions are a constant source of political conflict in any policy domain. A public problem can be thought of as "a condition or situation that affects a considerable number of people, produces needs or generates dissatisfaction among individuals or groups, for which relief or redress is sought."[36] Political actors may respond to problems for a variety of reasons, including fixing government or addressing market failures, delivering public goods, and ameliorating externalities—or, they may do nothing.[37]

Indeed, the lines by which we define the nature of a "public" problem are complex and blurry.[38] Scholars discuss the nature of the public in a relative or a subjective context that is based on who defines the problem. For instance, the idea of the "social construction of reality" holds that social problems come to be defined by groups based on their time, place, and context.[39] The "struggle for public ownership" seeks to establish jurisdiction over the policy area and assign policy domains.[40] In other words, for the residents of Carpentersville, Farmers Branch, and Hazleton, *whose* problem is illegal immigration? Is it a problem for the local government to address? Or, is it a problem for state or federal governments? These answers are the crux of policy debate.

The process of defining problems is political in nature. Political actors, both individual and groups, participate in the policy process to shape how the public comes to understand the varied dimensions of a problem. This process is often the source of political conflict. One common conflict that results is the competition for numerous definitions of a problem. According to Schattschneider, defining alternatives can redefine problems in different ways than actors intended.[41] Similarly, disagreements over the causes—or even the facts—of problems are typical sources of conflict. The corrective course of action, or the policy response, to the problem is yet another source of political disagreement. In some instances, the solution may be defined in the problem definition. Thus, the definitions themselves and their attributes form the politics of problem definition. Problems are not inherently self-defining or as clear as they may first appear.[42] If actors state that a city's problem is that there are too many immigrants, then what is it about having too many immigrants that is problematic? Are there concerns about crime, public services, housing, or language? Is the problem then that too many immigrants cause problems in those other areas of concern? Cobb and Elder capture this idea, asserting that, "Policy problems are not simply 'givens,' nor are they simply matters of the 'facts' of the situation."[43] So, the debate and strife in the suburbs centers on who defines what problems; when problems are defined; and how and why problems are defined.[44]

Communication framing is a useful framework for the analysis of problems and the politics of discourse. Iyengar writes, "The manner in which a problem of choice is 'framed' is a contextual cue that may profoundly influence decision outcomes."[45] Carpini goes on to note that "such alterations in the way information is presented (e.g., emphasizing certain facts over others, the choice of descriptive adjectives and adverbs, the amount and type of context provided, or the sounds and images included) can 'prime' recipients of the information in ways that affect both the issues they attend to (agenda-setting) and the construction of their specific opinions about these issues."[46] Indeed, information and its delivery matter. The characteristics of not only the content of the message but also the context can shape public opinion about the various dimensions of a problem. In an effort to influence political conflicts in defining problems, Cobb and Elder demonstrate that political actors employ rhetorical strategies and symbolic language to shape the frames of communication.[47] Accordingly, the framing of political conflict over problem definitions plays a role in the fight for local control of immigration policy. The way in which the legal dimensions are framed—communication tactics, language issues, suburban decline processes, and nativist backlashes—forms the basis for differences among actors in this debate. Thus, this framework provides a useful method for understanding how and why those differences evolved.

How do we examine how political conflicts evolve? David Easton asks, "What is the expressing function of politics?"[48] He argues that politics, as the authoritative allocation of values, allows us to identify the defining function of political life.[49] According to Easton, political systems create arrangements to carry out the defining function of government: to allocate values authoritatively. Politics, then, becomes the system by which institutions and actors can be analyzed.

As Figure 2.1 shows, we can apply this conceptual understanding to the political fight for local control of immigration policy. The demand for relief is defined as relief from illegal immigrants, relief from neighborhood, decline

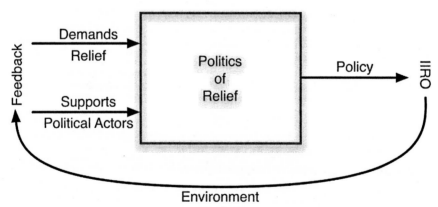

Figure 2.1.   Conceptualizing the Politics of Relief.

and relief from demographic change. Residents demand that their politicians confront the problem. The political actors establish numerous supports to navigate the politics of relief. The framing of the problem along many dimensions (legal, fiscal, civil rights, language, crime, rule of law, economic decline, and nationalism) then delineates the supporters and opponents of the policy design: the Illegal Immigration Relief Ordinance. The policy outcome, the failure, adoption, or implementation, is shaped by external environmental events like national attention. Next, the outcome leads to a policy feedback to determine again the demands and supports. This becomes a cyclical process as authoritative values are allocated.

This framework can be understood by way of Easton's three definitions of the authoritative allocation of values. First, the circumstances under which a public policy is authoritative occur when "people feel they must or ought to obey" the law. Second, public policies allocate, or distribute, the resources of government. Third, values are expressed by the people's attitudes and the actions of how goods and services are distributed among them. Of course, allocation decisions that are based on values are often the result of subjective decisions that depend on the context of the situation. In short, the study of the "politics" of the policy process—that is, the contextual circumstances by which the definitions of problems and solutions are defined—allows us to uncover the circumstances of the authoritative allocation of values in the political realm.[50] Residents and political actors in Carpentersville, Farmers Branch, and Hazleton authoritatively allocated the value that illegal immigration should be eliminated. Public intervention was called for to uphold these values and decisions.

NOTES

1. Michael Vitez, "Is a City America's Gatekeeper?" *The Philadelphia Inquirer*, March 13, 2007.

2. Despite the attention that *CNN* draws to the changing state of suburbia, the myth of suburbia still reigns in the scholarly literature and cultural public sphere. See Bernadette Hanlon, Thomas J. Vicino, and John Rennie Short, "The New Metropolitan Reality in the US: Rethinking the Traditional Model," *Urban Studies* 43, no. 12 (2006): 2129-2143.

3. See Jessica Ravitz, "5 Ways the Suburbs are Changing," *CNN*, December 21, 2011, accessed December 22, 2011, http://inamerica.blogs.cnn.com/2011/12/21/5 -things-we-now-know-about-suburbia.

4. William H. Frey, "Melting Pot Cities and Suburbs: Racial and Ethnic Change in Metro America in the 2000s," *The State of Metropolitan America*, (May 2011), Washington, DC: The Brookings Institution.

5. Alan Ehrenhalt, "Immigrants and the Suburban Influx," *Governing Magazine*, November 30, 2009.

6. Anthony Downs, *Opening Up the Suburbs: An Urban Strategy for America* (New Haven, CT: Yale University Press, 1973).

7. Jackson, *Crabgrass Frontier*, 3-11.

8. See generally Kevin M. Kruse and Thomas J. Sugrue, eds., *The New Suburban History* (Chicago: University of Chicago Press, 2006).

9. Rosalyn Baxandall and Elizabeth Ewen, *Picture Windows: How the Suburbs Happened* (New York: Basic Books, 2001); Barbara Kelly, *Expanding the American Dream: Building and Rebuilding Levittown* (Albany: State University of New York Press, 1993).

10. Jon C. Teaford, *The Rough Road to Renaissance: Urban Revitalization in America, 1940-1985* (Baltimore, MD: Johns Hopkins University Press, 1990).

11. Hayden, *Building Suburbia,* 5-30.

12. James Truslow Adams, *The Epic of America*, (New York: Little, Brown and Company, 1931): viii.

13. Thomas J. Sugrue, *The Origins of the Urban Crisis: Race and Inequality in Postwar Detroit* (Princeton, NJ: Princeton University Press, 1996).

14. Robert M. Fogelson, *Downtown: Its Rise and Fall, 1880-1950* (New Haven, CT: Yale University Press, 2001).

15. Robert Beauregard, *Voices of Decline: The Postwar Fate of U.S. Cities, 2nd ed. rev.* (New York: Routledge, 2003).

16. Thomas M. Stanback, Jr., *The New Suburbanization: Challenge to the Central City* (Boulder, CO: Westview Press, 1991).

17. Gregory Weiher, *The Fractured Metropolis: Political Fragmentation and Metropolitan Segregation* (Albany: State University of New York Press, 1991).

18. Dennis R. Judd and Paul Kantor, *Enduring Tensions in Urban Politics* (New York: Macmillan, 1992).

19. I have written extensively on the decline of suburbs. See John Rennie Short, Bernadette Hanlon, and Thomas J. Vicino, "The Decline of Inner Suburbs: The New Suburban Gothic in the United States," *Geography Compass* 1, no. 3 (2007): 641-656; Hanlon and Vicino, "The Fate of First-Tier Suburbs," 249-275; Thomas J. Vicino, "The Quest to Confront Suburban Decline: Political Realities and Lessons," *Urban Affairs Review* 43, no. 4 (2008): 553-581.

20. Richard Florida, "How the Crash Will Reshape America," *The Atlantic Monthly*, (March 2009): 44-56.

21. Hanlon, Short, and Vicino, *Cities and Suburbs,* 189.

22. John Iceland, *Where We Live Now: Immigration and Race in the United States* (Berkeley: University of California Press, 2009): 38-40.

23. See Park, Burgess, and McKenzie, *The City, vii-x*; Harris and Ullman, "The Nature of Cities," 7-17; Hoyt, "The Structure and Growth," 9-14.

24. Ibid.

25. Michael B. Katz, Mathew J. Creighton, Daniel Amsterdam, and Merlin Chowkwanyun, "Immigration and the New Metropolitan Geography," *Journal of Urban Affairs* 32, no. 5 (2010): 523-547.

26. Audrey Singer, ed., *Twenty-First Century Gateways*, 3-30; Elżbieta M. Goździak and Susan Forbes Martin, eds., *Beyond the Gateway: Immigrants in a Changing America* (Lanham, MD: Lexington Books, 2005).

27. Wei Li, *Ethnoburb: The New Ethnic Community in Urban America* (Honolulu: University of Hawaii Press, 2009). See also Emily Skop and Wei Li, "Asians in America's Suburbs: Patterns and Consequences of Settlement," *Geographical Review* 95, no. 2: 167-188.

28. Emily Hayes Skop, "Saffron Suburbs: Indian Immigrant Community Formation in Phoenix." Ph.D. dissertation, Arizona State University, 2002.

29. Charles Hirschman and Douglas S. Massey, "Places and Peoples: The New American Mosaic," in *New Faces in New Places: The Changing Geography of American Immigration*, ed. Douglas S. Massey (New York: Russell Sage Foundation, 2010): 1-19.

30. See generally Mark Ellis, "Unsettling Immigrant Geographies: US Immigration and the Politics of Scale," *Tijdschrift voor Economische en Sociale Geografie* 97, no. 1 (2006): 49-58; Monica Varsanyi, "Rescaling the 'Alien,' Rescaling Personhood: Neoliberalism, Immigration, and the State," *Annals of the Association of American Geographers* 98, no. 4 (2008): 877-896; David Delaney and Helga Leitner, "The Political Construction of Scale," *Political Geography* 16, no. 2 (1997): 93-97; Wayne A. Cornelius, "Controlling 'Unwanted' Immigration: Lessons from the United States, 1993-2004," *Journal of Ethnic and Migration Studies* 31, no. 4 (2005): 775-794; Benjamin J. Klebaner, "State and Local Immigration Regulation in the United States Before 1882," *International Review of Social History* 3, no. 2 (1958): 267-295.

31. Monica Varsanyi, ed., *Taking Local Control: Immigration Policy Activism in U.S. Cities and States* (Stanford, CA: Stanford University Press, 2010): 9-10.

32. Few scholars have studied the nature of these conflicts. On the likelihood to adopt IIROs, see Jill Esbenshade and Barbara Obzurt, "Local Immigration Regulation: A Problematic Trend in Public Policy," *Harvard Journal of Hispanic Policy* 20 (2008): 33-47; Kyle Walker and Helga Leitner, "The Variegated Landscape of Local Immigration Policies in the United States," *Urban Geography* 32, no. 2 (2011): 156-178. On policing, see Paul G. Lewis and S. Karthick Ramakrishnan, "Police Practices in Immigrant-Destination Cities: Political Control or Bureaucratic Professionalism?" *Urban Affairs Review* 42, no. 6 (2007): 874-900. On political ideology and attitudes toward immigration, Joel S. Fetzer, "Economic Self-Interest or Cultural Marginality? Anti-Immigration Sentiment and Nativist Political Movements in France, Germany, and the USA," *Journal of Ethnic and Migration Studies* 26, no. 1 (2000): 5-23; Elliott R. Barkan, "Return of the Nativists? California Public Opinion and Immigration in the 1980s and 1990s," *Social Science History* 27, no. 2 (2003): 229-283; Charles R. Chandler and Tsai Yung-mei, "Social factors influencing immigration attitudes: an analysis of data from the General Social Survey," *The Social Science Journal* 38, no. 2 (2001): 177-188; Adrian Pantoja, "Against the Tide? Core American Values and Attitudes Toward US Immigration Policy in the Mid-1990s," *Journal of Ethnic and Migration Studies* 32, no. 3 (2006): 515-531. On Spanish language issues, see S. Karthick Ramakrishnan and Tom Wong, "Partisanship, Not Spanish: Explaining Municipal Ordinances Affecting Undocumented Workers," in *Taking Local Control*, ed. Varsanyi, 73-96. On day laborers issues, see Varsanyi, "City Ordinances as

'Immigration Policing By Proxy:' Local Governments and the Regulation of Undocumented Day Laborers," in *Taking Local Control*, ed. Varsanyi, 135-156; Michael S. Danielson, "All Immigrations Politics is Local: The Day Labor Ordinance in Vista, California," in *Taking Local Control*, ed. Varsanyi, 239-254. On driver's licenses, see "Tired of Illegals: Immigrant Driver's Licenses, Constituent Letters, and Shifting Restrictionist Discourse in California," in *Taking Local Control*, ed. Varsanyi, 275-294. On regional growth, see Jill H. Wilson, Audrey Singer, and Brooke DeRenzis, "Growing Pains: Local Response to Recent Immigrant Settlement in Suburban Washington, DC," in *Taking Local Control*, ed. Varsanyi, 193-216; Owen J. Furuseth and Heather A. Smith, "Localized Immigration Policy: The View from Charlotte, North Carolina, A New Immigrant Gateway," in *Taking Local Control*, ed. Varsanyi, 173-192.

33. Monica W. Varsanyi, "Neoliberalism and Nativism: Local Anti-immigrant Policy Activism and an Emerging Politics of Scale," *International Journal of Urban and Regional Research* 35, no. 2 (2010): 295-311.

34. Caroline B. Brettell and Faith G. Nibbs, "Immigrant Suburban Settlement and the 'Threat' to Middle Class Status and Identity: The Case of Farmers Branch, Texas," *International Migration* 49, no. 1 (2011): 1-30.

35. This body of literature was published as I conducted the research for this book. The scarcity of topical studies in this domain reflects the timeliness of the IIRO policy debate.

36. David Leo Weimer and Aidan R. Vining, *Policy Analysis: Concepts and Practice, 5th ed.* (New York: Longman, 2010).

37. John M. Levy, *Essential Microeconomics for Public Policy Analysis* (Westport, CT: Praeger Publishers, 1994).

38. Chris Bosso, *Pesticides and Politics: The Life Cycle of a Public Issue* (Pittsburgh: University of Pittsburgh Press, 1987).

39. Edward Seidman and Julian Rappaport, *Redefining Social Problems* (New York: Plenum Press, 1986).

40. Joseph R. Gusfield, *The Culture of Public Problems: Drinking-Driving and the Symbolic Order* (Chicago: University of Chicago Press, 1981).

41. E. E. Schattschneider, *The Semisovereign People: A Realist's View of Democracy in America* (Hinsdale, IL: Dryden Press, 1960): 66-68.

42. David Dery, *Problem Definition in Policy Analysis* (Lawrence: University Press of Kansas, 1984).

43. Roger Cobb and Charles Elder, *Participation in American Politics: The Dynamics of Agenda-Building, 2nd ed.* (Baltimore, MD: The Johns Hopkins University Press, 1983): 172.

44. See E. E. Schattschneider, "Intensity, Visibility, Direction and Scope," *American Political Science Review* 51, no. 4 (1957): 933-942; Roger Cobb and Charles Elder, "The Politics of Agenda-Building: An Alternative Perspective for Modern Democratic Theory," *Journal of Politics* 33, no. 4 (1971): 892-915; Anthony Downs, "Up and Down with Ecology: The Issue-Attention Cycle," *The Public Interest* 28 (1972): 38-50; Deborah Stone, "Causal Stories and the Formation of Policy Agendas," *Political Science Quarterly* 104, no. 2 (1989): 281-300; and Christopher Bosso,

"The Contextual Bases of Problem Definition," in *The Politics of Problem Definition*, eds. David A. Rochefort and Roger W. Cobb (Lawrence: University Press of Kansas, 1994): 181-202.

45. Shanto Iyengar, *Is Anyone Responsible? How Television Frames Political Issues* (Chicago: University of Chicago Press, 1991): 11.

46. Michael X. Delli Carpini,"News from Somewhere: Journalistic Frames and the Debate over Public Journalism," in *Framing American Politics*, eds. Karen J. Callaghan and Frauke Schnell (Pittsburgh: University of Pittsburgh Press, 2005): 21-53.

47. Cobb and Elder, *Participation in American Politics*, 36-45.

48. See David Easton, *The Political System: An Inquiry into the State of Political Science* (New York: Knopf, 1953).

49. See also David Easton, *A Framework for Political Analysis* (Englewood Cliffs, NJ: Prentice-Hall, 1965).

50. John Kingdon's work also provides a useful framework to analyze the circumstances: problem, solution, and politics are "streams" that come together in a window of opportunity for policy action. See John Kingdon, *Agendas, Alternatives, and Public Policies, 2nd ed.* (New York: Addison Wesley, 1995)

Chapter Three

Setting the Stage

Local Histories and Contemporary Portraits

There is a fear of people or of things being different. There has been a kind of a collective amnesia about the way in which all of us ended up in this place called America.[1]

—*Ed Yohnka, Director of Communications and Public Policy of the ACLU of Illinois*

History offers society an archive of where we came from and offers a roadmap for where we might be headed. In his critique about Carpentersville's attempt to take local control of immigration policy, Ed Yohnka questioned the motivations of residents and politicians that supported the IIRO. He argued that native residents of suburbs were also descendants of immigrants. The irony, of course, is that the immigrants were primarily from Latin America instead of Europe, but the exclusionary nature of the IIRO hailed back to the days of the rules of Ellis Island. Yohnka's comments further remind us that the US is a nation of immigrants, just as President John F. Kennedy declared to Americans in the 1960s. Have we learned anything about this nation of immigrants? By looking back, we can better understand the circumstances that might influence the future.

LOCAL HISTORIES

Carpentersville, Farmers Branch, and Hazleton share similar histories of growth and development. They grew during the early-to-mid twentieth century. Figure 3.1 shows a map of these three places and their regional locations. How did these places grow and why? To set the stage for the contemporary policy debate, it is first necessary to consider the social, economic, and

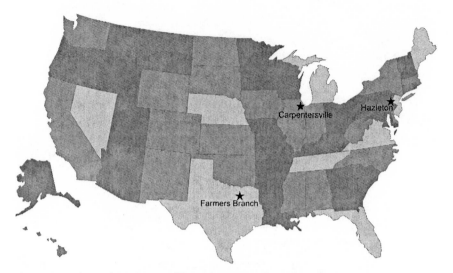

Figure 3.1.   Map of Carpentersville, Farmers Branch, and Hazleton.

political roles that influenced growth. We turn to an analysis of the historical patterns of development and then to a contemporary portrait.

Carpentersville

Today, Carpentersville is a bedroom suburb of Chicago; however, its legacy is more deeply rooted in agriculture. Located due east of the Fox River, the village is approximately 37 miles northwest of Chicago's Loop (see Figure 3.1). The city's area is 7.6 square miles.

Carpentersville was originally established in 1837. Charles and Daniel Carpenter, of Rock River, Mississippi, moved north and settled on the Fox River. They named the area Carpenter's Grove. Later, in 1851, Charles' son Julius Angelo Carpenter platted the land and founded the town of Carpentersville. The town's Main Street quickly developed with the arrival of local institutions, such as the Carpenter Store Building, a library, and a gristmill. Then, in 1877, the town incorporated.

There is a history of manufacturing employment and production in the suburb. The largest employer was the Illinois Iron and Bolt Company.[2] As an iron foundry, the company produced agricultural and transportation mechanisms. Other small blacksmith shops were also commonplace. These employment opportunities attracted numerous immigrants to Carpentersville during the late nineteenth century. In particular, during the 1870s and 1880s, German, Polish, and Swedish immigrants arrived in Carpentersville to work in the factories. These immigrants provided a new labor force for the town. By the early 1900s, some 2,000 residents were employed by local manufacturing companies.

Early twentieth century development in Carpentersville can also be linked to the development of regional transportation systems. During the early twentieth century, various forms of train service linked the region's western suburbs together and to downtown Chicago. As early as 1896, a network of electric trolley cars connected the village to other western suburbs in the Fox Valley region. These streetcars provided a direct route for residents of Carpentersville to a larger regional employer, the Elgin Watch Company. Also, they linked Carpentersville to transfer points on the Chicago Aurora and Elgin Railroad (CA&E). The streetcars operated continuously for 37 years until a severe tornado damaged the electrical wires over the Fox River Bridge in 1933. As the toll of Great Depression worsened, streetcar service was subsequently abandoned. However, the CA&E Railroad continued to operate until 1957, carrying passengers between the eastern and western parts of metropolitan Chicago.[3]

Carpentersville retained much of its character as a sleepy settlement until the mid-twentieth century. The arrival of the Interstate Highway System and other major roadways ushered a marked change in the developmental history of Carpentersville. Up until the end of the Second World War, Carpentersville remained isolated from the region, and its residents depended on slow railways for regional transport. The infrastructure of roadways in metropolitan Chicago, like many other regions, benefited immensely from the Federal-Aid Highway Act of 1956.[4] Commonly known as the Eisenhower Interstate System, federal funds poured into Chicago and its surrounding suburban jurisdictions. The construction of new roads paved the way for residents to "open up the suburbs" and settle in new territories outside of the central city.[5] Carpentersville was no exception.

The transformation of Carpentersville occurred with the development of Interstate 90 and State Roads 62 and 72. The Northwest Tollway, which is the stretch of I-90 from Chicago to the Fox Valley, is a 76-mile expressway that opened on August 20, 1958. The Interstate spans from southeast Wisconsin to the primary western suburbs of Rockford and Elgin, and then to Chicago.[6] Similarly, the construction (and later the maintenance) of state roads also played an important role in this pattern of suburban development. Illinois Routes 62 and 72 are illustrative cases for Carpentersville. In 1924, these routes were built and regularly expanded to serve as an east-west corridor from Carpentersville to the city limits of Chicago. They served as important precursors for the development of the Interstate system as they ran parallel to today's Interstate 90. Perhaps master planners Daniel Burnham and Edward

Bennett's prescient vision of this suburban expansion was inevitable. They held, "It needs no argument to show that direct highways leading from the outlying towns to Chicago as the center are of necessity for both; and it is also apparent that suburban towns should be connected with one another in the best manner . . . While good highways are of great value to the terminal cities, they are of even greater value to the outlying towns."[7] Indeed, these roadways facilitated the transformation of Carpentersville from a small village to a full-fledged suburban center.[8]

Carpentersville's mass suburban development did not begin until after the Second World War. In 1953, as a precursor to the village's suburbanization, local headlines proclaimed, "Big residential center to rise in Fox Valley . . . plan of town of 15,000 near Elgin."[9] This plan was to construct a new subdivision in the Meadowdale area of Carpentersville in the early 1950s. A local resident, Leonard W. Besinger, was responsible for the initial development and growth. He owned several thousand acres of land, which he used as a farm to breed horses. In 1949 and 1951, after his farm was destroyed by a series of severe fires, Besinger decided to develop the land. The Village of Carpentersville annexed his property and provided prime access to the Fox River for development. Besinger devoted the remaining years of the 1950s to expanding the suburban landscape of Carpentersville—from houses large and small to a state of the art regional mall and even a racing speedway.[10]

Upon the inauguration of Meadowdale, the *Chicago Tribune* observed, "Meadowdale of Carpentersville *is the largest and only development of its kind* to come into being as a complete town having its own shopping center, industrial development, executive homes, middle class homes, parks, play grounds, schools, churches, and community built by one man [emphasis added]."[11] Besinger further remarked, "So I started building and selling, and at the end of the first year we had sold more than 700 houses. After overcoming more trouble in the second year, we obtained VA financing and sold and built 700 units. Gradually the opposition faded and demand for homes in Meadowdale grew by leaps and bounds."[12] His development company estimated that the household incomes ranged between $4,700 and $6,900 in 1957, or approximately between $36,000 and $53,000 in today's dollars.[13] As the village quickly grew into a suburb, the first residents—and the first generation of suburbanites—were solidly middle-class residents.

Besinger's regional shopping mall provides further evidence of the development pressures to attract suburban residents—and indeed, his vision for a modern suburb.[14] In 1957, the Meadowdale Shopping Center opened in Carpentersville as one of the nation's largest indoor malls. It was built to not only serve the residents of Carpentersville and the Fox Valley but also the fast-paced suburbanization of Chicago during the 1950s. Developed on 50 acres, the mall had 45 stores and eventually grew to include some 120 stores, and there was ample parking for some 4,000 automobiles. The four anchor stores, Clark's, Carson Pirie Scott, Wieboldt's, and Woolworth's, established national retailers that would make Carpentersville a destination like in many other regions.[15] Such amenities made Carpentersville a desirable location to settle and call home during the first two decades after the Second World War.

The results were astounding. In 1950, the village's population was 1,523; and a decade later, it grew to 17,424 residents—a phenomenal growth rate of over 1,000 percent. Within two years, 1,700 prefabricated housing units and 6,000 housing dwelling units were constructed. Drawing on the strategies of William Levitt's housing development on Long Island, New York, Besinger sold as many as 60 houses per day.[16] Indeed, the demand for suburban living was great. "The average young American is tired of living in crammed city living quarters," Besinger argued. As word spread around of Carpentersville's growth, he further commented, "These people [the residents] are Meadowdale's best salesmen."[17] The foundation of suburban living grew stronger in subsequent decades, and developers like Besinger worked to supply a suitable housing stock for middle-class, white households.[18]

Carpentersville grew from its rural roots in the late 1800s to its legacy as a bedroom suburb of Chicago in the 1950s. Like many other urbanized settlements, the village initially grew based on its physical geography.[19] The settlement was located near valuable natural resources, such as the Fox River and the central business district of Chicago. The industrial heritage of iron manufacturing provided just enough jobs to sustain numerous generations of households for many years as a small village. However, larger economic transformations in the national economy, coupled with the World Wars, ushered in a new era of living for Carpentersville. The demand for new housing and the growth of family households meant that farms, agricultural land, and green spaces were quickly developed into suburban subdivisions of tract housing. Moreover, federal and state investments to build and improve transportation networks facilitated these growth patterns. The G.I. Bill only added to the growth of the suburbs, providing immense opportunities nationally for returning veterans to acquire a new house for very little money—and Carpentersville was no exception.[20] Real estate and development entrepreneurs like Leonard Besinger capitalized on these circumstances. The transformation to a suburb became a reality by the midpoint of the twentieth century.

Farmers Branch

Farmers Branch is an inner-ring suburb of Dallas; it shares a northern border with the central city. Situated in northwestern Dallas County, the city is approximately 15 miles from Dallas's central business district (see Figure 3.1). The city's area is 12 square miles.

Farmers Branch was originally settled between 1841 and 1843.[21] During that period, Thomas Keenan, Isaac B. Webb, and William Cochran received land grants from the Peters Colony to settle the area.[22] Later, residents migrated from the Midwest and Southeast, particularly from Illinois, Indiana, Missouri, and Kentucky. Originally the settlement spanned the land between White Rock Creek to the east, the Elm Fork of the Trinity to the west, the Dallas County Line to the north, and Cedar Springs to the south. The area was first named Mustang Branch as a reference to the mustang grapes that grew along the creek. But as the settlers later discovered rich soil and abundant land to grow crops, they renamed the area Farmers Branch.

The city has a historical legacy that is largely based on farming. For most of its history, Farmers Branch was primarily an agricultural and farming settlement. For the duration of the nineteenth century, the population remained at approximately 100 residents. As the first generation, they earned a living and survived off of the land's rich soil. Cattle and sheep grazed the land. Cotton yields were abundant. The supply and production of meat and leather was high. Various fruits and vegetables were grown. These successes not only made Farmers Branch an attractive place, but they also served as a precursor to future development.

The local economy continued to expand throughout the nineteenth century. Farmers Branch claims a number of "economic firsts" in greater Dallas. For example, in 1845, William Bowles built and opened the first blacksmith shop. Then, in 1849, James A. Smith built the first cotton gin in the region. Also, a gristmill was built. These new production sites fueled the economic expansion of the city. But, more importantly, they created employment opportunities for a growing settlement. As a result, this attracted numerous national migrants and immigrants to Farmers Branch.

These settlers also built the city's first social, economic, and cultural institutions. At the beginning of the twentieth century, the population stood at 300 residents. By the early 1900s, Farmers Branch had emerged as a shipping center for grain and cotton. Many new stores were constructed, including a millinery, a lumberyard, a grocery store, and the city's first major bank, the Riddle Banking Company. Public infrastructure was also developed, including electricity, telephone connections, telegraph service, a post office, and a public school.

The development of regional transportation networks also influenced the early development of Farmers Branch. During the early twentieth century, train service linked the city to Dallas and to the Midwest and Southwest. In 1871, the Dallas and Wichita Railway Company was chartered to span 100 miles to Wichita, connecting the region's rich minerals together. John Neely Bryan began construction a year later, but the Panic of 1873 halted construction for five years. The railway was later sold to the Texas and Pacific Company, then again sold to the Missouri, Kansas and Texas Railway Company in 1881. When service began a decade later, Farmers Branch benefited immensely. The city was connected by heavy rail to the south to Dallas and to the north to Wichita. Its location was ideal because it served as a stopover for arriving and departing passengers and goods.[23] The city witnessed more economic and population growth; more than 300 residents had arrived by the 1900s.

In 1924, Farmers Branch was connected to electric rail service. The Texas Interurban Railway commenced electric rail service between Dallas and Denton, and the city benefited with a stop in its commercial center. The rail service was the first local option for cheap and convenient commuter options. Not only were business trips useful, but leisure trips were also made accessible for the first time. However, the rail was short lived. Service ceased in 1932.[24]

For the first half of the twentieth century, Farmers Branch remained a small outpost on the fringe of Dallas. With the exception of the railroad, the city was largely isolated from the Metroplex. Residents relied on slow railways for access to regional transport. The arrival of the interstate roadways stands out as the most important historical factor in the development of Farmers Branch. The Federal-Aid Highway Act of 1956 funded a large infrastructure of expressways and highways in the Metroplex.[25] The Eisenhower Interstate System provided substantial federal funding for Dallas, Fort Worth, and the surrounding suburban jurisdictions. This facilitated the outward movement from the central city of Dallas—Farmers Branch was now even more accessible.

The transformation of Farmers Branch occurred with the development of US Highway 77 and later Interstates 35E and 635. The Stemmons Freeway in Dallas, which is the stretch of I-35E from downtown Dallas to the north, is a 97-mile expressway that opened on August 3, 1959. The final stretch was completed on August 15, 1963 and connected Dallas to Farmers Branch and ultimately to the state line. The I-35E is the split of I-35 on the eastern side of the Metroplex, while I-35W is the split on the western side, near Fort Worth.[26] Similarly, the LBJ Freeway, or I-635, was constructed in 1959 as a spur of the I-35E to form a loop around eastern Dallas. The 37-mile spur meets the northern portion of the Stemmons Freeway in Farmers Branch.

The location of these highways proved to be a critical factor in the suburban development of Farmers Branch. The city was situated at the junction of I-35E and I-635. This prime location meant that the city became a meeting point for business and leisure travelers, and more importantly, a site for shipping goods. The ease of access to numerous highways fueled the city's growth. Perhaps Texas highway planners understood the long-term impact of the supply and demand of highways and the ultimate suburban expansion. In the late 1950s, they observed, "Texas is far ahead of all other states in construction (mileage) in the 40 billion dollar interstate system with more than 591 miles completed . . . Texans travel an average of 102 million vehicles miles daily."[27] They also noted that the growth and future demand to use highways would continue to grow. "Even now with the Texas highway expansion program increasing rapidly, the traffic burden remains heavy. By 1970, it is estimated that there will be 5.6 million autos in Texas and they will be traveling at least 150 million miles per day."[28] Indeed, the growth and subsequent expansion of these highways transformed Farmers Branch from a small rural town to a full-fledged suburban center.[29]

Farmers Branch's mass suburbanization began with the subdivision of land for the development of tract housing after the Second World War. The city was incorporated on February 23, 1946, and a home-rule charter was granted a decade later. Then, on March 16, 1959, the city's territory grew to its current size by adding approximately 2,000 acres, when the land on the west side was annexed.[30] During this period, early signs of Farmers Branch's suburbanization were omnipresent in local news throughout Dallas. Headlines declared, "Farmers Branch's Farming Dwindles."[31] Indeed, Dallas's booming industries—manufacturing, home development, gravel pits, oil, and dairies—provided valuable jobs for the growing middle class in the Metroplex. Demand for new, quality housing surged.

Numerous real estate speculators and developers saw opportunity in Farmers Branch, including former Dallas County Commissioner Tom W. Field, Farmers Branch Mayors William Dodson, Lawson Lewis, and H. O. Good, and businessman A. Webb Rogers. These men, active in both elected politics and as independent business owners, emerged as important boosters for the new city. The coalition acted as a growth regime to collectively promote the growth of Farmers Branch.[32] Locally, they began to advance the idea of living in Farmers Branch as a suburban utopia, with easy access to transportation, planned shopping centers, attractive and safe houses, and clean water. These men harnessed their businesses and personal relationships to build an infrastructure for the city. Mayor Dodson oversaw the building of a city hall, firehouse, and community center. Mayors Good and Lewis built a water system, connected the city to natural gas and electricity grids, and developed a sewer system. The city was then ready for housing. Tom W. Field reflected, "All this represents startling change . . . Our last cotton gin is gone and I remember when we ginned 4,500 bales . . . now all of this old cotton land is covered with industry and homes."[33]

The results were astounding—and profitable. In a single decade, land values soared 700 percent, from $125 per acre in 1940 to $1,000 per acre in 1950. The next challenge was to attract homebuilders and retail shopping developers. With an infrastructure in place, developers began to flock to Farmers Branch, as opportunities to build soared. One of the earliest and most successful suburban developments was Valwood Park. The Cato Corporation, headed by C. Grady Cates, Jr., developed and built this neighborhood, which served as the first residential anchor for the young city. Cates, and his colleagues Henry Kersey, K. D. Lewis, and E. P. Lamberth, were prominent homebuilders in the Metroplex. The sheer scale of this planned community created incentives for these builders to work together. Their goal was to make Valwood Park the region's largest modern suburban community. A 500-acre tract north of the historic town core, Valwood Park featured 3,500 new housing units, a shopping center, parks, schools, and churches. Houses were priced from $8,750 to $16,000, and they featured three bedrooms, a two-car garage, and a large kitchen. Veterans paid no down payment, and others paid only $175 to secure an FHA loan.[34] At the peak of construction, developers sold many units daily. Upon completion a decade later, the entire development cost $30 million. The 7,000 new residents of Valwood Park propelled Farmers Branch's families into the middle class.[35]

The growth was remarkable. In 1950, prior to incorporation of Farmers Branch, the population was 915. In the period of one decade, Farmers Branch grew by over 1,400 percent. The population in 1960 was over 13,000. The foundation of suburban living was poured and remained stable for decades. Developers such as Gates, Kersey, Lewis, and Lamberth built a healthy supply of affordable, decent housing units for middle-class, white households.[36]

Farmers Branch was not only transformed into a modern suburb, but it was built with a pioneering spirit. The city grew "with all the vigor of youth, courage and foresight."[37] In fact, observers noted that there were "no slums, no shacks, no underprivileged wards of society" in Farmers Branch.[38] The typical new residents of the city consisted of a young family, husband and wife, small children, and an annual average household income of approximately $7,500. The *Dallas Morning News* captures the essence of the climate in Farmers Branch, observing that "[The community] has suburban beauty and freshness with city convenience and opportunity."[39]

Farmers Branch developed from its rural roots in the late 1800s to its legacy as a bedroom suburb of Dallas in the 1950s. Like so many other communities, the city's early growth was based on its physical geography.[40] Strategically located near the railroads that carried goods and people in and out of Dallas, Farmers Branch harnessed its location to grow. The production of goods like cotton and leather provided a steady stream of jobs. As the twentieth century progressed, the Second World War ushered in a new way of life in Farmers Branch. Returning war veterans needed new housing to grow their families. The area of farms and agricultural land that would later become Farmers Branch was rapidly subdivided for the construction of tract housing. The G.I. Bill provided financial support for returning veterans to purchase new homes for very little money, and new residents of Farmers Branch benefited from such public support.[41] Also, state and federal investments helped to build and improve transportation infrastructure within the suburb as well as the greater region. By taking advantage of these circumstances, real estate developers built a modern community. By the midpoint of the twentieth century, Farmers Branch flourished into a full-fledged suburb. A suburban economy was born, and new residents nurtured its growth.

Hazleton

Hazleton is located in Luzerne County. The city sits on Spring Mountain and is located between the Delaware and Susquehanna Rivers. Hazleton is approximately 25 miles south of Wilkes-Barre and 90 miles north of downtown Philadelphia (see Figure 3.1). The city's area is six square miles.

The development of Hazleton was a function of circumstance rather than design. For most of its history, Hazleton was primarily a small outpost in central Pennsylvania. In 1780, approximately 50 soldiers originally settled the area during the Revolutionary War. Then, by the turn of the nineteenth century, it became a convenient location for sojourners to rest on the Susquehanna River. They navigated the Lehigh Valley and rested along the river, eventually settling in present day Hazleton and calling it home. During the early 1800s, the area remained an isolated settlement with very few residents. Advances in the economy, transportation, and housing would later impact the region's population and its legacy. This progress allowed the area to later incorporate as a borough in 1857. Then, in 1891, Hazleton was incorporated as a city.

Local businessmen and entrepreneurs played important roles in growing the economy and employment base. The discovery of coal and the development of the coal mining industry became the keystone of Hazleton's regional economy. In 1818, Josiah White and Erskine Hazard founded one of the earliest collieries, the Lehigh Valley Coal Company, which focused on building railroad and canal infrastructure to transport coal. Then, in 1836, industrialist Ario Pardee formed the Hazleton Coal Company. Later, during the mid-1850s, Eckley Coxe developed Eckley Miners Village and built numerous collieries in and around Hazleton. These leading industrialists were the coal barons of Hazleton. Together these companies employed some 20,000 residents, who produced several million tons of coal annually. Indeed, Hazleton was the "jewel" of the coalfields.[42]

Plentiful employment opportunities resulted in the exponential growth of Hazleton's population. German and Irish immigrants arrived in Hazleton during the 1840s and 1850s. Many worked in the mines and established roots in the community. Then, in the following six decades, numerous immigrants arrived from Italy, Poland, and Russia. Hazleton became a city of immigrants. Although employment in the mining industry carried health risks, hazardous conditions, and low wages, immigrants flocked toward these opportunities. Despite the circumstances, the city's population grew from 4,000 residents in 1860 to 12,000 in 1890. Immigration was the primary driver of that growth.

The growth of nearby patch towns influenced development in Hazleton. Also known as "company towns," these early suburbs were usually villages, townships, or boroughs that surrounded Hazleton. The corporate entities of nearby collieries constructed them. John Garner observes, "Industrialists took a genuine interest in the welfare of their workforces, and attempted to provide a model environment."[43] Places like Hazle Townships, West Hazleton, and Coleraine provided an industrial and residential setting for workers. Houses, schools, churches, stores, and bars were developed to offer residents the amenities of a larger city. This allowed companies to ensure that employees lived close to work in working-class or middle-class neighborhoods.[44]

The development of regional transportation systems in Hazleton was an integral part of the success of the coalmining industry. A synergetic relationship between the railroads and mining industries developed during the early nineteenth century. The first railroad to connect Hazleton to a network originated from neighboring Weatherly on the Lehigh Valley Railroad (LVRR). In 1850, the railroad's construction began after businessman Asa Packer invested in the company. The rail service connected central and southeastern Pennsylvania to the important Penn Haven Line, thus providing access to numerous coalmining sites and other larger cities. In 1907, the LVRR built a station in Hazleton, and it operated until 1961.

Trolley tracks, too, played a role in developing the early suburbs in and around Hazleton. The Lehigh Traction Company, pioneered by coal financier Alvan Markle, built a local network of rails for trolley service during the first half of the twentieth century. Rail diesel cars and electric trolleys were primarily utilized through the city limits and surrounding areas. Similarly, the Interstate Highway System connected Hazleton to other places. Two key Interstate highways shaped development in Hazleton. Constructed between 1959 and 1970, Interstate 80 spans 311 miles along the east-west corridor of Pennsylvania. Interstate 81 spans 232 miles along the north-south corridor of Pennsylvania. Located five miles south of I-80 and at the intersection of I-81,

Hazleton was ideally situated as a transit center for the manufacturing and distribution of goods. By the 1950s, buses had replaced most street trolleys, and shortly thereafter, automobiles became the principal mode of transportation.

The metropolitan development of Hazleton began in the early 1900s. Hazleton's population reached 25,000 in 1940, which was twice the population only three decades before. Residents generally settled in the outer neighborhoods of Hazleton, and nearby boroughs benefited from the extension of the trolley tracks and roadways. From the 1880s to the 1930s, residential areas were built featuring track development of new, single-family housing units. In particular, Hazleton's housing stock that was constructed during the two decades of the twentieth century was arranged on a grid pattern. It was composed of single-family units on small plots of green space. Some 5,000 units, or about half of the city's housing units, were built in this style. Hazleton's outer neighborhoods were built as an early form of streetcar suburbia.[45]

Summary

The history of Carpentersville informs us about the roles of private land speculators and public policies that aimed to boost the supply of the housing stock. Until 1970, population and housing growth in places like Carpentersville was the norm of suburban development and economic stability. Farmers Branch illuminates the historical roles of early suburban settlement patterns. Market-driven development and pro-growth government policies resulted in a population boom. From the period of 1950 to 1970, the suburban development of Farmers Branch created economic stability for the baby boom generation. However, since the initial growth and early prosperous years, divergent patterns of the social and economic fabric grew in subsequent decades. Hazleton's history is rooted in the anthracite coalfields. Since its incorporation, the city flourished as an industrial city and a destination for new immigrants searching for upward mobility. As economic prosperity grew, the city emerged as a financial and industrial hub as new firms were established. From the 1840s until the 1940s, Hazleton created jobs that resulted in a larger population base. Investments in transportation, housing, and social institutions made it a desirable place to live. Hazleton's early suburbs developed and provided residents with a middle-class life. Throughout this period of growth, the city's spatial form changed from a small urban environment to a suburban setting. Yet, the decline of the coal industry and loss of manufacturing jobs ushered in a challenging postwar era for the city. Thus, in postwar Hazleton, the development of a new economy and population center became the primary economic and political issue for policymakers.

In Carpentersville, Farmers Branch, and Hazleton, the boom period ended several decades ago. By 1970, the growth of these local economies faded.

Population growth and housing development stagnated accordingly. Then, the arrival of a new wave of immigrants provided local leaders with a divisive issue that stirred the emotions of local residents.

CONTEMPORARY PORTRAITS

Portraits of the socioeconomic composition of Carpentersville, Farmers Branch, and Hazleton provide useful benchmarks to demonstrate how these communities evolved in the context of the contemporary suburban landscape. These portraits also connect local histories to today's socioeconomic conditions because they characterize the processes of neighborhood change and demonstrate patterns of suburban decline. The realities of socioeconomic change in the neighborhoods of these towns framed the manner in which residents defined the problem of immigration and the various policy alternatives. This contemporary portrait draws on an examination of data from all of the census tracts in each place in this study. It is a spatial analysis that spans four decades from 1970 onward.[46] Tables 3.1, 3.2, and 3.3 show a summary analysis of the data. The analysis is organized thematically along four dimensions: 1) population characteristics, 2) household income dynamics, 3) the nature of the housing stock, and 4) the structure of the labor force.

Population Characteristics

The population characteristics tell us about the demographic structure of the suburban communities. Let us consider the characteristics of the size, foreign-born status, race, and ethnicity of the population.

Carpentersville's population had reached a plateau by 1970, and it remained largely stagnant from 1970 to 1990. In 1970, the population was 26,310, and it grew slightly to 27,748 by 1990, which was an increase of 5.4 percent in over 20 years. However, during the 1990s, the village experienced a large increase in its population. The number of residents grew by 47 percent, to 40,902 in 2000. A decade later, the population receded slightly by 3,758 residents, or by 9.1 percent. Meanwhile, the village population was not aging in place; that is, residents were not living in the same place for many years. Between 1970 and 2009, less than 5 percent of the population was over the age of 65.

Similarly, Farmers Branch's population reached a plateau by 1970, and it too remained largely stagnant from 1970 to 1990. In 1970, the population was 27,588, and by 1990, it had only grown slightly to 28,737, which was an increase of 4 percent over two decades. Yet, during the next decade, Farmers Branch experienced a population boom. By 2000, the number of residents grew by 18 percent, to 34,043. A decade later, 7,866 residents left the city,

Table 3.1. Analysis of Socioeconomic Structure of Carpentersville, 1970 to 2009[a]

	1970		1980		1990		2000		2009	
	Number	Percent	Number	Percent	Number	Percent	Number	Percent	Number	Percent
Total Population	26,310	N/A	25,870	N/A	27,748	N/A	40,920	N/A	37,162	N/A
Foreign-Born Population	919	3.5%	1,545	5.9%	2,461	8.8%	8,961	22.0%	12,023	32.4%
Over 65 Population	648	2.4%	571	2.2%	1,464	5.2%	2,060	5.0%	1,725	4.6%
Non-Hispanic White	26,279	99.9%	24,939	96.3%	24,197	87.2%	30,819	75.3%	25,493	68.6%
Non-Hispanic Black	11	0.0%	125	0.0%	1,032	3.7%	2,051	5.0%	1,713	4.6%
Hispanic or Latino[b]	1,078	4.0%	2,232	8.6%	3,823	13.8%	13,181	32.2%	17,576	47.3%
Average Household Income[c]	$63,580	N/A	$59,127	N/A	$71,399	N/A	$78,786	N/A	$69,163	N/A
Per Capita Income	$15,340	N/A	$17,278	N/A	$22,189	N/A	$26,124	N/A	$21,267	N/A
Poverty	1,226	4.7%	1,681	7%	2,471	8.9%	3,198	7.8%	3,493	9.4%
Owner-occupied housing units	5,231	82.3%	5,231	68.3%	6,338	75.6%	9,945	82.5%	9,062	83.0%
Renter-occupied housing units	1,124	17.7%	1,782	23.3%	2,040	24.3%	2,102	17.4%	1,850	17.0%
Housing units built pre-1970	N/A	N/A	N/A	N/A	N/A	N/A	N/A	N/A	5,991	48.3%
Manufacturing employment	5,223	50.2%	5,900	48.6%	5,584	40.8%	5,552	29.9%	3,984	23.0%
Unemployment	286	2.7%	753	5.8%	910	6.2%	1,003	5.1%	1,381	5.4%

[a] Source: *Decennial U.S. Census of Housing and Population; American Community Survey (ACS) 2005-2009 (Data Release 2010)*. See Appendix 2 for further explanation of the author's calculations of the data.

[b] Hispanic or Latino of any race and ethnicity.

[c] All figures are calculated as 2009 dollars.

Table 3.2. Analysis of Socioeconomic Structure of Farmers Branch, 1970 to 2009[a]

	1970		1980		1990		2000		2009	
	Number	Percent	Number	Percent	Number	Percent	Number	Percent	Number	Percent
Total Population	27,588	N/A	28,723	N/A	28,737	N/A	34,043	N/A	26,177	N/A
Foreign-Born Population	457	1.6%	1,573	5.4%	4,205	14.6%	9,385	27.5%	7,035	26.9%
Over 65 Population	712	2.6%	1,379	4.8%	2,459	8.6%	3,664	10.6%	3,401	12.9%
Non-Hispanic White	27,318	99.0%	26,706	92.9%	23,398	81.4%	25,946	76.2%	14,288	54.2%
Non-Hispanic Black	92	0.0%	386	1.3%	1,481	5.1%	1,584	4.7%	815	3.1%
Hispanic or Latino[b]	1,427	5.2%	2,159	7.5%	5,697	19.8%	12,703	37.3%	12,091	45.8%
Average Household Income[c]	$71,276	N/A	$69,583	N/A	$66,083	N/A	$78,815	N/A	$72,406	N/A
Per Capita Income	$20,178	N/A	$26,725	N/A	$27,574	N/A	$31,312	N/A	$27,258	N/A
Poverty	755	2.7%	1,355	4.8%	2,261	8.0%	2,369	7.0%	2,382	9.1%
Owner-occupied housing units	5,949	78.6%	5,949	54.4%	6,286	56.1%	7,075	55.6%	6,278	66.8%
Renter-occupied housing units	1,622	21.4%	4,549	41.6%	4,829	43.4%	5,614	44.2%	3,121	33.2%
Housing units built pre-1970	N/A	N/A	N/A	N/A	N/A	N/A	N/A	N/A	6,046	61.6%
Manufacturing employment	4,505	38.4%	5,821	33.8%	4,131	25.5%	3,846	21.7%	1,597	12.1%
Unemployment	281	2.3%	389	2.2%	992	5.8%	733	4.0%	1,184	8.2%

[a] Source: Decennial U.S. Census of Housing and Population; American Community Survey (ACS) 2005-2009 (Data Release 2010). See Appendix 2 for further explanation of the author's calculations of the data.

[b] Hispanic or Latino of any race and ethnicity.

[c] All figures are calculated as 2009 dollars.

Table 3.3. Analysis of Socioeconomic Structure of Hazleton, 1970 to 2009[a]

	1970		1980		1990		2000		2009	
	Number	Percent	Number	Percent	Number	Percent	Number	Percent	Number	Percent
Total Population	30,426	N/A	27,318	N/A	24,730	N/A	23,264	N/A	21,853	N/A
Foreign-Born Population	1,188	3.9%	833	3.0%	619	2.5%	857	3.6%	3,256	14.9%
Over 65 Population	4,399	14.5%	5,481	20.0%	5,920	24.0%	5,135	22.0%	4,299	19.7%
Non-Hispanic White	30,388	99.8%	27,113	99.2%	24,264	98.1%	22,058	94.8%	18,251	83.5%
Non-Hispanic Black	16	0.0%	13	0.0%	46	0.0%	194	0.0%	655	3.0%
Hispanic or Latino[b]	42	0.0%	71	0.0%	334	1.3%	1,077	4.6%	5,207	23.8%
Average Household Income[c]	$40,937	N/A	$43,276	N/A	$43,348	N/A	$49,751	N/A	$41,978	N/A
Per Capita Income	$14,332	N/A	$17,351	N/A	$24,730	N/A	$22,195	N/A	$17,937	N/A
Poverty	3,136	10.3%	2,626	10.0%	3,292	13.4%	3,262	14.2%	3,933	18.0%
Owner-occupied housing units	6,143	58.6%	6,549	60.1%	6,379	60.3%	6,045	59.0%	5,547	60.6%
Renter-occupied housing units	4,333	41.3%	4,213	39.1%	4,195	39.7%	4,205	41.0%	3,603	39.3%
Housing units built pre-1970	N/A	N/A	N/A	N/A	N/A	N/A	N/A	N/A	9,939	91.6%
Manufacturing employment	5,572	45.7%	4,135	37.5%	3,353	31.9%	2,641	27.5%	2,195	24.1%
Unemployment	501	3.9%	853	7.2%	678	6.1%	674	6.5%	814	8.2%

[a] Source: *Decennial U.S. Census of Housing and Population; American Community Survey (ACS) 2005-2009 (Data Release 2010).* See Appendix 2 for further explanation of the author's calculations of the data.

[b] Hispanic or Latino of any race and ethnicity.

[c] All figures are calculated as 2009 dollars.

for a 23 percent population loss. Meanwhile, unlike Carpentersville, the city's population was aging in place. Between 1970 and 2009, there was nearly a five-fold increase of the population over the age of 65.

In 1970, Hazleton's population was 30,426, and by 1990, it had declined to 24,730, nearly a 19 percent decrease over two decades. The city's population had peaked and then had declined in every decade since 1970. Yet during the 1990s, the city's population loss was modest. The number of residents shrank by 6 percent to 23,264 in 2000. As of 2009, the population had continued to recede. Overall, during the course of four decades, approximately one-third of the population was lost. Meanwhile, since 1990, like Farmers Branch, the city's population had aged in place. For three decades, nearly a quarter of the population was over the age of 65.

The patterns of foreign-born population growth differed slightly in the three cities, but in all three towns, the foreign-born population increased significantly between 1970 and 2009. In Carpentersville, the foreign-born population grew from 4 percent (1,000) in 1970, to 9 percent in 1990, to 22 percent by 2000, and to 33 percent by 2009. In Farmers Branch, the foreign-born population grew from 2 percent in 1970 (500), to 5 percent in 1980, to 15 percent in 1990, to 25 percent (8,000) in 2009, despite the fact that 2,000 foreign-born residents had left during the previous decade. In Hazleton, the foreign-born population was 4 percent (1,188) in 1970 and declined for 30 years before growing again in the first decade of the century to 15 percent in 2009.

In all three towns, the proportion of foreign-born residents who were not citizens was surprisingly high: 70 percent in Carpentersville, 70 percent in Farmers Branch, and 65 percent in Hazleton, so only slightly more than one-third of the foreign-born population were naturalized citizens. The percentage of foreign-born households in which Spanish was the only language spoken was also high: 44 percent in Carpentersville, 40 percent in Farmers Branch, and 20 percent in Hazleton.

The proportion of non-Hispanic white residents gradually declined in these towns as the foreign-born, primarily Hispanic or Latino, population grew. The black population consistently remained a low proportion of residents in all three towns, so the dramatic foreign-born growth added greatly to racial and ethnic diversity in these communities.

Household Income Dynamics

The household income dynamics tell us about the income level of households, the distribution of household income, and poverty status among residents in Carpentersville, Farmers Branch, and Hazleton.

Carpentersville's mean household income grew slightly throughout the period, from $63,580 in 1970, to $69,163 by 2009, which was a 9 percent increase over four decades.[47] In Farmers Branch, mean household income essentially remained stagnant for four decades, growing a mere 1.5 percent from $71,276 four decades ago to $72,406 in 2009.[48] In working class Hazleton, household income grew from $40,937 in 1970 to $41,978 by 2009, which was a 2.5 percent increase over 40 years.[49] Household income barely kept up with the cost of living.

However, per capita household income was significantly lower than the mean income in all three towns and showed a pattern of growth and decline.[50] In Carpentersville, 1970 per capita income was $15,340, and it increased gradually until peaking at $26,124 in 2000, declining to $21,267 by 2009. In Farmers Branch,[51] 1970 per capita income was $20,178, and it grew gradually until peaking at $31,312 in 2000, declining to $27,258 by 2009. By comparison, per capita household income was significantly lower than the mean income. In Hazleton, 1970 per capita income was $14,332, and it increased gradually until 1990, when it peaked at $24,730, declining to $22,195 by 2000—by 2009, it declined again to $17,937.[52] In all three towns, the large difference in the mean income and per capita income suggests an uneven distribution of income among households, as concentrations of high-income and low-income households illuminate economic disparities among residents.

Regarding the poverty status among residents, the number of residents living in poverty consistently grew during the time period. In 1970, 1,226 residents, or 5 percent, lived in poverty in Carpentersville. Four decades later, nearly 3,500 residents lived in poverty, which was a 185 percent change in the number of residents in poverty. In Farmers Branch, the number and proportion of residents living in poverty has consistently grown since 1970. In fact, it had more than tripled by 2009. In 1970, 755 residents, or 2.5 percent, lived in poverty. Four decades later, 2,382 residents lived in poverty. In 1970 and 1980 in Hazleton, 3,136 residents, or 10 percent, lived in poverty. Four decades later, nearly 4,000 residents lived in poverty, which was a 25 percent change in the number of residents in poverty. Similarly, the proportion of residents living in poverty had increased in all three towns by 2009 to high levels: 10 percent in Carpentersville, 9 percent in Farmers Branch, and 18 percent in Hazleton.

The household income dynamics of Carpentersville, Farmers Branch, and Hazleton improved slightly in the decades following 1970 until the turn of the century, when signs of economic decline and increases in poverty became well apparent.

Nature of the Housing Stock

The nature of the housing stock describes the housing tenure, age, and size of housing development.[53] In 2009, there were 11,472 housing units in Carpentersville. With the exception of the 1980s, the large majority of housing units were owner occupied. In 1970, 82 percent of units, or 5,231 housing units, were owner occupied. By 2009, the proportion remained nearly the same; 83 percent of units, 9,062 housing units, were owner occupied. Whereas the majority of residents were homeowners, a small minority rented housing units. During the 1980s and 1990s, one-quarter of residents rented; otherwise, less than one-fifth of residents rented in the 1970s and in the 2000s and beyond.

The age and size of the village's housing stock was generally quite old and small in the suburban context. In terms of age, in 2009, more than half of all housing units were over half of a century old. Specifically, 54 percent, or 6,226 units, were built prior to 1970. In contrast, 24 percent, or 2,719 units, were built in the 2000s alone. Conversely, approximately one-quarter of the housing stock was built in the 1950s. In terms of size, nearly one-third of housing units had two or fewer bedrooms, and fully 80 percent, or 9,175 housing units, had three or fewer bedrooms.

Figure 3.2 and Figure 3.3 contrast the dramatic differences in the nature of Carpentersville's housing stock. On the one hand, Figure 3.2 shows that new housing units were developed during the 2000s. These large houses are in good structural condition and well kept and maintained. On the other hand, Figure 3.3 shows the state of the older housing units that were constructed at

Figure 3.2.   Photo of new housing stock in Carpentersville.

Figure 3.3.   Photo of old housing stock in Carpentersville.

least a half of a century ago. At best, these small houses are in fair structural condition and well kept. At worst, these houses are in very poor structural condition and lack upkeep or maintenance. Either way, the trend shows that there is a general lack of reinvestment in the housing stock.

In Farmers Branch, there were 7,571 housing units in 1970. The large majority of housing units were owner occupied. In 1970, 78 percent of units, or 5,949 housing units, were owner occupied. By 2009, two trends were apparent. First, there was very little growth in the owner-occupied housing stock. There were approximately 300 units added, suggesting that very little development occurred. Second, the proportion of owner-occupied units shifted dramatically. Four decades later, the proportion declined to two-thirds owner occupied. The housing stock of renter-occupied households doubled during this period, such that just over one-third of housing units (3,121) were renter occupied in 2009.

In the suburban context, housing stock was old and small. Approximately two-thirds of all housing units were over half of a century old. Specifically, 62 percent, or 6,046 units, were built prior to 1970. In contrast, few housing units were constructed recently. Forty percent of the housing stock was built in the 1950s or 1960s. In terms of size, nearly one-third of housing units had two or fewer bedrooms, and nearly 80 percent, or 7,745 housing units, had three or fewer bedrooms. There are stark differences in the nature of Farmers Branch's housing stock. There is some new development of housing units, which offer many of the same amenities found in other new suburban subdivisions. But there is a large stock of older housing units that are a half-century old. In some cases, these small houses are in fair structural condition and maintained. At worst, these houses are in very poor structural condition and lack maintenance. In either case, the trend shows that there is a general lack of reinvestment in the housing stock.

Hazleton's housing stock was composed of 9,150 housing units in 2009. The housing tenure remained consistent over four decades. In 1970, 58.6 percent of units, or 6,143 housing units, were owner occupied. By 2009, the proportion remained nearly the same; 60.6 percent of units, 5,547 housing units, were owner occupied. Similar trends were apparent in the renter-occupied housing units. Approximately 40 percent of housing units were rented from 1970 through 2009.

The city's housing stock was generally quite old and small as compared to the other towns. In 2009, nine out of 10 housing units, approximately 10,000 units, were built prior to 1970. Few units were constructed after 1970, and only 130 units were constructed during the 2000s. Nearly half of the city's housing stock, 5,206 units, was constructed prior to 1939. In terms of size, nearly half of housing units had two or fewer bedrooms, and 83 percent

Figure 3.4.   Photo of aging housing stock in Hazleton.

Figure 3.5. Photo of small housing stock in Hazleton.

had three or fewer bedrooms. Figures 3.4 and 3.5 illustrate the nature of Hazleton's housing stock. In Figure 3.4, the aging condition of the housing is displayed. Figure 3.5 shows the smaller size of the multi-family housing units. While some houses still retain a solid structural condition, others suffer from a decaying condition from a lack of upkeep or maintenance. There is a general lack of housing reinvestment.

This nature of the housing stock in Carpentersville, Farmers Branch, and Hazleton depicts some growth but an overall pattern of decline. Inklings of suburban decline grew increasingly apparent as the quality and supply of the housing stock varied.

Labor Force Structure

The labor force structure defines the industries that employ residents as well as the employment status. The historic legacy of Carpentersville's manufacturing sector is evident in the distribution of jobs. In 1970, over half of all residents held manufacturing jobs. By 2009, less than one-quarter of residents worked in the sector. Nearly 2,000 jobs were lost during this period. Manufacturing employment peaked in 1980, when nearly 6,000 residents held jobs. During this economic transition, growth in other employment sectors, such as services in retail, education, and health, grew markedly. The share of unemployed residents in the labor force was small for four decades. In 1970, less than 3 percent of residents in the labor force were unemployed. In 2009, approximately 5 percent of residents were unemployed.[54]

In Farmers Branch, the distribution of jobs shows that manufacturing employment was historically strong. In 1970, manufacturing employment reached its peak. Forty percent of residents worked in the sector, but by 2009, the manufacturing employment fell to a mere 12 percent. Nearly 3,000 jobs were lost during this period. The economic transition to the service sector, as well as the growth of the Sunbelt, influenced Farmers Branch.[55] The share of unemployed residents in the labor force nearly quadrupled. In 1970, less than 3 percent of residents in the labor were unemployed. In 2009, over 8 percent of residents were unemployed.[56]

Hazleton's legacy as a center of manufacturing activity is evident in the distribution of jobs. In 1970, nearly half of all residents held manufacturing jobs. By 2009, one-quarter of residents worked in the sector. There were 3,377 jobs lost during this period. During this economic transition, growth in the service sector occurred. The share of unemployed residents in the labor force grew incrementally for four decades. In 1970, 4 percent of residents in the labor force were unemployed; yet by 2009, over 8 percent of residents were unemployed.[57]

LEARNING FROM THE PAST ABOUT TODAY

Looking back at the historical development of suburbs opens a window into the social, economic, and political environments that influenced how communities grew. Only from an understanding of how a place grew can we begin to understand the dynamics of decline. In Carpentersville, Farmers Branch, and Hazleton, residents and their neighborhoods were transformed from their historic legacies as small settlements to the suburbs we know today. Undoubtedly, it is evident that these communities are different places than they were after the Second World War as well as the 1970s when the changes slowly began to form. Like so many other aging suburbs, they face a mid-life crisis today. Residents in these communities turned to their politicians to develop policies to respond to these dynamic changes.

At the beginning of the twenty-first century, Carpentersville's population comprised a majority of white, non-Hispanic residents as well as a large minority of Mexican Americans who arrived during the 1970s. In the 2000s, concerns emerged about the "growth of an illegal immigrant population."[58] In 2007, two members of the legislative council introduced an ordinance to eliminate the perceived large illegal immigrant population. The ordinance, dubbed the Illegal Immigration Relief Ordinance, sought to "establish penalties for the employment of unlawful workers and the harboring of illegal aliens in the Village of Carpentersville, and to provide for cooperative enforcement of federal immigration laws by the Village police department."[59]

The national media quickly descended upon Carpentersville as a debate raged over how to deal with the issue of immigration. The suburb was morphed into a microcosm for the national debate over immigration policy. Thousands of residents packed into village hall to attend numerous council meetings to express support or protest the ordinance. Rhetoric about the policy debate evolved into public concerns over issues like neighborhood stability and housing decline, public infrastructure decline, and increased crime. Supporters of the ordinance blamed an illegal immigrant population for these conditions. In contrast, protesters blamed the economy and public disinvestment for these problems. The ordinance was tabled indefinitely, and the policy failed to be adopted.

In 2009, Farmers Branch's population was approximately 27,000 residents, of which over one-third of residents were Hispanic or Latino. The persistent growth of the Hispanic population and the emergence of suburban decline brought on community tensions between white and non-white residents. Prompted by these shifts in the community, City Councilman Tim O'Hare introduced three separate ordinances, and they were passed unanimously into law between 2006 and 2008. First, Ordinance 2892 was a comprehensive local law that sought to prohibit landlords from renting to illegal immigrants; declared English as the city's official language; and authorized local police to collaborate with US Immigrant and Customs Enforcement (ICE) to detain and remove illegal immigrants from the city. A clause to prohibit the employment of illegal immigrants in the city was considered but later rejected. Then, Ordinance 2903 was the result of a direct special election, in which residents voted in favor of the ordinance by a margin of 68 percent. Last, Ordinance 2952 was implemented as a revised version of the previous ordinances to streamline and shift the verification of residency in households from landlords to the city. While legal challenges arose, local policymakers revised ordinances to skirt judicial injunctions on previous ordinances. Subsequently, long-term mayor Bob Phelps's reservations about the ordinances, coupled with threats of violence against his family, led him to retire. Chief sponsor of the ordinances, City Councilman Tim O'Hare, was then elected mayor, giving him a political mandate to take local control of immigration policy.

Today, many Hazleton residents share an identity with greater Philadelphia, and its environment and people are suburban in nature. The population hovers around 25,000. Hazleton's economic base has suffered in the postwar era. In 2000, the city was composed primarily of white residents. Approximately 93 percent of residents were white, non-Hispanic, and 5 percent were Hispanic. However, during the 2000s, there was tremendous growth in the Hispanic population; recent estimates suggest that the city is approximately one-third Hispanic. The arrival of light manufacturing plants, like Cargill Meatpacking Solutions, provided new employment opportunities for the city's Hispanic residents.

In light of these social and economic transformations, the city's new demographic structure, coupled with significant socioeconomic decline, created significant tensions between the historically white population and the newly arrived Hispanic population. These tensions culminated in 2006 when the mayor, Lou Barletta, proposed an ordinance to stop illegal immigration. The mayor estimated that nearly half of the city's Hispanic residents were illegal. The city council passed the Illegal Immigration Relief Act by a four-to-one vote in July 2006. The ordinance sought to put pressure on businesses, landlords, and social services that worked with illegal immigrants. The ordinance would deny licenses to commercial entities that employed illegal immigrants; fine landlords $1,000 for each illegal immigrant in a rental property; and declare English the official language of the city. Upon the passing of the ordinance, the mayor, who wore a bulletproof vest to the signing, commented, "[to] the illegal citizens, I would recommend they leave . . . what you see here tonight, really, is a city that wants to take back what America has given it."[60] The ordinance was challenged, and the judiciary issued a stay that prevented the implementation of the ordinance. The city continues to suffer from socioeconomic decline. In short, tensions persist.

These historical and contemporary analyses frame the circumstances of how the problems emerged among differences in neighborhoods. These results demonstrate the unevenness of growth and decline in the context of suburbia. The inklings of socioeconomic decline were apparent by the end of the twentieth century, and public problems began to emerge in these once idyllic suburbs. These trends certainly support what Lucy and Phillips aptly call the "next urban crisis," and "with their small, outmoded, and deteriorating housing, many post-World War II bedroom suburbs are in urgent need of help."[61] In the end, these dramatic social and economic changes created an environment ripe for political tensions. Ed Yohnka's claim that suburbanites suffered from a "collective amnesia" of the nation's history would become the starting point defining public problems and solutions in the fight for the local control of immigration policy.

NOTES

1. Sophia Tareen, "Immigration Proposals Divide Illinois Village." Associated Press, August 4, 2007.

2. J. A. Carpenter founded the Illinois Iron and Bolt Company in 1864. The company was later purchased by Star Manufacturing to produce agricultural machinery. Star remained in Carpentersville until 1977. See archival papers, Dundee Historical Society, 2009.

3. Larry Plachno, *Sunset Lines: The Story of the Chicago Aurora & Elgin Railroad: 2-History* (Polo, IL: Transportation Trails, 1989): 160-215.

4. See Public Law 84-627, June 29, 1956. See also, Mark H. Rose, *Interstate: Express Highway Politics, 1939-1989, Revised Edition* (Knoxville: University of Tennessee, 1990): 85-94.

5. Downs, *Opening Up the Suburbs*, 1-12.

6. Interstate 90 was funded with a $415 million bond issued by the Illinois State Tollway Commission.

7. Daniel Burnham and Edward Bennett, *Plan of Chicago* (Chicago: Chicago Plan Commission, 1909): 40-42; Carl Smith, *The Plan of Chicago: Daniel Burnham and the Remaking of the American City* (Chicago: University of Chicago Press, 2006): 71-110.

8. Owen D. Gutfreund, *Twentieth-Century Sprawl: Highways and the Reshaping of the American Landscape* (New York: Oxford University Press, 2005): 7-60.

9. Al Chase, "Big Residential Center To Rise In Fox Valley," *Chicago Daily Tribune*, March 1, 1953, A7.

10. Besinger built the Meadowdale International Speedway to commemorate his love of racing. The 3.27-mile track opened on September 13, 1958, and the last race was held on July 8, 1968. Declining infrastructure and safety concerns led to the track's closure. Remnants of intact speedway are located in the Raceway Woods County Forest Preserve in Carpentersville.

11. Subsequent suburban communities were developed in this fashion, most notably Columbia, Maryland. See Ann Forsyth, *Reforming Suburbia: The Planned Communities of Irvine, Columbia, and The Woodlands* (Berkeley: University of California Press, 2005): 107-160.

12. "Small Village Takes the Lead in Home Building," *Chicago Daily Tribune*, June 24, 1956.

13. The Bureau of Labor Statistics began calculating the Consumer Price Index in 1913. For estimates, see *Historical Statistics of the United States to 1970*, Table E135-166, Washington, DC: US Government Printing Office.

14. Richard Longstreth, *The American Department Store Transformed, 1920-1960* (New Haven, CT: Yale University Press, 2010).

15. Joseph M. Siry, *Carson Pirie Scott: Louis Sullivan and the Chicago Department Store* (Chicago: University of Chicago Press, 1988): 3-12.

16. Kelly, *Expanding the American Dream*, 21-34.

17. Chase, "Big Residential Center," A7.

18. The suburbs were largely monolithic developments in terms of race and class from 1950 to 1970. See Louis H. Masotti and Jeffrey K. Hadden, eds., *The Urbanization of the Suburbs: Urban Affairs Annual Review, Vol. 7* (Beverly Hills, CA: Sage Publications, 1973). Of course, there were examples of noted diversity; however, these were exceptions to the general patterns. After 1970, this pattern changed dramatically as the suburbs diversified. See Louis H. Masotti and Jeffrey K. Hadden, eds., *Suburbia in Transition* (New York: New Viewpoints, 1974).

19. William Alonso, *Location and Land Use: Toward a General Theory of Land Rent* (Cambridge, MA: Harvard University Press, 1964).

20. Glenn Altschuler and Stuart Blumin, *The GI Bill: The New Deal for Veterans* (New York: Oxford University Press, 2009): 179-204.

21. Georgia Myers Ogle, *Elm Fork Settlement: Farmers Branch and Carrollton, Commemorative Ed.* (Austin, TX: Eakin Press, 1996).

22. Peters Colony was an area of land in North Texas. It was an empresario grant by the Republic of Texas in 1841. The grant included twenty American and English investors that were led by William S. Peters. See Harry E. Wade, "Peters Colony," *Handbook of Texas Online*, Texas State Historical Association, accessed October 10, 2011, www.tshaonline.org/handbook/online/articles/uep02.

23. The Katy Railroad Historical Society and Museum, Denison, Texas, accessed October 10, 2011, http://katyrailroad.org and http://www.redriverrailmuseum.org. See also Lisa C. Maxwell, "Farmers Branch, TX," *Handbook of Texas Online*, Texas State Historical Association, accessed October 10, 2011, www.tshaonline.org/handbook/online/articles/hef01.

24. Robert A. Rieder, "Electric Interurban Railways," *Handbook of Texas Online*, Texas State Historical Association, accessed October 10, 2011, www.tshaonline.org/handbook/online/articles/eqe12.

25. See Public Law 84-627, June 29, 1956. See also, Mark H. Rose, *Interstate: Express Highway Politics, 1939-1989, Revised Edition* (Knoxville: University of Tennessee, 1990): 85-94.

26. Interstate 35 is a 1,568-mile expressway that begins in Texas and ends in Minnesota. Approximately 504 miles span Texas. See Federal Highway Administration, "Table 1 Main Routes of the Dwight D. Eisenhower National System Of Interstate and Defense Highways," accessed October 10, 2011, www.fhwa.dot.gov/reports/routefinder/table1.htm.

27. Texas Department of Transportation, 1959, "Stemmons Freeway Dallas Brochure." Austin, TX.

28. Ibid.

29. Owen D. Gutfreund, *Twentieth-Century Sprawl: Highways and the Reshaping of the American Landscape* (New York: Oxford University Press, 2005): 7-60.

30. See Table III-3: West Side Development Potential By Land Use, City of Farmers Branch Comprehensive Plan (1989): 17.

31. Walter Robinson, "Farmers Branch's Farming Dwindles," *Dallas Morning News*, July 29, 1950, Section 4, 1.

32. Clarence N. Stone, *Regime Politics: Governing Atlanta, 1946-1988* (Lawrence: University Press of Kansas, 1989): 1-12.

33. Robinson, "Farmers Branch's Farming Dwindles," 1.

34. Real estate classified advertisements, *Dallas Morning News*, November 22, 1959, 23.

35. "Housing development will cost $30,000,000," *Dallas Morning News*, November 14, 1954, 1.

36. The suburbs were largely monolithic developments in terms of race and class from 1950 to 1970. See Herbert J. Gans, *The Levittowners: Ways of Life and Politics in a New Suburban Community* (New York: Pantheon Books, 1967): 153-184.

37. Lynn Landrum, "Farmers Branch Growing." *Dallas Morning News*, November 24, 1958, 4.

38. Ibid.

39. Ibid.

40. Alonso, *Location and Land Use*, 1-17.

41. Altschuler and Blumin, *The GI Bill*, 179-204.

42. Tony Wesolowsky, "A Jewel In the Crown of Old King Coal Eckley Miners' Village," *Pennsylvania Heritage Magazine* 22, no. 1 (1996): 30.

43. John S. Garner, ed., *The Company Town: Architecture and Society in the Early Industrial Age* (New York: Oxford University Press, 1992): 4.

44. Richard W. Funk, *Around Hazleton* (Charleston, SC: Arcadia Publishing, 2005): 10-14.

45. Warner, *Streetcar Suburbs*, 1-14. See also Sam Bass Warner and Andrew H. Whittemore, *American Urban Form* (Cambridge, MA: The MIT Press, 2012).

46. Other recent studies have employed similar techniques to examine patterns of suburban decline. See Bernadette Hanlon, "The Decline of Older, Inner Suburbs in Metropolitan America," *Housing Policy Debate* 19, no. 3 (2008): 423-455. This analysis utilizes census place-level and tract-level from 1970 to 2000 as well as the American Community Survey, 2005-2009. See Appendix 2.

47. Mean household income is reported in 2009 constant dollars.

48. Ibid.

49. Ibid.

50. Per capita household income is reported in 2009 constant dollars.

51. Ibid.

52. Ibid.

53. The ACS 2005-2009 data are discussed. As the most current data available, they report the most accurate portrait of today's housing stock.

54. It should be noted that since ACS data represent a rolling average over five years, the employment data do not fully account for the recession of 2008. See William H. Lucy, *Foreclosing the Dream: How America's Housing Crisis Is Reshaping Our Cities and Suburbs* (Chicago: APA Planners Press, 2010): 1-30.

55. Carl Abbott, *The New Urban America: Growth and Politics in the Sunbelt Cities, Revised Edition* (Chapel Hill: University of North Carolina Press, 1987): 36-59.

56. It should be noted that since ACS data represent a rolling average over five years, the employment data do not fully account for the recession of 2008. See Lucy, *Foreclosing the Dream*, 1-30.

57. Ibid.

58. Alex Kotlowitz, "Our Town," *The New York Times*, August 5, 2007.

59. Village of Carpentersville *Illegal Immigration Relief Ordinance* was proposed on September 26, 2006, and tabled July 4, 2007, by the President of the Village Board of Trustees.

60. Associated Press, "Pennsylvania City Passes Anti-Illegal Immigrants Law," July 13, 2006.

61. Lucy and Phillips, "Suburban Decline," 55-62.

Chapter Four

Inklings of a Public Problem

Among these symbols of American nationality are holding middle class values and tastes, being law-abiding, and being patriotic. Immigrant "others" are viewed as the lawbreaking underclass who are disloyal to this country.[1]

—*Caroline B. Brettell and Faith G. Nibbs*

In the early 2000s, tensions among residents of Carpentersville, Farmers Branch, and Hazleton were quite palpable. At first glance, these tensions appeared to be related to many different issues—the provision of public services, population diversity, the arrival of new immigrants, housing stock decline, aging infrastructure, crime, and low-quality public services. However, upon further examination, they evolved as the policy debate developed over the local issue of illegal immigration. Emotions grew strong as socioeconomic conditions declined. Dissatisfied with the current state of affairs in their towns, residents set out to define the public nature of these problems. By the mid-2000s, residents and policymakers were ready to design public policy responses to the public nature of the problems in their communities.

According to Brettell and Nibbs, the problem identification and subsequent policy responses are, in part, the result of a threat to middle-class living that immigrants present to suburbanites.[2] As early as the 1900s, the historic nature of suburbia's isolation from the urban condition, such as poverty, minority populations, crime, and infrastructure decay, meant that residents on the metropolitan fringe were monolithic in terms of race and class.[3] From the 1970s onward, as the suburbs grew, so did the diversity of residents. In the midst of this suburban transformation, some communities embraced this diversification but many did not.[4] By the end of the twentieth century, residents of Carpentersville, Farmers Branch, and Hazleton faced the challenge of coping with such changes. Immigrants presented economic threats, safety threats, and social threats. They challenged the suburban way of life. Residents were apprehensive and turned to their local politicians to halt these threats and confront what they viewed as public problems. As Baldassare argued, "Trouble in paradise" arrived.[5]

Guiding the following discussion, Tables 4.1, 4.2, and 4.3 show a matrix of the problem streams. We can draw on policy theory to examine how such problems were defined through an analysis of the streams of definitions, solutions, and politics. Let us now consider the evolution of the problems in the fight for local control of immigration policy.

IMMIGRANTS

The arrival of new immigrants in Carpentersville presented problems for its residents. The magnitude of the number of new immigrants was unsettling for many residents, especially because these residents perceived the new immigrants as illegal. One village trustee declared, "There is a ghost population of 10,000 people in this village."[6] In the fall of 2006, Trustee Judy Sigwalt

Table 4.1.   Problem Stream Matrix in Carpentersville

Problem Theme	Problem Statements	Problem Attributes
Immigration	"There is a ghost population of 10,000 people in this village." "This is a crisis, enough is enough."	Crisis
Public services	"This is unfair to our residents, to be forced to shoulder the burden of scofflaws."	Undeserving population
Housing	"There are too many overcrowded, dilapidated, and vacant houses in Carpentersville."	Severity and incidence
Crime	"Gangs in Chicago have been expanding out of the city limits over the past decade. Chicagoland suburbs have seen a dramatic rise in gang activity."	Causal stories and incidence
Flags	"Once here legally, immigrants should strive to Americanize themselves. Not fly their homeland's flag."	Symbols
Suburban decline	"Carpentersville is old, falling apart, and getting poorer."	Proximity
No problem	"There is no problem."	Do nothing

Table 4.2. Problem Stream Matrix in Farmers Branch

Problem Theme	Problem Statements	Problem Attributes
Immigration	"Illegal immigrants are destroying our community."	Crisis
Housing	"A single-family home is for a single family, not a hotel for six or seven individuals."	Severity and incidence
Crime	"Drive-up shootings aren't supposed to happen in the suburbs."	Causal stories and incidence
Suburban decline	"We need more than a facelift."	Proximity
No problem	"There is no problem."	Do nothing

argued that the "ghost population" represented all of the illegal residents living in Carpentersville. She estimated that over one-quarter of the village's residents were illegal. In one small phrase, Carpentersville had *too many* illegal immigrants.

Vivid descriptions and characterizations of the "problem population" shaped how public problems were defined. Both Trustees Sigwalt and Humpfer defined and ultimately championed the problem as a crisis. Armed with political crisis rhetoric, instead of evidence and data, the problem was publically defined in terms of scale and proportion. At events around the village, from community centers to village board meetings, they exclaimed, "Enough is enough." Similarly, they employed ultimatums to define the risks of *not* acting on the village's crisis. Humpfer regularly spoke about his fear: "If we do not pass this law . . . Carpentersville will [become] a sanctuary city. Illegal aliens will flood our town."[7] In essence, the sheer scale of the problem defined the public imperative to act.

Table 4.3. Problem Stream Matrix in Hazleton

Problem Theme	Problem Statements	Problem Attributes
Immigration	"There are too many illegal aliens in the City of Hazleton."	Severity and incidence
Public services	"Any money and resources being spent on illegals is being spent in the wrong place."	Fairness and equity
Crime	"When you have violent crimes committed, it takes away and chews at our quality of life."	Causal stories and incidence
Suburban decline	"Hazleton is an old city that's falling apart."	Proximity
No problem	"There is no problem."	Do nothing

In suburban Farmers Branch, many immigrants had settled in the previous two decades. By the end of the first decade of the 2000s, nearly half of the population was Hispanic or Latino, and about one-third was foreign born. This was a dramatic departure from the demographic structure of the sleepy, white, middle-class suburb of Farmers Branch prior to this period. This social transformation troubled many residents since the magnitude of the change was so marked. Long-time residents branded the new immigrants as illegal residents. A simple problem definition was developed: *too many illegal immigrants resided in Farmers Branch*. This definition emerged as the crux in the public discourse about the issue.

Suburbanites also identified immigrants' use of a foreign language—namely Spanish—as a problem in their community. They blamed the problem on the growth of an illegal immigrant population. One resident asserted, "I grew up there and it saddens me to see what it [Farmers Branch] has become. I am tired of hearing Spanish in the streets and trying to figure out if someone understands what I'm saying."[8] Another resident reflected that, "I can still remember going to high school with Hispanic kids, but back then, they were more like us . . . not like today's foolish kids."[9] Indeed, immigrants were portrayed as the population that created the city's problems. Residents and policymakers made poignant characterizations about how nearly all the immigrants in the city were illegal. The mayor's definition, for example, further refined the scope of the problem. Mayor Tim O'Hare held, ". . . You can't find a city anywhere in the country where 60 percent of its population is comprised of people who are in the country illegally and the city to be a thriving, dynamic, growing, and economically viable city."[10] In other words, illegal immigrants inhibit suburban growth. According to residents, such public dialogue persuasively made the case to promote growth by confronting the problem of illegal immigration. The scale of the problem was all-encompassing; it served as a call for public action.

In Hazleton, some 5,000 Latinos had arrived by the end of 2009, and approximately 15 percent of residents were immigrants. A dramatic change in the demographic structure of the city had occurred. Formerly, Hazleton was nearly an exclusively white, working-class city. The quick population change worried many residents. They labeled the city's new population as illegal residents. Longtime residents of Hazleton felt that too many immigrants—many illegal—had moved into their city. The public discourse became focused on this problem definition.

In Hazleton, as in Farmers Branch, the proliferation of Spanish was emblematic of the larger problem of the growth of the residency of illegal immigrants. Spanish-speaking residents were keenly aware of the stereotype of Latinos as illegal immigrants. One resident remarked, "We're all guilty by association if we speak Spanish."[11] Witold Walczak, an attorney for the ACLU, echoed these sentiments. He said, "Those with brown skin and thick accents are coming under suspicion, even if they're citizens. The overwhelming feeling I find in Hazleton is sadness."[12] Latinos who spoke Spanish were cast as the root of the city's problems. Residents and policymakers characterized the importance of learning the English language. The mayor's arguments reflected this importance. Barletta argued, "We're sending the wrong message in America. We are not helping immigrants by making it easier *not* to learn the English language . . . My grandparents came from Italy. Do you think they would have learned English if they were able to get by speaking Italian? . . . This is *our* country and English is *our* language."[13] This public dialogue persuasively made the case to residents that the problem of illegal immigration was related to language.

Public Services

In Carpentersville and Farmers Branch, public services became a big issue. A public problem can be identified by assigning causation or blame to a particular population. Labeling a population as undeserving is one method of blaming a group of residents that share a set of common characteristics, such as skin color or foreign-born status. In Carpentersville, Trustees Humpfer and Sigwalt were deeply troubled because of the financial issues associated with providing public services to a population that they characterized as not paying taxes. They immediately identified these residents as the problem population. Illegal immigrants represented an increased *public* burden for the village. That public burden needed to be addressed with a public policy. A burden such as this, they argued, made illegal immigrants dependent on a local government to provide basic welfare services.[14] Thus, policy alternatives can be accordingly proposed and defended as a rational response to the problem.[15]

In a series of well-publicized appearances, Trustee Paul Humpfer complained about the burden that illegal immigrants posed to the village, regarding the level, quality, and cost of public services. He said that schools were so overcrowded that it costs the village over $7,700 to educate each student. Humpfer said that if a mere 1,300 students were illegal immigrants, the village would take on an additional $10 million in education expenses. Plus, Humpfer complained that local hospitals were busting with people seeking basic health care. He regularly cited that "$372,000 was written off the village's coffers because collection agencies could not find *these people* [emphasis added]."[16] For Humpfer and his supporters, "these people" were a burden to the village and did not deserve the public services that other residents enjoyed.

Indeed, residents responded to the trustee's comments. "I was raised in Carpentersville. My old neighborhood is now at least half Mexican. . . . The issue is that rooms are rented out and then too many people are then living in too small of a space. The landlord does not pay taxes on these tenants while costs are driven up in the schools and the extra load on [Carpentersville]."[17] Humpfer and other supporters argued that illegal immigrants did not deserve public services like schools and hospitals because they broke the law and did not pay taxes. It was unfair to other residents that paid taxes. Only law-abiding citizens deserved such public services. He summed it up: "This is unfair to our residents, to be forced to shoulder the burden of scofflaws."[18]

In Farmers Branch, the quality of public services, such as police protection, trash collection, schools, and hospitals had diminished as demands had increased. As in Carpentersville, the political actors argued that the new population of immigrants placed more frequent demands on these services to deal with increasingly more severe problems. On the other hand, advocates argued that new immigrants revitalized a decayed downtown with locally owned shops and restaurants. The public discourse on public services reflected the scope of the problem.

During the 2000s, problems with Farmers Branch's public services grew more frequent and severe in nature, leading to the definition and framing of a public problem. Mayor Lou Barletta led the charge to define the problems with the city's services. In a simple problem statement, he said, "Illegal aliens are destroying our city."[19] He argued that an unfair burden was placed on the city's residents, since illegal immigrants did not pay taxes but utilized the police force, schools, and the local hospital. Mayor Barletta said, "I'm not denying that other people commit crimes, but in a small city, any money and resources being spent on illegals is being spent in the wrong place."[20] Problems were also related to the public school system. Barletta claimed that classroom instruction costs related to the provision of English as a Second Language grew from $500 in 2000 to over $1 million in 2007.[21] Residents also complained about overcrowding at Hazleton General Hospital, the city's only facility. Barletta's sentiment on the fairness and deservingness of public services captured residents' feelings on the issue. He said, "Our budget is for people who pay their taxes . . . the illegals are not paying their taxes, their fair share."[22] These types of complaints about public services occurred frequently, and angry residents and politicians argued that such problems had grown too severe to ignore any longer.

Housing

Carpentersville and Farmers Branch shared another issue regarding housing, such as overcrowding, lack of upkeep, and vacant units. These were defined as severe and frequent problems in the towns. Clear statements about the problem framed the issue: "There are too many overcrowded and vacant houses in Carpentersville," and "There are too many dilapidated houses in Carpentersville."[23]

The public discourse on housing defined this problem. Trustee Humpfer's graphic comment, "Some homes are so overcrowded, people are living in garages," captured the attention of many residents.[24] Similarly, Trustee Sigwalt echoed a frequent sentiment that "too many illegals don't take care of their homes."[25] One resident observed, "Every day I see illegals that urinate in their front lawns. It's disgusting."[26] Another resident complained, "I'm tired of seeing homes with tall grass and broken windows."[27] Last, the increase in vacant units and foreclosures served to exacerbate the severity. Foreclosures dramatically increased over the previous decade from approximately 200 units annually to nearly 1,000 units annually.[28]

Public statements in Farmers Branch about housing problems were also framed unequivocally, and they reflected the scope of the problem. Problems related to the physical decay of housing units, which plagued many neighborhoods throughout the city. Scattered trash, loud noises at night, lack of parking, overcrowding, and lack of maintenance were among the chief complaints. Residents also worried about the value of their homes. One resident exclaimed, "When you paint your house some fluorescent or garish color scheme, you negatively affect my home value."[29] Overcrowding of housing units, too, was a common complaint. "A single-family home is for a single family, not a hotel for six or seven individuals."[30] The rise of vacant units and foreclosures aggravated the severe nature of the housing problem. Foreclosures increased annually during the 2000s. Such types of complaints occurred frequently, and angry residents argued that such problems had grown too severe to ignore any longer. The frequency and severity of problems with the housing stock in Carpentersville and Farmers Branch permitted political actors and residents to frame the issue as a public problem.

Crime

Stories are powerful and can have lasting effects as they shape the policy agenda.[31] Telling stories illuminates the dimensions of a problem, and they also focus attention toward the need for a policy intervention by the public nature of a problem and its impacts.[32] Stories told about the criminal activities of illegal immigrants in Carpentersville, Farmers Branch, and Hazleton defined the public nature of the problem.

In the early 2000s, a series of widely reported crimes focused residents' attention on the problem of crimes that illegal immigrants committed in Carpentersville. The stories abound. A drunk driver rear-ended a car into a minivan, which killed a mother of three. A resident was struck and killed in a crosswalk by an illegal immigrant who fled the scene of the crime. The owner of a local diner and his family were kidnapped and held at gunpoint for ransom. Stories that politicians, the press, and others told worried residents and raised concerns about the development of a public problem.

Moreover, stories about organized gang activity in Carpentersville frightened many residents and further focused attention to the issue. Village residents first became aware of gangs when numerous properties were defaced with graffiti among competing gangs. The issue persisted.[33] Graffiti was spread across the village by local rivaling gangs, which began "taking a toll in Carpentersville and on its residents."[34] Then, residents were shocked to learn about coordinated raids by village police, Illinois state police, and the FBI. The Latin Kings gang allegedly had been recruiting illegal immigrants and dealing cocaine in Carpentersville.[35] For many residents, the memory of a Carpentersville as a safe place had faded, and it was replaced by stories about crime and illegal immigrants. These crimes, committed within a short time span, caused many residents to focus their attention and define a public problem.

Numerous acts of crime and violent activities shaped the public discourse about issues facing Farmers Branch. Residents began to worry about violent crime after learning about the shooting and killing of a police officer in Houston. Juan Leonardo Quintero shot and killed Officer Rodney Johnson when he was arrested after a routine traffic stop. Quintero was an illegal immigrant. In a nationally televised interview, Houston's Police Chief Harold Hurtt indicted the federal government's failure of protecting the nation's borders. Hurtt asserted, "The subject [Quintero] was deported [in 2004], and yet he came back, so if the government fulfilled their responsibility of protecting the border we would probably not be standing here today."[36] Politicians, the press, and concerned residents reiterated this story that told similar accounts of other events to make the case for a public problem. Residents yearned for the era when their city was a safe, quiet suburb of Dallas.

In Hazleton, a rapid increase in criminal activity shaped the public discourse about crime, and several high-profile crimes drew attention to the problem. Mayor Lou Barletta and other political actors called for a policy intervention to address a problem. In particular, several key events triggered the definition of crime as a public problem. In 2002, a coordinated drug raid with federal authorities and local police in Hazleton indicted 20 individuals for trafficking narcotics. For the city's residents, this event shed light on the issue of gang violence and the drug trade. For years, members of two rival gangs transported a variety of drugs from the Dominican Republic to New York to Hazleton. Dubbed Operation Coal Cracker, the police raid seized 500 grams of crack cocaine and 16,000 tablets of Ecstasy, which were valued at $50,000 and $400,000, respectively. US Attorney Thomas A. Marino said, "That's a lot of drugs taken off the street. I am convinced we saved a lot of lives."[37] Similarly, Ed Harry, Hazleton Police chief noted, "None of them [suspects] were homegrown."[38] City officials were quick to assert that illegal immigrants were responsible for these crimes.

Other violent crime events focused public attention to the problem, too. In 2006, two men shot and killed 29-year-old Derek Kichline on a suburban street in Hazleton, Pennsylvania. He was shot at point-blank range in between his eyes; there was no motive. The defendants were illegal immigrants, and all charges were dropped about a year later. At the same time, a 14-year-old illegal immigrant fired numerous rounds from a gun into a crowded playground. Mayor Barletta defined illegal immigration as a public problem after the killings of Hazleton residents. "If others had done their jobs by keeping this murderous thug and his cohorts out of the country, out of Hazleton, Derek Kichline may still be alive today. It makes me angry," Barletta said. "It really does. It makes me hurt, disappointed, and I can only imagine how it makes the Kichlines feel."[39]

Residents began to notice that as the demographic composition of Hazleton changed over the previous decade, the dynamics of crime shifted notably. They perceived that crime was more intense and frequent; the arrival of new immigrants was often associated with the change in the nature of crime. Hazleton's most violent and visible offences were largely committed by Latinos, which fueled resentment among native residents and immigrants. Resident Mary Ann Feno said, "In this area, people need to blame someone."[40] Another resident said that her family left Hazleton for another suburb because "Hazleton has turned into a Little Harlem."[41]

Indeed, the drug raid, murders, and other violent crimes reinforced these perceptions. Robert Ferdinand, Hazleton's Chief of Police, observed that there was "a certain cold-bloodedness to it [crime] that we had never seen before."[42] Mayor Barletta agreed and said, "When you have violent crimes committed, it takes away and chews at our quality of life. I don't need numbers . . . the people in my city don't need numbers." Politicians, the press, and concerned residents reiterated these stories that told similar accounts of other events to make the case for a public problem. Longtime Hazletonians remembered their city as a safe place to raise a family. As stories emerged about violent crime that illegal immigrants had committed, ensuring public safety became a policy issue that joined the political agenda. For the native residents of Carpentersville, Farmers Branch, and Hazleton, too many illegal immigrants committed crime. For policymakers, controlling the illegal immigrant population was the answer.

Flags

Symbols define public problems as well. They provide powerful messages and convey meaning in policy debates. Symbolic politics "rais[e] public concerns about an issue, then offe[r] an apparently effective policy response that assuages public concerns."[43] As Figure 4.1 shows, flags were prominently displayed in Carpentersville's neighborhoods during the time of the policy debate.

Flags—both American and other nations' flags—emerged as dividing lines in the debate over immigration policy. To show support for the IIRO policy proposal, residents flew the American flag on their houses or yards. To show opposition to the IIRO policy proposal, residents flew the Mexican flag. A few residents flew both flags. According to these residents, they wanted to show their legacy of legal immigration and assimilation in the United States while honoring their past at the same time.[44]

The flags came to symbolize many things. The American flag symbolized freedom, security, patriotism, and ultimately the American Dream. Residents said that it demonstrated the struggles of their previous relatives who immigrated to the United States, worked hard, learned English, and sustained a middle-class living. Similarly, the Mexican flag symbolized the large presence of Mexicans in Carpentersville and their path toward the American Dream as well.

Figure 4.1.   Photo of US flag in a Carpentersville neighborhood.

However, the display of national flags presented problems for the residents. Trustee Sigwalt, an ardent supporter of the symbol of the American flag, regularly asked residents, "Are you tired of seeing the Mexican Flag flown above our flag?" She told *The New York Times*, "You have Americans giving up on their own country." Sigwalt often times carried photographs with her that showed the desecration of the American flag. Carpentersville's changes forced her neighbors out of town, and their household junk was thrown to the curb, which included a flag—"a symbol of surrender."[45] A Carpentersville resident's comments best sums up the symbolic nature of the flag, "Once here legally, immigrants should strive to Americanize themselves. Not fly their homeland's flag. They left that third world cesspool. Time to forget it."[46]

Suburban Decline

The analysis of census data demonstrates that Carpentersville, Farmers Branch, and Hazleton had transformed from suburbs of growth to suburbs in decline. In the three most recent decades, there was a slow and steady loss of jobs. Employers and employment opportunities in the areas all but disappeared, and incomes declined. Infrastructure and housing was old and not maintained. Such trends are symptoms of the structural decline of places.

In Carpentersville, roads had not been paved for 50 years. Elementary and secondary school buildings had not been renovated since the boom of the first suburban generation. Sewer and storm water drains were cracked to a point beyond repair. Parks lacked basic upkeep.

Farmers Branch's public infrastructure was also old and required maintenance. Roads, sewers, storm water drains, and schools lacked upkeep, and they had not been renovated since the city's initial boom in the 1950s. The new infrastructure that many early residents of Farmers Branch took for granted was now located in the outer suburbs. Communities like Farmers Branch were left behind in the quest for public investment in suburbs.

The story in Hazleton was the same; its heyday was long gone. The city's physical landscape and socioeconomic status of its residents had declined since the 1940s. Roads, sewers, storm water drains, and schools required renovation—many lacked any reinvestment since the city's boom ended in the 1940s. Communities like Hazleton were left behind, as public investment for development moved into the metropolitan fringe.

Older, bedroom suburbs across the United States experienced similar patterns of decline. A recent report from the Brookings Institution confirms these trends.[47] One-fifth of the nation's residents live in declining suburbs, in counties such as Kane, Dallas, and Luzerne. Once home to a growing population, flourishing economies, and well-maintained neighborhoods, these suburbs now suffer from decay like their central city counterparts.

While questions abound surrounding the causes of suburban decline, there is little doubt that suburban communities face substantial social and economic challenges. The dramatic growth of today's older suburbs has shifted outward to outer-ring suburbs and exurbs. The decentralization of growth and the population movement toward the metropolitan fringe became influential factors in the socioeconomic decline of suburbs.

By the turn of the twenty-first century, the problem of suburban decline was widespread. Throughout the Midwest and Rustbelt, older and smaller cities and suburbs became victims of their own early growth for two reasons.[48] The deindustrialization of the Rustbelt drained cities of millions of middle-class jobs that led to lower wages.[49] The movement outward to newer suburbs drained these places of residents and commercial activity.[50] The migration of people and jobs to the Sunbelt vacuumed the remaining strength and vitality of these places.[51]

Despite strong evidence of the phenomenon of suburban decline, policymakers did not view the set of problems as issues related to a structural and spatial process of the socioeconomic decline of a suburban community. Rather, these problems were framed jointly as problems of illegal immigration. Strong support for public intervention allowed for the establishment of a political agenda. A window of opportunity then opened for local legislative action. In the end, local policymakers designed several solutions to confront these problems, and ultimately they adopted IIROs. Regan Cooper, the executive director of the Pennsylvania Immigration and Citizenship Coalition aptly summed it up: "There is one thing we all agree on. Our immigration system is badly broken."[52]

For Carpentersville, Farmers Branch, and Hazleton, the native residents and immigrants alike worried about these patterns of decline. The residents saw the problem as a "proximate" problem, which was localized at the municipal level.[53] They sought answers to their problems and turned toward local government for solutions.

In the fall of 2006, Paul Humpfer and Judy Sigwalt, trustees of the Village of Carpentersville, introduced the Illegal Immigrant Reform Act (IIRO) to confront what they believed to be the problem: the growth of illegal immigrants in their village. In addition to the violence and gang activity, Humpfer and Sigwalt raised other issues associated with the growth of immigrants in the village. In fact, they capitalized on the national dissatisfaction with the lack of comprehensive immigration reform to raise these concerns. Among them, Humpfer and Sigwalt argued that immigration problems included the overcrowding of housing, the lack of English speakers, the display of the Mexican flag, the lack of jobs, and the loss of community investment. Humpfer explained, "I don't like that it turns into that I'm somehow against Hispan-ics. . . . I want to deal with the crime and the overcrowding in our town. And we're doing anything we can to influence the outcome nationally."[54]

In the summer and fall of 2006, some 1,000 miles south of Carpentersville, politicians and residents of Farmers Branch debated the merits of an IIRO for their city. Approximately one-third of the city's residents were Hispanic or Latino when the debate erupted over the proposal to adopt local immigration policies. Former City Councilman Tim O'Hare led the fight to take local con-trol of Farmers Branch. He argued that illegal immigrants had taken over his city. O'Hare supported a comprehensive ordinance with the following mea-sures: declare English the official language; authorize local police to enforce federal immigration laws; prohibit the employment of illegal immigrants; and prohibit landlords from renting to illegal immigrants. On November 13, 2006, the city council passed and later amended several ordinances to implement an IIRO. The employment ordinance was not passed; however, all other ele-ments of the IIRO were passed. Months later, the residents of Farmers Branch voted for the IIRO by referendum. It passed by over a two-to-one margin.

In the subsequent mayoral election, O'Hare was swept into office as he campaigned largely on the successful vote, adoption, and implementation of the city's IIRO. As O'Hare noted, he would do "what's right" for Farmers Branch. In this context, the residents and politicians alike agreed that the IIRO preserves local values and protects residents from immigrants. This case demonstrates the legislative success of the IIRO proposal. Overwhelm-ing agreement on the definitions of the public problem of immigration facili-tated this success. While the housing ordinance of the IIRO was temporar-ily stayed until further judicial review, the remaining elements of Farmers Branch's IIRO remained intact and popular.

Moving east to the heart of the Rustbelt, the City Council of Hazleton passed a comprehensive IIRA on July 13, 2006. For Mayor Lou Barletta, Kichline's murder inspired him to champion the ordinance. On the city's crime, he said that "the killing marked the beginning of a crime spree, much of it by people who should not have been in Hazleton to begin with. . . . Let's understand there are people around the world that want to hurt us."[55] Bar-letta's concerns also grew beyond crime. He argued that illegal immigrants contribute to overcrowded classrooms and failing schools, create fiscal hard-ships on hospitals and other public services, and destroy neighborhoods and quality of life. Political and community support for the IIRO was strong and passed without much conflict.

These are the stories of three communities and their fight for local control of immigration policy. In the cases of Carpentersville, Farmers Branch, and Hazleton, the policy entrepreneurs believed that their communities were at risk of becoming havens—or sanctuaries—for illegal immigrants. These communities had reached crossroads. They were faced with the realities of demographic change and socioeconomic decline. Political decisions and public policies were crafted in response to these changes. The adoption and implementation of IIROs were attempts by these communities to reject the growth of an immigrant population and the decline of a native, white population, and at the same time, they failed to accept the declining socioeconomic status of their residents. In short, this debate is about whether communities embrace or reject these realities. The fate of these communities, then, rests in the reconciliation of democratic values and the diversity of people and the economy.

The case of Carpentersville centers on the political tensions and policy debates as a consequence of the growth of immigration. This is the story of how one suburb confronted its large-scale demographic changes in a short two-year period: 2006 to 2008. During the 2000s, Carpentersville residents Judy Sigwalt and Paul Humpfer grew increasingly concerned about the decline in the quality of neighborhoods, and the widely held perception that illegal immigration was rampant. They were elected to the village's board of trustees as the "All American Team," after nearly 2,000 households received a flier that read, in part:

> Are you tired of waiting to pay for your groceries while Illegal Aliens pay with food stamps and then go outside and get in a $40,000 car? Are you tired of paying taxes when Illegal Aliens pay NONE! Are you tired of reading that another Illegal Alien was arrested for drug dealing? Are you tired of having to punch 1 for English? Are you tired of seeing multiple families in our homes? Are you tired of not being able to use Carpenter Park on the weekend, because it is over run by Illegal Aliens? Are you tired of seeing the Mexican Flag flown above our Flag? If so, vote for the All American Team![56]

Indeed, their message resonated with many residents of Carpentersville. Frustrated residents concerned about the quality of their neighborhoods elected the "All American Team" to the board of trustees.[57] The team subsequently had widespread political support to improve the quality of life in Carpentersville. Sigwalt and Humpfer were soon confronted with the question of how to accomplish their platform issue. Their answer was to craft legislation to limit illegal immigration.

Armed with a political mandate, Sigwalt and Humpfer set out to tackle the village's problems concerning the issue of immigration. In 2006, the two trustees together introduced the Illegal Immigration Relief Ordinance (IIRO). The ordinance, modeled on the City of Hazleton, Pennsylvania's ordinance, would *locally* regulate businesses, landlords, and police enforcement to curb the presence of illegal immigrants in the village. As one of the first—and harshest—local legislative proposals put forth by a local jurisdiction, the nation looked upon the case of Carpentersville with great interest and intrigue.

The case of Farmers Branch focuses on these very tensions. Political and policy debates ensued over the local regulation of immigration. This case chronicles the experience of how an aging suburb confronted the issue of demographic change and socioeconomic decline. In the fall of 2006, City Councilman Tim O'Hare led the fight to resolve these tensions. O'Hare was increasingly concerned about the decline of Farmers Branch in the 2000s. He regularly argued that "the city's older neighborhoods face not only the problem of poorly maintained properties, but also a rising crime rate, declines in property values or growth in valuations less than the rate of inflation, and lowered performance of local schools as the influx of non-English speaking students continues."[58] O'Hare often spoke of his "duty to protect" Farmers Branch, and immigration policy became a core issue for him.

With growing political support, O'Hare explained that ". . . the citizens of Farmers Branch . . . are concerned, worried, upset, frustrated and downright mad that President Bush and the Executive Branch of the United States government has and is totally failing in the enforcement of the Immigration Act as it relates to the influx of illegal aliens."[59] This message resonated with the majority of residents in Farmers Branch. It served as a call to action for O'Hare and the city council.

The policy evolved between 2006 and 2008 from an iterative process of three designs. The original policy design was presented as Ordinance 2892, and it was unanimously adopted on November 13, 2006, during a city council meeting. The ordinance mandated that any potential tenant submit proof of citizenship or residency *before* renting an apartment within the city limits. This ordinance was passed jointly with Resolution 2006-130 and a related motion. Resolution 130 declared English as the official language of the city, and a motion was also passed that directed the city to pursue participation in the federal 287(g) program to expand local policing powers over the apprehension of illegal immigrants.

Next, on January 11, 2007, US District Court Judge Bruce Priddy issued a temporary restraining order to delay the enforcement of Ordinance 2892. The city council accordingly repealed Ordinance 2892 and adopted a revised version named Ordinance 2903. This ordinance remained largely the same as 2892; however, it called for a referendum vote on May 12, 2007. It passed with 68 percent of residents supporting the ordinance; yet 10 days later, a temporary restraining order was issued to halt the implementation of Ordinance 2903. Finally, on August 29, 2008, US District Court Judge Sam Lindsay issued a final judgment, which permanently stopped the ordinance's enforcement.

Then, rather than appeal Ordinance 2903, the city council adopted Ordinance 2952 as the third version of the city's IIRO. This third ordinance was revised to address the US District Court's legal concerns. Largely based on Ordinance 2903, the third ordinance was designed to shift the burden of verification of legal status of tenants from the landlord to the city. Farmers Branch would issue licenses to tenants to demonstrate legal residency in the United States. The new ordinance was also expanded to include any type of property rented, including not only apartment or multi-family units but also single-family rental units. Ordinance 2952 remains an adopted law that awaits implementation.

While the fight for local control of immigration policy in Farmers Branch still persists some six years later in federal courts, the local debate consisted of: (1) a political fight over the politics of problem definition, (2) a policy debate over the public responses and solutions, and (3) a public discourse about how to provide residents "relief" from illegal immigrants.

The case of Hazleton deals with these social, economic, and political tensions. In 2006, Mayor Lou Barletta decided to act after a spree of high-profile crimes. A 14-year-old was arrested for shooting a gun in a crowded playground. Crack cocaine was sold in playgrounds and near schools. Then, Derek Kichline was murdered in front of his house. Illegal immigrants committed these crimes. Barletta's reaction was somber. He remarked, "I had lost control of our city, and I knew then that we couldn't control what was happening."[60] These crimes were triggering events. They focused the public's attention to a problem, and political actors dedicated themselves to setting the political agenda. The problem was illegal immigration, and the solution was to take control of local immigration policy.

Mayor Barletta argued that the crimes might not have occurred had national immigration policy been effective. In other words, the failure to regulate national borders resulted in the migration of criminals to the United States. Barletta regularly argued that he had a duty to protect his city. He said, "I took an oath of office to protect the people here in the city of Hazleton, and that's just what I'm doing. I'm not going to wait and sit back and wait for somebody else to do it for us. We're going to take action and we'll let the cards fall where they may."[61] Indeed, Barletta and the Hazleton City Council took action. Drawing on the experience of San Bernardino, California, Barletta discovered a policy proposal that could locally regulate illegal immigration. The proposal was largely a function of an organization named Save Our State. Founded by Jim Turner, the nationalist group lobbied for an IIRO that would "ward off the threat from inferior cultures who would turn ours into a third world cesspool."[62] The Hazleton proposal was primarily based on an IIRO that had failed to be adopted by the San Bernardino City Council.

In 2006, Hazleton's Illegal Immigration Relief Act (IIRA) was introduced to the city council. As a rationale for introducing a local immigration law, Barletta maintained that the IIRA would solve the city's problems that illegal immigrants had created. Throughout the year, political support grew for Barletta's policy proposal. He pledged to make Hazleton "one of the toughest cities in America for illegal aliens."[63] This message resonated with the majority of the city's native residents, and the law was adopted on July 13, 2006. The fight for local control of immigration policy ensued, as legal challenges prevented the law's implementation. The local fight consisted of: (1) a political fight over the politics of problem definition, (2) a policy debate over the public responses and solutions, and (3) a public discourse about how to provide residents "relief" from illegal immigrants.

POLICY DESIGN:
THE ILLEGAL IMMIGRATION RELIEF ORDINANCES

By 2006, social and economic tensions among residents of Carpentersville, Farmers Branch, and Hazleton were quite palpable. Residents were angry, and private enterprises and community organizations were similarly frustrated with the issues. In response, political actors successfully made the case that the growth of an illegal immigrant population was a *public* problem. The problem of illegal immigration was successfully set on the political agenda. The IIROs were crafted to be a comprehensive policy design to meet as many aspects of the problem definition as possible.

According to Carpentersville's IIRO, the policy goal was "to adopt policies and procedures to deter and prevent unauthorized employment, harboring of illegal aliens, and criminal activity by illegal aliens."[64] Furthermore, the ordinance sought "to establish penalties for the employment of unlawful workers and the harboring of illegal immigrants in the Village of Carpentersville, and to provide for cooperative enforcement of federal immigration laws by the Village police department."[65] Hence, through the establishment of financial, civil, and criminal penalties—that is, rules and regulations—the main policy design aimed to deter the undesirable behaviors of those living and working in the village as illegal immigrants.

The stated policy goal of Farmers Branch's IIRO was to provide for "residential occupancy licenses; verification of aliens' immigration status with the federal government consistent with federal law; offenses; enforcement; judicial review; a penalty."[66] The ordinances aimed to establish disincentives for the harboring of illegal immigrants in the city. At the same time, they would permit the cooperative enforcement of federal immigration laws by the city's police department. Through the establishment of rules and regulations, namely financial, civil, and criminal penalties, the policy design sought to deter the housing of illegal immigrants and related crimes.

The policy goal of the Hazleton IIRA was "to secure . . . the right to live in peace free of the threat of crime, to enjoy the public services provided by this city without being burdened by the cost of providing goods, support and services to aliens . . . and to be free of the debilitating effects on their economic and social well being imposed by the influx of illegal aliens."[67] In addition, the act was "empowered and mandated by the people of Hazleton to abate the nuisance of illegal immigration by diligently prohibiting the acts and policies that facilitate illegal immigration in a manner consistent with federal law and the objectives of Congress."[68] By establishing financial, civil, and criminal penalties, the policy design was intended to prevent nuisance behaviors, such as residing and working in the city as an illegal immigrant.

In all three towns, policymakers, advocates, and supporters designed a comprehensive policy solution to confront the *local* problems through regulation of *local* housing rules, *local* employment rules, *local* policing, and an official *local* language. Tables 4.4, 4.5, and 4.6 show a matrix of the solution stream. The matrix lists these solutions and describes the ordinances' provisions. These provisions can be analyzed in the context of how they would address the various elements of the problem definition.

There were two primary arguments for the localization and descaling of immigration policy from national levels to sub-national levels.[69] First, supporters of the IIROs argued that the federal government had failed to address the rise of illegal immigration. In other words, they held, "The state and federal government lack the resources to properly protect the citizens of the Village of Carpentersville from the adverse effects of unauthorized employment, harboring of illegal aliens, and the activities of criminal aliens."[70] Farmers Branch Mayor Tom O'Hare repeatedly echoed this rationale. He said, "You have to remember when we first started talking about this it wasn't discussed in presidential debates, this wasn't discussed in senatorial elections, and everybody stayed away from it."[71]

The second argument for descaling immigration policy to the local level was that the stated public problems were local problems, which thus merited local responses. During a Carpentersville village meeting, one resident exclaimed in support of the IIRO, "It's a neighborhood problem," while another resident shouted, "It's time to take back our own neighborhoods."[72] The Farmers Branch IIRO echoed the sentiment: "The benefits and protections provided through the HUD citizenship and immigration status certification processes would also benefit the city [and] to protect the health, safety, and welfare of its citizens."[73] The Hazleton IIRA mirrored the justification: "Il-

Table 4.4. Solution Stream Matrix in Carpentersville

Name	Date(s)	What	Who	How	Why
Illegal Immigration Relief Ordinance	2006-2007	Comprehensive ordinance for local control of immigration policy	Village	Establish rules and regulations for criminal and civil behaviors	Limit number of illegal immigrants in Carpentersville
1. Housing	2006-2007	Verify the residency status of tenants	Landlords	Establish criminal and civil rules, regulations, and penalties through Village Community Development	Limit residential opportunities for illegal immigrants
2. Commercial	2006-2007	Verify the residency status of employees	Businesses	Establish criminal and civil rules, regulations, and penalties through Village Business Development	Limit commercial opportunities for illegal immigrants
3. Police	2006-2007	Verify the residency status of residents and enforce criminal and civil rules	Police	Police enforcement of criminal and civil rules	Limit local crime and enforce federal immigration laws
4. Language	2007	Declare English as the official language of Carpentersville	Village	Exclusive use of English by Village Trustees and Village Manager	Encourages assimilation of immigrants into the community
Carpentersville Improvement Commission	2007 - Present	Assist residents to understand the importance of property maintenance as it pertains to the general welfare, safety and aesthetics	Volunteers and Trustees	Annual projects "Adopt-a-Block," "Graffiti Deterrent Project," and "Paint-a-Thon"	Connect volunteers and needs to make Carpentersville a better place to live today and tomorrow
Community Response Team	1998 - Present	Prevent and act upon illegal gang and drug activity	Police	Police, Village Trustees, and Village Manager	Make Carpentersville a safer community to live, work, and play

Table 4.5. Solution Stream Matrix in Farmers Branch

Name	Date(s)	What	Who	Rationale	Status
Ordinance 2892	2006	Law to require landlord to verify the residency status of tenants; adopted by City Council	Landlords	Establish criminal and civil rules, regulations, and penalties to limit residential opportunities for illegal immigrants	Limit residential opportunities for illegal immigrants
Ordinance 2903	2007	Law to require landlord to verify the residency status of tenants; adopted by referendum vote	Landlords	Establish criminal and civil rules, regulations, and penalties to limit residential opportunities for illegal immigrants	Revision of Ordinance 2892; not in effect
Ordinance 2952	2007 - Present	Law to require City to verify the residency status of tenants in single and multi-family units; revised by City Council	City	Establish criminal and civil rules, regulations, and penalties to limit residential opportunities for illegal immigrants	Revision of Ordinance 2903; restraining order
Motion of City Council	2006	Declare English as the official language of Farmers Branch	City	Exclusive use of English in public institutions	Encourage assimilation of immigrants into the community

Table 4.6. Solution Stream Matrix in Hazleton

Name	Date(s)	What	Who	How	Status
Ordinance 2006-10	July 13, 2006	Comprehensive IIRA	Landlords, employers, and city	Establish criminal and civil rules, regulations, and penalties to limit residential and employment opportunities for illegal aliens	Declared unconstitutional and enjoined on July 26, 2007
Ordinance 2006-18	September 21, 2006	Law to provide criminal sanctions for harboring illegal aliens	Landlords and city	Establish criminal and civil rules, regulations, and penalties for providing a residence for illegal aliens	Revision of Ordinance 2006-10; Declared unconstitutional and enjoined
Ordinance 2006-19	September 21, 2006	Declare English as the official language of Hazleton	City	Exclusive use of English in public institutions	Encourage assimilation of immigrants into the community
Ordinance 2006-35	December 13, 2006	Law to establish a registration program for residential rental properties	Landlords and city	Establish criminal and civil rules, regulations, and penalties for providing a residence for illegal aliens	Revision of Ordinance 2006-10 and 2006-18; Declared unconstitutional and enjoined
Ordinance 2006-40	December 28, 2006	Law to provide criminal sanctions for harboring illegal aliens	Landlords and city	Adds implementation and process section	Revision of Ordinance 2006-18 and 2006-25; Declared unconstitutional and enjoined; under appeal[1]

[1] See *Lozano, et al., v. City of Hazleton, July 27, 2007* for the United States District Court for the Middle District of Pennsylvania, and September 9, 2010 Case No. 07-353 for United States Court of Appeals for the Third Circuit.

legal immigration leads to higher crime rates, subjects our hospitals to fiscal hardship and legal residents to substandard quality of care, contributes to other burdens on public services, increasing their cost and diminishing their availability to legal residents, and diminishes our overall quality of life."[74] Let us now turn to an analysis of common elements in each of the town's policy design.

Residential Housing and Landlords

All three pieces of legislation sought to prohibit anyone from harboring or employing illegal immigrants. The Carpentersville IIRO specifically stated, "The provision of housing to illegal aliens is a fundamental component of harboring."[75] Furthermore, the village emphatically declared that "unlawful employment, the harboring of illegal aliens in dwelling units in the Village, and crime committed by illegal aliens harm the health, safety and welfare of authorized US workers and legal residents in the Village."[76]

In Farmers Branch, Ordinance No. 2892 was defined as "an ordinance amending chapter 26, businesses, article iv apartment complex rental, mandating a citizenship certification requirement pursuant to 24 cfr 5 et seq.; providing for enforcement; providing a penalty; providing a severability clause; providing an effective date; and declaring an emergency."[77] The city's IIROs stated clearly that "widespread concern of future terrorist attacks following the events of September 11, 2001, landlords and property managers through the country have been developing new security procedures to protect their buildings and residents."[78]

Ordinance 2952 would establish definitions of residency status, residential occupancy licenses, and standards of offenses, enforcement, and judicial review. The ordinance provides three definitions for the policy's target population: (1) an alien is any person not a citizen or national of the United States; (2) a lessor is any person who leases or rents a multi- or single-family dwelling unit; and (3) an occupant is any person age 18 or older who resides in the rented or leased dwelling unit. Each occupant would be required to purchase a residential occupancy license accompanied by a signed declaration of legal residency.[79] The ordinance would criminalize the occupancy of a dwelling unit without a license.

Hazleton's IIRA specifically stated, "It is unlawful for any person or business entity that owns a dwelling unit in the City to harbor an illegal alien in the dwelling unit, knowing or in reckless disregard of the fact that an alien has come to, entered, or remains in the United States in violation of law."[80] Moreover, the IIRO clearly declared, "To let, lease, or rent a dwelling unit to an illegal alien, knowing or in reckless disregard of the fact that an alien has come to, entered, or remains in the United States in violation of law, shall be deemed to constitute harboring."[81]

The policy design for all three towns was an attempt to decrease, or even eliminate, the illegal immigrant population. By diminishing the size of the housing supply, the actions would push illegal immigrants out of the towns and into other jurisdictions. Both Carpentersville and Hazleton placed the responsibility for enforcement directly on the landlord. Under the IIRO, Carpentersville would initiate an inquiry to the landlord such that documents would be provided to the local government to demonstrate proper legal residency in the US. Failure to do so would result in a financial penalty of $100 per day, per adult tenant. Successive violations could result in criminal proceedings. Likewise, the Hazleton Code Enforcement Office would respond to complaints of harboring illegal immigrants. Failure to comply would result in suspension of the landlord's rental license. Subsequent violations would result in a $250 fine per violation. In Farmers Branch, since both the occupant and the lessor were required to attain a license, both could lose their licenses and face criminal prosecution under the ordinance. The local police and building inspectors would be responsible for enforcement. It would be unlawful for any person or business to provide housing.

Carpentersville's ordinance went a step farther and also put additional burdens on businesses and residents who provided a domicile to an illegal immigrant, knowingly or unknowingly. Residents or businesses could be charged with harboring an illegal immigrant and would be subject to criminal and civil penalties. Additionally, Carpentersville established teams and commissions to address the issues of overcrowding of tenants in dwelling units and physical upkeep. First, the village's zoning enforcement would carry out occupancy laws through verification of residency requirements by landlords. Second, the Carpentersville Improvement Commission would address lack of maintenance of houses and apartments. The commission, which began as a volunteer committee of residents, evolved into a village commission to take the lead on painting houses, mowing lawns, removing snow, cleaning streets, and removing debris and graffiti. This collective housing strategy, as IIRO supporters argued, would limit the harboring of illegal immigrants in the village.

While existing federal laws already prohibit the harboring of illegal immigrants, the initiatives in Carpentersville, Farmers Branch, and Hazleton were intended to duplicate, or reinforce, these federal laws.[82] By doing so, the towns hoped to curb the number of places that illegal immigrants could call home.

Local Business and Employment Practices

Both Carpentersville and Hazleton focused on prohibiting anyone from employing illegal immigrants. The Carpentersville IIRO specifically stated, "Unlawful workers and illegal aliens, as defined by this ordinance and state and federal law, do not normally meet such conditions as a matter of law when present in the Village. State and federal law require that certain conditions be met before a person may be authorized to work or reside in this country."[83] In addition, the village put forth "It is unlawful for any business entity to recruit, hire for employment, or continue to employ, or to permit, dispatch, or instruct any person who is an unlawful worker to perform work in whole or part within the Village."[84]

The Hazleton IIRA held that "it is unlawful for any business entity to recruit, hire for employment, or continue to employ, or to permit, dispatch, or instruct any person who is an unlawful worker to perform work in whole or part within the City."[85] Plus, the city further mandated, "Every business entity that applies for a business permit to engage in any type of work in the City shall sign an affidavit, prepared by the City Solicitor, affirming that they do not knowingly utilize the services or hire any person who is an unlawful worker."[86] Accordingly, if a business in either town were to employ a worker who is an illegal immigrant, knowingly or unknowingly, then that business would be in violation of the law and thus subject to criminal and civil penalties.

Under both IIROs, the communities would require that local businesses sign an affidavit certifying that its employees are legal residents in the United States. Failure to comply would result in the suspension of the communities' business license, and subsequent violations would result in financial penalties and the revocation of the license or permit to conduct business in the city. The burden to comply would rest entirely on the employer.

Yet, according to existing federal statutes and codes, it is already mandated that employers submit proper residency status of its employees to demonstrate the legal eligibility to work in the United States.[87] Both ordinances duplicate the federal codes on a local level of government, such that they would further deter illegal immigrants from seeking work in Carpentersville or Hazleton.

Arguments in support and opposition were commonplace in the development of the policy design. For instance, Rudolfo Garcia, the owner of a local specialty grocery store in Carpentersville, expressed concern about the IIRO's business provision. He said, "My business is 100 percent Hispanic. Who do you think brings in the money to the town?"[88] But, Trustee Paul Humpfer dismissed these concerns and offered a regular rebuttal to business owners. He continued to simply frame the problem as "too many illegal aliens work in Carpentersville."[89]

Local Policing of Illegal Immigrants

Carpentersville and Farmers Branch both opted to allow for the local police enforcement of federal laws because according to the Carpentersville IIRO, it is in the "best interests of and will serve and benefit the health, safety and welfare of the public and law-abiding business entities and property owners."[90] Both towns authorized participation in the Immigration and Nationality Act Section 287(g) program, a federal program that permits local police forces to act as agents of the US Department of Homeland Security to detain and transfer a person who is found to be an illegal immigrant.[91]

Carpentersville's IIRO precisely stated, "The state and federal government *lack the resources to properly protect the citizens* of the Village of Carpentersville from the *adverse effect* of unauthorized employment, harboring of illegal aliens, and the activities of criminal aliens [emphasis added]."[92] By empowering local police officers to verify citizenship and immigration status of any person found to be in violation of the law, the towns would be able to control, in effect, the illegal immigrants who commit crime. The Carpentersville IIRO additionally proposed to mandate the village's participation in numerous federal programs to enforce federal laws by legislating such participation, including the US Department of Homeland Security's Basic Pilot Program[93] and Secure Communities, which enables local police forces to share information about detained persons in local custody for US deportation.[94]

In essence, the Carpentersville IIRO empowers the community to take control over the policing of *all* US immigration policies at the scale of its jurisdiction. In support of the 287(g) program, village trustee Judy Sigwalt said the village's participation was important "to keep the federal government on its toes. If nothing else, this lets the federal government know that we're not backing off on anything that pertains to helping communities deal with illegal immigration. We cannot become complacent now and become silent."[95] However, opponents of the IIRO disagreed. Trustee Jim Frost argued, "It seems to me that trying to tell the federal government what to do is not in the best interest of anybody."[96]

The City of Farmers Branch entered into a Memorandum of Agreement (MOA) with the Department of Homeland Security on October 15, 2009.[97] Gary Greer, the city manager of Farmers Branch, and John Morton, the assistant secretary of Immigration and Customs Enforcement (ICE), signed the MOA that stipulated the terms and provisions of the 287(g) partnership. The MOA empowered designated local law enforcement personnel of the Farmers Branch Police Department (FBPD) as deputized agents of the federal government to detain criminal aliens in custody for other charges. Specifically, the MOA established a provision to nominate, train, certify, and authorize FBPD officers to enforce federal immigration functions. The policy design was to "enable the FBPD to identify and process immigration violators and conduct criminal investigations under ICE supervision."[98] Moreover, the purpose of the policy was stated to "enhance the safety and security of communities by focusing resources on identifying and processing for removal of criminal aliens who pose a threat to public safety or a danger to the community."[99]

Policymakers in both towns held that federal and state government had failed to keep residents safe from illegal immigrants. The outcome would effectively mean that the cities would hold the police power to apprehend and expel illegal immigrants in the city. The local police forces would carry out federal immigration law.

The English Language

Carpentersville, Farmers Branch, and Hazleton all attempted to adopt English as their official language. As the local immigration policy debate continued, numerous residents began to worry about the growth of the Spanish language—speaking, reading, listening, and writing—throughout their towns. Native residents were preoccupied about the spread of the Spanish language; they felt threatened. In Farmers Branch, the city was a bilingual place by the 2000s. Its neighborhoods, businesses, schools, and churches conducted affairs in both Spanish and English—and in some instances, exclusively in Spanish. In Hazleton, Spanish was the language of record throughout some of the city's residential and commercial areas.

In all three communities, a number of citizens argued that English is the common language of the United States. Carpentersville proponents of the cause were supported by the state, since Illinois had adopted English as the state's official language, providing further support for the proponents of the measure. In Farmers Branch, a supporter declared, "English language is the common language of the City of Farmers Branch, of the State of Texas and of the United States." Likewise, in Hazleton they declared, "The English language is the common language of the City of Hazleton, of the Commonwealth of Pennsylvania and of the United States,"[100] and they declared that English "removes barriers of misunderstanding and helps to unify the people . . . and helps to enable the full economic and civic participation of all its citizens" by unifying residents.[101] Stating that English is the *common* language inherently reassured local policymakers that there was nothing *uncommon* about their resolution.

Others argued that public costs would be reduced and efficiency increased, and rights of English-only speakers would be preserved. Above all, residents would benefit economically and culturally from the exclusive adoption of

English. In Carpentersville, Fox Valley Citizens for Legal Immigration Chair Bob Sperlazzo strongly supported these arguments. He summarized that an official language would "send a message that there are responsibilities and benefits to living here. One of them is to speak English."[102]

In contrast, opponents in Farmers Branch and Carpentersville argued the measure was useless and did not solve any problems. Other residents argued that the measure was a waste of city business, while still others held that it would promote discrimination against all Hispanics and Latinos, which would ultimately deter growth. Still others argued simply that the ordinance was discriminatory and would result in the racial profiling of Spanish speakers. For example, one Carpentersville resident summarized the opposition argument: "This debate is about language, but everybody knows it's about much, much more. This is about racism."[103]

In Farmers Branch, supporters developed and distributed t-shirts that read, "This is America. Please Speak English." This slogan was so popularized that supporters began to sell the shirts to raise revenue for the city's legal defense fund to fight judicial challenges of the IIRO.[104] Opponents countered with a similar slogan that read, "I'm American and I speak Spanish. I'm not a criminal!"

In Hazleton, since residents associated the Spanish language with illegal immigration, there was little public debate about the official language policy. Joe Yannuzzi, president of the Hazleton City Council, frequently reminded residents, "This is not a discussion" and "This is not up for debate."[105] Hazleton Mayor Barletta suggested that the language issue was just a side issue: "English has nothing to do with immigration. . . . We're really just trying to protect the English language."[106]

Ultimately, in Carpentersville, the seven village trustees refused to vote on the IIRO, and the ordinance was tabled indefinitely. Residents raised concerns about the costs of legal challenges and the further social divisions among neighborhoods. While the English-only measure was proposed as a separate policy from the IIRO, it was nonetheless debated within the context of the IIRO. In the midst of the IIRO, this measure was the only policy that was immediately debated and passed; the others failed to move forward.

Despite the fact that 40 percent of residents of Carpentersville speak Spanish, there was strong support for the measure. On June 19, 2007, more than 100 people attended the village board meeting in which the board of trustees voted to change the proposal from an ordinance to a resolution. The change made the proposal non-binding. The resolution passed by a vote of five to two, with Village President Bill Sarto and Trustee Linda Ramirez-Sliwinski dissenting. Sarto called the resolution "pointless" and said, "It changes nothing."[107] Furthermore, Ramirez-Sliwinski said, "[W]hen the resolution singles out 40 percent of the community, this is not good for the whole community."[108] But, Sigwalt, as a strong supporter of the English-only ordinance, countered by saying, "Even though a resolution is just fluff, we are still making a statement."[109] Since the declaration was a non-binding resolution, there was no mandate or legal authority for enforcement.

On November 13, 2006, the Farmers Branch City Council unanimously approved Resolution 130 to adopt English as the official language of Farmers Branch. Mayor Bob Phelps then read the full resolution in the city's record during the meeting. Even though 43 percent of the residents of Farmers Branch spoke Spanish, there was strong support for the measure. The resolution to declare English the official language of Farmers Branch was a binding resolution. It mandated the legal authority for public enforcement.[110]

On September 23, 2006, the Hazleton City Council adopted Ordinance 2006-19 to declare English as the official language of the city. The official declaration was proposed and adopted separately from the IIRO. The English-only declaration was proposed and adopted separately from the IIRO.

The adoption of these resolutions became a symbol in the design of local legislation to address illegal immigration. It demonstrated the role of symbolic politics in the debate for a policy design and solution. The policies were crafted to serve as a symbol for the preservation of a language and thus the status quo. It also reminds us that the conformity of a national language symbolizes the national interests of American identity. In this case, language presents a challenge—or even a threat—to the collective American identity. Espenshade asserts, "Important symbols of American nationality may evoke anti-immigrant attitudes."[111] Schmid holds that a "renewed hostility toward language minorities" has risen during the past two decades.[112] In Carpentersville, Farmers Branch, and Hazleton, this hostility was aimed at Spanish speakers. The English-only resolutions attempted to legislate this hostility.

PUBLIC PROBLEMS AND POLICY RESPONSES

The arrival of the 2000s ushered in a new era of socioeconomic realities in Carpentersville, Farmers Branch, and Hazleton. These towns were faced with numerous shifts in the demographic structure, economic status of residents, employment opportunities, housing stock, crime, and public infrastructure. Stagnation and decline characterized these transitions. For residents, the concurrent settlement of immigrants made these changes more pronounced. In consequence, local politicians framed these changes as public problems that required public responses—that is, public policies to address these issues.

The solution policy streams were developed to address the public definitions related to the problem of illegal immigration. Local policymakers developed a policy design to address each of the elements of the problem definition. The IIROs sought to curtail illegal immigration in four primary ways, which included the regulation of residential housing and landlords, the regulation of local business and employment practices, the local policing of illegal immigrants, and the declaration of English as an official language. The solution was designed to minimize the residential opportunities for illegal immigrants by prohibiting landlords from renting to this population as well as shifting the burden of tenant verification of residency status to landlords.

Similarly, the solution was also designed to minimize the employment opportunities for illegal immigrants by prohibiting businesses from employing this population as well as shifting the burden of employee verification of residency status to businesses. The IIROs empowered the local police forces to enforce immigration laws to the fullest extent. Last, English was declared the official language. Collectively, these policies bundled together as the IIROs were designed to implement a solution to reduce the problems of illegal immigration.

The policymakers in Carpentersville—namely Trustees Judy Sigwalt and Paul Humpfer—crafted a solution and cosponsored legislation to address the problems as they so defined. The key political actors agreed on the policy design, which facilitated the development of the IIRO. However, the other Village Trustees—namely, Bill Sarto and Linda Ramirez-Sliwinski—opposed the policy design. "It's [the IIRO] driven a wedge between our community," said Village President Bill Sarto.[113] In contrast, Village Trustee Judy Sigwalt countered, "We have fought very hard and very long. We have said repeatedly it is not about race. It is about what is legal and illegal. And it's all these other people playing the race card."[114] Such disagreements led, in part, to various political struggles about the local control of immigration policy. In Farmers Branch, then Councilman Tom O'Hare, with the unanimous support of the city council, crafted a set of solutions and designed legislation to address the problems of illegal immigration. Members of the city council all agreed on the problems, and they all agreed on the solutions. There was a common sentiment that the federal government had failed to deal with illegal immigration in communities like Farmers Branch. Mayor O'Hare said, "If you're not here legally, you're breaking the law, and we want to be a city that upholds the law."[115] In Hazleton, policymakers crafted a solution and introduced legislation to address the public problems in Hazleton. The political actors agreed on the policy design and consequently adopted the law.

Boisterous politicians made their positions on illegal immigration obvious. Judy Sigwalt, a trustee of Carpentersville, emphatically stated, "We're not backing down. We're not going away . . . It's only going to be a matter of time before some lawyers or attorneys figure out a way to reword and make this ordinance stick and hold up under the law."[116] Then, Mayor Tim O'Hare affirmed, "Farmers Branch is a town of law and order . . . a patriotic, American-loving town. . . . I think this is important for America. It's important to show other cities and towns that you can make a difference, you can stand up for what's right."[117] Mayor Lou Barletta persistently reminded the nation that he would make Hazleton "one of the toughest cities in America for illegal aliens" for illegal immigrants.[118]

Opponents were just as vocal. "There is a fear of people or of things being different," said Ed Yohnka, Director of Communications and Public Policy of the ACLU of Illinois.[119] Iván Vázquez, a resident of Farmers Branch, proclaimed, "You're afraid of being Hispanic in this city. Who wants to stay here if they don't like you? I'll move."[120] Cesar Perales, President and General Counsel, Puerto Rican Legal Defense and Education Fund captured the sentiments of the opponents by warning, "These ordinances are nothing more than an officially sanctioned witch hunt . . . Hazleton intends to aggressively search out and identify every single immigrant within its boundaries, assess their immigration status by a lawless process in which the immigrant has no say, and expel those who do not pass the test."[121]

And so a fierce and chaotic local battle was brewing as the public nature of problems was defined and as solutions were designed. Residents, politicians, community leaders, and advocacy groups argued about the varied dimensions of "relief" from illegal immigrants. Ultimately, to understand how power was used to influence this debate, it is necessary to analyze the politics stream—the politics of relief.

NOTES

1. Brettell and Nibbs, "Immigrant Suburban Settlement and the 'Threat' to Middle Class Status and Identity," 1-30.

2. Ibid.

3. Katharine L. Bradbury, Anthony Downs, and Kenneth A. Small, *Urban Decline and the Future of American Cities* (Washington, DC: Brookings Institution Press, 1982): 4-10.

4. Mark Baldassare, *Trouble in Paradise* (New York: Columbia University Press, 1986).

5. Ibid.

6. Larrisa Chinwah, "Village's Debate Begins" *Daily Herald,* September 28, 2006.

7. "10 Questions for Paul Humpfer," *Free Republic* Blog, accessed October 27, 2006, www.freerepublic.com/focus/f-news/1727583/posts.

8. Anonymous, "Letters to the Editor," *Dallas Morning News*, August 24, 2006.

9. Ibid.

10. Branch Bulletin, City of Farmers Branch, "Tim O'Hare: The Interview," April 6, 2011.

11. Anonymous personal interview, June 8, 2007.

12. Milan Simonich, "Hazleton Ordinance Aimed at Illegal Immigrants Put Mayor at Center Stage," *Pittsburgh Post-Gazette*, August 27, 2006.

13. Lou Barletta, "Immigration Panel," *Conservative Political Action Conference*. Washington, DC, February 11, 2011, accessed January 28, 2012, www.npitv.com/374.

14. Anne Schneider and Helen Ingram, "The Social Construction of Target Populations: Implications for Politics and Policy," *American Political Science Review* 87, no. 2 (1993): 334-347.

15. Deborah A. Stone, "Causal Stories and the Formation of Policy Agendas," *Political Science Quarterly* 104, no. 2 (1989): 281-300.

16. Personal interview, Larrisa Chinwah, May 7, 2009.

17. "Kristi," *Free Republic* Blog, accessed October 28, 2006, www.freerepublic.com.

18. "10 Questions for Paul Humpfer," *Free Republic* Blog, October 27, 2006.

19. Testimony, Lou Barletta, US District Court for the Middle District of Pennsylvania, Scranton, March 14, 2007.

20. Simonich, "Hazleton Ordinance Aimed," 1.

21. Jennifer Ludden, "Local Immigration Law Challenged by ACLU," *All Things Considered National Public Radio*, March 12, 2007.

22. Staff, "Hazleton Mayor Who Cracked Down in Illegal Immigrants Takes US House Seat," *Associated Press*, December 14, 2010.

23. Personal interview, Trustee Ed Ritter, May 8, 2009.

24. "10 Questions for Paul Humpfer," *Free Republic* Blog, October 27, 2006.

25. Carpentersville Village Board of Trustees meeting, September 19, 2006.

26. Anonymous personal interview, May 8, 2009.

27. Ibid.

28. "Trends in Kane County," RealtyTrac, September 8, 2011, www.realtytrac.com.

29. Stephanie Sandoval, "Grocer Rumor Raises Racial Tensions in FB," *Dallas Morning News*, March 27, 2007.

30. Anonymous, "Letters to the Editor," *Dallas Morning News*, August 24, 2006.

31. Deborah A. Stone, *Policy Paradox: The Art of Political Decision Making* (New York: W. W. Norton, 1997).

32. Ibid.

33. It is estimated that the following gangs have operated in Carpentersville: Latin Kings; Imperial Gangsters; Gangster Disciples; Four Corner Hustlers; Maniac Latin Disciples; Spanish Cobras; Surenos 13; and Latin Angels, accessed September 8, 2011, www.chicagogangs.org.

34. Glorida Carr, "Gang Graffiti: 'Tagging' Takes Toll in Carpentersville," *Courier News Sun*, August 29, 2003.

35. Ray Quintanilla, "Drug Bust Nets Alleged Suburban Gang Leaders," *Chicago Tribune*, April 26, 2007.

36. Michael Von Fremd, "Cop Killing Sparks Immigration Debate," *ABC News*, September 25, 2006, accessed September 8, 2011, http://abcnews.go.com/GMA/story?id=2487004#.Txs-92PUOPA.

37. Bob Laylo, "Police: Drug Rings, Killer Nabbed," *The Morning Call*, September 4, 2002.

38. Ibid.

39. Wade Malcolm, "Barletta: 'Illegal Aliens Got Away With Murder,'" *Citizens Voice*, July 7, 2007.

40. Dan Gilgoff, "A Town in Need of a Tomorrow," *US News and World Report*, December 12, 2002.

41. Ibid.

42. Ellen Barry, "City's Immigration Law Turns Back Clock," *Los Angeles Times*, November 9, 2006.

43. Elaine B. Sharp, "Paradoxes of National Antidrug Policymaking," in *The Politics of Problem Definition*, eds., Rochefort and Cobb, 109.

44. Anonymous personal interview, May 7, 2009.

45. Anonymous personal interview, May 8, 2009.

46. "The immigration Debate: Carpentersville, IL Setting Its Stage," accessed September 9, 2011, http://samaha.wordpress.com/2006/10/11/the-immigration-debate-carpentersville-il-setting-its-stage/.

47. Robert Puentes and David Warren, "One Fifth of America, A Comprehensive Guide to America's First Suburbs" (February 2006): The Brookings Institution, Washington, DC.

48. See Jon Teaford, *The Metropolitan Revolution: The Rise of Post-Urban America* (New York: Columbia University Press, 2006).

49. See Barry Bluestone and Bennett Harrison, *The Deindustrialization of America: Plant Closings, Community Abandonment, and the Dismantling of Basic Industry* (New York: Basic Books, 1984).

50. Jackson, *Crabgrass Frontier,* 3-11.

51. See Bernard L. Weinstein and Robert E. Firestine, *Regional Growth and Decline in the United States: The Rise of the Sunbelt and the Decline of the Northeast* (New York: Praeger Publishers, 1978).

52. Amy Worden, "Ruling Awaited in Hazleton Immigration Case," *The Philadelphia Inquirer*, March 23, 2007.

53. Rochefort and Cobb, eds., *The Politics of Problem Definition*, 21.

54. Kristi Jac, "10 Questions for Paul Humpfer," *The Free Republic*, October 27, 2007.

55. Simonich, "Hazleton Ordinance," 1.

56. Anonymous campaign material, 2007.

57. Judy Sigwalt was first elected to the Village Board of Trustees in 1999. Paul Humpfer was first appointed to the Village Board of Trustees, and he was later elected.

58. Sandoval, "Illegal Migrant Proposal Stirs Passions," 1B.

59. Ibid.

60. Lou Barletta, Forum on Immigration, Temple University School of Law, Philadelphia, March 31, 2010.

61. John Gibson, "Hazleton, Pennsylvania, Mayor Cracking Down on Illegal Immigrants," *Fox News*, June 21, 2006, accessed November 1, 2008, www.foxnews .com/story/0,2933,200452,00.html#ixzz1lL29xUZ8.

62. Jim Turner, "Immigration," Save Our State, accessed December 1, 2010, http://saveourstate.info.

63. Michael Powell and Michelle Garcia, "Pa. City Puts Illegal Immigrants on Notice," *The Washington Post*, August 22, 2006.

64. See Appendix 1.

65. Village of Carpentersville Illegal Immigration Relief Ordinance Preamble.

66. City of Farmers Branch Ordinance No. 2952, not dated.

67. City of Hazleton Illegal Immigration Relief Act §2(F).

68. City of Hazleton Illegal Immigration Relief Act §2(D).

69. Varsanyi, ed., *Taking Local Control*, 1-30.

70. Village of Carpentersville Illegal Immigration Relief Ordinance §1(B)(4).

71. Branch Bulletin, "Tim O'Hare: The Interview," 1.

72. Political rally in Carpentersville, Illinois, October 16, 2007.

73. City of Farmers Branch Ordinance No. 2903, May 22, 2007.

74. Ibid.

75. Village of Carpentersville Illegal Immigration Relief Ordinance §1(B)(6).

76. Village of Carpentersville Illegal Immigration Relief Ordinance §1(B)(3).

77. City of Farmers Branch Ordinance No. 2892, Preamble, November 13, 2006.

78. City of Farmers Branch Ordinance No. 2892, November 13, 2006.

79. According to the ordinance's provisions, it would be a crime to make any false statement under Title 18 U.S.C. §1324(e).

80. City of Hazleton Illegal Immigration Relief Act §5(A).

81. City of Hazleton Illegal Immigration Relief Act §5(A)(1).

82. See 8 U.S.C. §1324(a)(1)(A).

83. Village of Carpentersville Illegal Immigration Relief Ordinance §1(B)(3).

84. Village of Carpentersville Illegal Immigration Relief Ordinance §2(B).

85. City of Hazleton Illegal Immigration Relief Act §4(A).

86. Ibid.

87. See 8 U.S.C. §1373.

88. Larrisa Chinwah, "A Question of Too Much Law? Business Owners, Landlords Decry Ordinance" *Daily Herald,* October 8, 2006, 1.

89. "10 Questions for Paul Humpfer," *Free Republic* Blog, October 27, 2006.

90. Village of Carpentersville Illegal Immigration Relief Ordinance §1(B)(5).

91. See 8 U.S.C. §1357(g).

92. Village of Carpentersville Illegal Immigration Relief Ordinance §1(B)(4).

93. See Illegal Immigration Reform and Immigration Responsibility Act (1996) P.L. 104-208, Division C, §403(a) and 8 U.S.C. §1324(a). The Basic Pilot Program, also known as "E-Verify," is a voluntary federal program of the US Department of Homeland Security used to verify the residency status of immigrants through numerous identification systems.

94. This program seeks to: (1) identify criminal aliens through modernized information sharing; (2) prioritize enforcement actions to ensure apprehension and removal of dangerous criminal aliens; and (3) transform criminal alien enforcement processes and systems to achieve lasting results. See US Department of Homeland Security, "Secure Communities: A Comprehensive Plan to Identify and Remove Criminal Aliens Strategic Plan," July 21, 2009.

95. Larrisa Chinwah, "Tonight's Immigration Debate: Police Training Village Officials to Seek Federal Funding for Specialized Training of Officers," *Daily Herald,* December 5, 2006.

96. Ibid.

97. It took approximately three years of local and federal planning before the 287(g) application was completed.

98. City of Farmers Branch, Texas and ICE Memorandum of Agreement, accessed November 23, 2011, www.ice.gov/doclib/foia/memorandumsofAgreementUn derstanding/r_287gfarmersbranchpd101509.pdf.

99. Ibid.

100. City of Hazleton Official English Ordinance 2006-19 §2(A).

101. City of Hazleton Official English Ordinance 2006-19 §2(B).

102. Village Board of Trustees meeting, April 17, 2007.

103. Ibid.

104. City of Farmers Branch Legal Defense Fund, accessed December 22, 2006, www.farmersbranchlegaldefensefund.com.

105. Thomas Espenshade, "Unauthorized Immigration to the United States," *Annual Review of Sociology*, 21 (1995): 210.

106. Wade Malcolm, "Hazleton Council Ready to Consider Revised Ordinance," *Citizens' Voice*, September 8, 2006.

107. Larrisa Chinwah, "Carpentersville makes English official," *Daily Herald,* June 20, 2007.

108. Ibid.

109. Ibid.

110. Under certain circumstances, such as the protection or promotion public health, sanitation, and safety; the promotion of trade or tourism; or the collection of debts, the use of another language is permitted.

111. Espenshade, "Unauthorized Immigration to the United States," 195-216.

112. Carol Schmid, *The Politics of Language: Conflict, Identity, and Cultural Pluralism in Comparative Perspective* (New York: Oxford University Press, 2001): 8.

113. Sophia Tareen, "Immigration proposals divide Illinois village," *USA Today,* August 4, 2007.

114. Ibid.

115. Sandoval, "Illegal Migrant Proposal Stirs Passions," 1B.

116. Sophia Tareen, "Immigration Proposals Divide Illinois Village." *Associated Press,* August 4, 2007.

117. Anna M. Tinsley, "Farmers Branch Keeps Up Illegal-Immigration Fight," *Fort Worth Star Telegram,* April 25, 2010.

118. Michael Powell and Michelle Garcia, "Pa. City Puts Illegal Immigrants on Notice," *The Washington Post*, August 22, 2006.

119. Sophia Tareen, "Immigration Proposals Divide Illinois Village." *Associated Press*, August 4, 2007.

120. Stephanie Sandoval, "Groups Decry FB Law," *Dallas Morning News*, November 15, 2006.

121. "Coalition Returns to Court Over Harsh Anti-Immigrant Law in Hazleton," ACLU Press Release, October 30, 2006, accessed November 1, 2008, www.aclupa .org/pressroom/coalitionreturnstocourtove.htm.

Chapter Five

The Politics of Relief

This country has a large Latino population and millions of Latinos live here without legal permission. However, the great majority live quietly, raise families, obey the law daily, and do work for our country. For all that they contribute to our welfare, they live in constant dread of being apprehended as [undocumented immigrants] and being evicted, perhaps having their families disrupted. As unsatisfactory as this situation is it is the immigration scheme we have today . . . This is a national problem, needing a national solution.[1]

—*Opinion, US Court of Appeals for the Fifth Circuit, March 21, 2012*

The case is definitely not over.[2]

—*Kris Kobach, Attorney, March 22, 2012*

We need only look to the history of the progression of the legal battle to understand the fierce support and staunch opposition to IIROs. Responding to the latest ruling that IIROs usurp federal laws, Kris Kobach declared that the fight was not over. As lead counsel for the plaintiffs in the Hazleton case, Kobach emerged as a national spokesperson for relief ordinances for many other jurisdictions including Farmers Branch and Carpentersville. The majority of politicians and residents of Farmers Branch and Hazleton continued to utilize public resources for the fight to implement their ordinances. Despite numerous judicial setbacks, the supporters continue the political fight for policy adoption. This chapter examines how relief politics shaped these fights.

The fight for local control of immigration policy was about, at its core, the need of a native population to gain relief *from* a foreign-born population. The relief stemmed from the perceptions of the problems that illegal immigrants, and more broadly illegal immigration, brought into the community.

It was further complicated as native residents perceived not only illegal immigrants as threats but also all immigrants, and especially native residents of Hispanic origin. Accordingly, this relief came in the form of a loosely joined set of public policies known as IIROs. Such ordinances allegedly diminished the threat to middle-class living and the threat of suburban decline that immigrants presented to the native population. The IIRO became a vehicle to provide relief from these threats.

Relief politics defined the struggle for power to gain local control of immigration policy. As Kingdon aptly notes, "The political stream flows along according to its own dynamics and its own rules."[3] Relief emerged as the political dynamic in this debate. The political stream converged on the problem and solution streams as the process that ultimately would determine the outcome of the debate. The problem stream comprised a set of definitions that characterized the nature of the problems and the relationship to the public. The solution stream produced the IIRO policy design as a potential public law that could solve the problem. It was designed to be the "tactic" or "method" to carry out a set of desired values to regulate the presence of illegal immigrants. The problem and solution streams joined together to move toward policy adoption and an implementation process. Residents wanted to control their own political agenda, adoption, and implementation of immigration policies. Whether they supported or opposed the IIRO, residents sought to control their own destiny over the policy issue of immigration. Thus, what determines whether residents seek the ability to set their own course and how?

The politics of relief are about the processes that confront these questions. The answers rest on the political arguments and arrangements that are made by residents who seek relief. I identify seven political frames in the context of relief politics: the legal frame, the rule of law, the intergovernmental frame, the communication frame, the language frame, the suburban decline frame, the judicial frame, and the nativist frame. These frames explain the struggle for political power and relief of the immigration problem. The evolution of the IIRO debate can be analyzed through an examination of these frames.[4]

To develop an understanding about how the IIRO was proposed, debated, and ultimately whether it was either adopted or failed in these three towns, it is necessary to uncover the politics that influenced the policy debates. Now, drawing on a discourse analysis of events and various key informant interviews, I turn to an analysis of the politics of relief by drawing on the context of political frames in Carpentersville, Farmers Branch, and Hazleton.[5]

CARPENTERSVILLE

On October 3, 2006, a crowd of nearly 2,000 people protested in opposition to the IIRO in front of the Carpentersville Village Hall during a board of trustees meeting.[6] This was the largest rally of its kind in Carpentersville's history. After the meeting, Trustee Sigwalt proudly declared, "The support is there now that [news of the IIRO] has traveled across the country. That support was not there before. We are talking good old-fashioned politics, taking it back to the grassroots, to the people."[7] Her statement captured the essence of the politics of relief. The debate over "relief" was about grassroots politics and "taking it back" to the people. Indeed, the IIRO galvanized political activity for both supporters and opponents. Specifically, I examine the individual actors as displayed in Table 5.1 and the group actors as displayed in Table 5.2.

The Legal Frame

Relief politics were expressed on the legality of immigration and the illegal immigrant. Political discourse about law and order, bureaucratic implementation, and intergovernmental affairs shaped the legal frame. Residents, elected officials, and advocates contributed to this discourse.

"Illegal means illegal" was the most frequent argument that IIRO supporters articulated. Pam McConnell, a member of the Illinois Minuteman Project, asserted, "It is important for people to follow the law. It is law and order and without the law, there is no order."[8] Yet others argued that the ordinance would be unconstitutional on human rights grounds. Opponents commonly argued, "No human being is illegal." Frank Scarpelli summarized, "The Fair Housing Act says we have to treat everyone equally as legal, law abiding citizens. We cannot deny someone on what we feel or believe. It has to be a proven fact in a court of law that they are illegal."[9]

Supporters and opponents also told stories about the legal history of immigration. In a village board meeting, Carpentersville resident Michael Williams stood at the public comment podium and said, "I am Polish. If you're Polish, and you're in the United States illegally, I want you to go back to Poland. I'm making a point here. It doesn't matter if you're Polish, German, Mexican, or who you are. If you're not here legally, I want you gone. Period."[10] IIRO opponents disagreed. According to another Carpentersville resident, "A hundred years ago when the Irish came here, facing political persecution, they were told they were scum. They were told that they weren't welcome. They were told that they were going to ruin the nation."[11] These stories were commonplace, and they were told to argue for and against illegal immigration.

Various ranking bureaucrats in local government also shaped the legal frame. Village attorney James Rhodes remained silent about the legal matters. According to local residents and the IIRO opposition, his silence was a tacit endorsement of the IIRO. During the debate, Rhodes did not answer

Table 5.1. Politics Stream Matrix: Individual Actors in Carpentersville

Who	Role	IIRO Position	Relief Frame(s)	Quote
Bill Sarto	Elected President, Village of Carpentersville	Oppose	Legal, fiscal, civil rights	"It's [the IIRO] downright discriminatory and unconstitutional."
Linda Ramirez-Sliwinski	Elected Trustee, Village of Carpentersville	Oppose	Legal, fiscal, civil rights	"I am afraid that if we pass this ordinance it could affect our bond applications and insurance coverage."
Tom Roeser	President, Otto Engineering	Oppose	Housing and zoning	"Legal or illegal, you're going to have that problem."
Judy Sigwalt	Elected Trustee, Village of Carpentersville and IIRO Co-Sponsor	Support	Legal, language, crime, economic	"For too long, people have been passing the buck and saying it is the federal government's problem and it is not up to us."
Paul Humpfer	Elected Trustee, Village of Carpentersville and IIRO Co-Sponsor	Support	Legal, language, crime, economic	"I have seen an increase in gang activity, crime, overcrowding, and I am concerned there are illegal aliens living in the village."
Bob Sperlazzo	President, Fox Valley Citizens for Legal Immigration	Support	Legal, language, crime	"Carpentersville residents suffer under the weight and fear of the matter [illegal immigration] before us."
Grant Crowell	Videographer	None	Communication and transparency	"[C]arpentersville, Illinois, has become a laughingstock by the rest of the U.S. and the world today."
Larissa Chinwah	Reporter, The Daily Herald	None	Transparency and good government	"I was looking for straight answers...it's a reporter's job."
Alex Kotlowitz	Contributor, The New York Times Magazine	None	Transparency and good government	"All immigration politics is local, and complicated, nasty, and personal."

Table 5.2. Politics Stream Matrix: Group Actors in Carpentersville

Who	Role	IIRO Position	Relief Frame(s)	Quote
American Civil Liberties Union	Interest group	Oppose	Legal and civil rights	"Misguided, divisive and expensive anti-immigrant strategy…[an] unconstitutional and unwise approach"
National Council of La Raza	Interest group	Oppose	Legal and civil rights	"Take the hate out of the immigration debate in Carpentersville."
Carpentersville Community Alliance	Pressure group	Oppose	Business interests	"The IIRO will kill our local businesses."
Carpentersville Catholic Churches	Interest group	Oppose	Human rights	"Every member of our community deserves dignity and respect."
Latinos Unidos	Interest group	Oppose	Legal and civil rights	"We need to vote and show that they will no longer be the only scapegoat for the country's immigration problems."
Illinois Coalition for Immigrant and Refugee Rights	Pressure group	Oppose	Human rights	"Carpentersville demonizes immigrants."
Save Carpentersville	Pressure group	Support	Crime and economic	"Our neighborhoods have deteriorated enough."
Chicago Minutemen	Pressure group	Support	Legal and nativist	"We must take back our country."
Illinois Minutemen	Pressure group	Support	Legal and nativist	"Illegal immigrants are a toxic threat to Americans."
Americans for Legal Immigration PAC	Interest group	Support	Legal, language, crime, economic	"Americans fighting back to control and reserve illegal immigration."
Fox Valley Citizens for Legal Immigration	Pressure group	Support	Legal, language, crime, economic	"How many more people will be harmed or killed by criminal aliens?"

phone calls, nor did he offer comment or clarification on the implications. A confidential memorandum was sent to the trustees regarding his legal opinions, but that memo was not made public, and it remains sealed. Similarly, Dave Neumann, the village's police chief, entered the debate when he said that his police officers would be able to enforce the ordinance with the support of federal training.[12] Furthermore, Village Manager Craig Anderson said of the IIRO, "It's [the IIRO] meant to send a message to the new Congress that there's an immigration role to be played on the local level."[13] The positions of bureaucrats quietly influenced village trustees and further divided the village.

In the context of the legal frame, intergovernmental relations also played a part. Residents and elected officials raised numerous questions about whether immigration policy was an intergovernmental affair or not. Who legislates immigration policy? Whose responsibility is it to enforce immigration law? Who pays? Such questions drove the legal frame.

Debates were poignant. During a village board meeting on June 19, 2007, the issue of jurisdiction and intergovernmental relations erupted into a loud and voluminous discussion. In particular, tempers flared among elected officials. Village President Sarto's positions were clear and unwavering. He held that immigration policy was specifically and only in the federal domain. In a village board meeting, he declared, "Immigration laws are federal laws."[14] Sarto furthermore argued that "there's [sic] things that municipalities can and can't do. The point is that the issue of illegal immigration is already a federal issue because the deferral laws dictate the policy as to who is allowed to come into this country and who isn't."[15] In contrast, Trustees Sigwalt and Humpfer strongly argued otherwise. Trustee Humpfer countered to Sarto, "States, municipalities are passing laws for conduct within their own jurisdictions. . . . So I kind of take exception to what you say 'it doesn't affect us at a local level.'" Then, Sigwalt added, "For too long, people have been passing the buck and saying it is the federal government's problem and it is not up to us."

The politics of issues on intergovernmental affairs were divisive. Supporters of the IIRO argued that if other municipalities were enacting laws, so could Carpentersville. The argument was based on government failure to do something about the problem. Trustee Sigwalt captured the essence of this argument, holding, "Our federal government is failing to take action."[16] Supporters also argued that the IIRO made sense given the demographic composition of the village; Carpentersville was over 40 percent Hispanic. Opponents strictly argued that the federal jurisdiction of immigration policy was a constitutionally mandated function of a federated system of government. "It's [the IIRO] unsound. Federal law is not enforceable at the local level. That's why we have the FBI and federal marshals. If they are able to pass it in the first place, the advantage would be to bring enforcement to a local level," said local attorney Ronald Roeser.[17] Either way, the legal frame did not provide relief.

The Communication Frame

Relief politics were expressed by utilizing new forms of political communication. Various actors and organizations harnessed emerging technologies to communicate political messages. Internet distribution of public meetings, blogging, and electronic media were methods employed to influence the debate. These messages framed how the problem and solution definitions were used in political ways to determine the level of support for the IIRO.

The video distribution of public village meetings via the Internet had a strong influence on the political debate. Between 2006 and 2008, the board of trustees meetings were filmed and then placed online through YouTube. The online video transmission of legislative meetings brought a wider audience into the IIRO, although the wider dissemination of these meetings was not without controversy. Village President Sarto strongly argued that filming and streaming YouTube videos was a waste of time and resources. Furthermore, he said, "Carpentersville residents just don't watch web videos."[18]

Others disagreed. In a spirit to promote democratic ideals, Carpentersville resident activist Grant Crowell began filming the village board meetings. Crowell forcefully argued,

> Online video is the best tool for good government today, and good exposure for politicians willing to embrace it. All politicians on the White House level and Congress realize it. Local governments are in the best position to benefit from it, if they mean to do good. But if they have lots of bad stuff going on, then they won't want to allow for video of their activities, because that's the most objective form of transparency. Video can't make government honest, but done right it can expose dishonesty in government (and far better than the local newspaper media, which in Carpentersville is totally clueless themselves with investigative journalism using online video).[19]

Indeed, Crowell hoped to improve the quality and frequency of "good government" interactions between the residents and the village by filming meetings. However, others lacked Crowell's civic-minded nature. For example, Sarto placed blame for the village's problems on Crowell for posting unfavorable online videos on YouTube. Crowell commented:

> Sarto blamed the town's problems on my unfavorable online videos. The new Village President also told me recently that [he] will refuse to do online video,

telling me it [has] caused them nothing but trouble. What they fail to realize is that online video is not the cause of any of their problems. It holds up a mirror, and if there was good government, it would make people want to fix those problems.[20]

However, video distribution can make a difference in the politics of policy issues. In their comprehensive study of E-government, Blackstone, Bognanno, and Hakim assert, "Citizens are able to learn easily about their public officials' voting and activities. Transcripts and real-time video transmission of meetings and hearings are available. All of that increases accountability and transparency, thus enhancing democracy."[21]

Other forms of communication can also play a role, including blogging and electronic daily news. Blogging also played an important role in the communication frame. "Bloggers openly take sides and form alliances with other players who are also seeking to shape the public agenda . . . they advocate clearly for one candidate or policy outcome over another."[22] Similarly, others argue that blogs increasingly play an important role in the political debates and policy outcomes. David Perlmutter argues that blogs provide a venue for actors to provide an alternative perspective to the mainstream media, to help society, to influence public opinion, and to help a cause.[23] Three political blog sites of Bill Sarto, Save Carpentersville, and Carpentersville Action Network emerged as political venues in the agenda setting, problem definition, and political processes. Like other actors in the policy process, bloggers "possess agendas . . . they seek to place those agendas before the public and compel other players to address them."[24] Blogging, for supporters and opponents, ignited the strong emotions in the debate. These blogs did just that.[25]

As the village's political executive, Bill Sarto regularly blogged throughout his term in office. Sarto's blog closely chronicled the IIRO debate and served not only as a source of information but also as a forum for him to express his opposition to the IIRO. According to Sarto, his blog was

> [d]edicated to providing you with the best possible news and events that are taking place in our Village. My goal is to keep you informed of all happenings that are pending. I want you to know the good things that continue to go on in Carpentersville. At this site you will NOT find GOSSIP or controversy. What you will find is NEWS. You will be allowed to make comments: I want to hear what YOU have to say.[26]

The other two blogs, Save Carpentersville and Carpentersville Action Network, emerged as two forums of support and opposition for the IIRO. They, too, chronicled the legislative progress of the IIRO and the related political happenings. Popular threads such as "lowlights" and "trouble with Carpentersville" stand out as issues related to the problem of immigration and the policy proposals. In many cases, public comment from village board meetings continued on these blogs for several years.

The anonymous nature of the blogosphere further exacerbated the veracity of this form of political communication. These venues served as a virtual platform for IIRO supporters and opponents to restate positions and political arguments as well as a place to organize groups. As Sarto aptly held, "I've decided that it's time to keep our residents informed of what is happening outside of the political squabbles that have been going on for far too long. The public has a right to know what is happening in the Village." Indeed, each of these blogs set out to accomplish these goals.

Persistent electronic and print coverage about the IIRO also framed the politics of relief. The regional daily newspaper of Chicago's western suburbs, *The Daily Herald*, provided frequent and in-depth coverage on the issue. Print copies and free access online also spread the word and helped to keep the issue on the political agenda by charting the political conversation about the debate about problem definition to policy design and political responses.

Residents did not always approve of this visibility and increased public attention. "The DH [*Daily Herald*] and [Larrisa] Chinwah are really bad for the Village of Carpentersville. They don't report half of what's really happening in the meetings, only a slanted view. . . . I thought a reporter was supposed to be objective? There is very little objectivity in the Chinwah articles. Why can't the DH hire an American Citizen to write the C'ville [Carpentersville] news anyway?"[27] In response to such criticism, Chinwah responded, "It's a shame that there is so much aggression and misinformation about the immigration debate in this country. In all of the Village Board of Trustees meetings that I've attended, supporters of the ordinance primarily rely on nativist arguments. My job is to report the truth: what occurs and what people tell me."[28] Similarly, a cover article in the *New York Times Magazine* by Alex Kotlowitz brought national attention to the debate in Carpentersville and further empowered supporters and opponents. National attention and scrutiny arrived.

In short, new forms of communication—specifically electronic media—shaped the politics of relief in the immigration debate in Carpentersville. Whether online videos, blogging, or electronic news, the rapid dissemination of political news through various formats allowed for the framing of specific information-related news about immigration and its policy dimensions. The communication frame brought the political debates into the living rooms and home offices of most residents of Carpentersville. Above all, it fostered political participation for residents who may not have otherwise participated.

The Language Frame

Relief politics were expressed by the value and preservation of the English language.[29] The ability to speak English and use the language daily emerged as a benchmark in the determination of whether an immigrant was illegal as well as the degree to which immigrants had assimilated into society. In other words, by supporting the IIRO, proponents of the law facilitated the identification of native Spanish speakers as potential illegal immigrants, or at least, as immigrants that were not integrated into the village. So relief from the Spanish language—in addition to preserving the use of English—also framed the politics of the IIRO debate.

Bob Sperlazzo, the chair of the Fox Valley Citizens for Legal Immigration, led the movement to declare English as the official language of Carpentersville. From 2006 to 2008, he regularly presented vociferous arguments on a monthly basis at village board meetings. He argued, "Declaring English the official language is essential and beneficial to the village . . . leads to the realization of the American Dream . . . [is] common sense government . . . [and] sends a message that there are responsibilities and benefits to living here. One of them is to speak English."[30] Sperlazzo further argued, "English is the glue that unites races, colors, creeds, and it is vital to assimilation." He called for an end to "linguistic welfare."[31] IIRO supporters rallied behind Sperlazzo. Relief from illegal immigrants also came to symbolize relief from the Spanish language. In contrast, opponents argued that since the nation's founding, the United States has been a multi-lingual, multi-cultural nation. The declaration of an English-only law would be a "threat to American liberties and a threat to the principles on which the United State had been created for years before."[32]

For the duration of the 2007 legislative year, activists for and against an English-only law sparred with one another. Residents rallied and disrupted board meetings, as public comments were offered on a monthly basis about the English and Spanish languages. Finally, in June, the village board passed a non-binding resolution to declare English the official language.

The Suburban Decline Frame

Relief politics also centered on the social and economic threats of illegal immigrants: to the village, to the residents, and to the region. Fears of residential and demographic change dominated the suburban decline frame. Specifically, long-term residents worried about the socioeconomic status of new residents, namely immigrants, legal or illegal. Carpentersville residents and employers worried about a loss of population, an increase in poverty, and diminishing property values. They also worried that new residents would contribute to an increase in crime, an increase in unemployment, and a decline in the stability of neighborhoods. For worried residents, the IIRO was the answer to these problems.

By 2000, Carpentersville was an aging suburb with symptoms of decline even before the IIRO policy debate. The suburb's declining public infrastructure presented many problems for residents and local policymakers. In addition to demographic changes, infrastructure decline further exacerbated residents' worries. Financial concerns about the IIRO were copious. Prior to the IIRO proposal, the village was already burdened by the costs of the decline problems. Trustee Ramirez-Sliwinski expressed, "I am afraid that if we pass this ordinance it could affect our bond applications and insurance coverage. It will affect us in many, many ways, not just the immigrants in the village, but all of the residents."[33] Trustee Humpfer further echoed, "Illegal immigrants are hitting citizens in the pocketbook" for the services they use without paying taxes.[34]

Residents framed this process of social and economic change as suburban decline. For them, increased social diversity and changes in the economic structure demonstrated a threat to the way of life. Coupled with a decaying public infrastructure and the potential costs associated with maintenance, the decline of suburban Carpentersville was an imminent threat to the middle class way of life.

The Nativist Frame

Relief politics were expressed by nativist fears of others in the form of xenophobic attitudes and behaviors. The nativist frame focused on the political characterization of immigrants in the public discourse. Nativist politics or policies favored the interests of established residents over those of immigrants. Nativists aimed to reestablish or preserve long-term cultural traits, thoughts, and lifestyles in order to limit the assimilation of immigrants into the community. In the context of Carpentersville, political phrases, terminology, and public ownership shaped the nativist frame. So, framing the issue of immigration in distinct ways shaped the debate and its outcome.

Phrases become politicized through repetition and common use in everyday language. They are used for a power advantage to shape public opinion over policy debates. Phrases in Carpentersville were used in newspapers, community meetings, neighborhood associations, rallies, and village board meetings. Phrases such as "we're tired" and "enough is enough" embodied the nativist attitudes in this debate—and served as a policy rationale for relief. The repetition of phrases like these became spoken symbols of the politics of relief. For instance, Trustee Sigwalt made one of the strongest nativist arguments. She yelled in a board meeting, "Capitol Hill has got to sit up and take notice that the American people aren't going to take it anymore. We can't afford it anymore, and I think that we should move forward and support those other brave communities that have said, 'enough is enough.' I believe we owe it to our residents—our taxpaying residents—to hear what they have to say."[35]

Political terminology also mattered. Actors used specific terms to identify and define the problem population. According to Lina Newton, "Official rhetoric ensures that policy nomenclature is often not politically neutral."[36] Political actors in Carpentersville commonly used three terms to refer to the foreign-born population of Carpentersville. First, "illegal immigrant" was used to refer to a person and their legal status. Second, "illegal alien" was used to refer to the legal status exclusively. Third, "undocumented resident" or "undocumented immigrant" was used to refer to the action of a person. These terms were thinly veiled political statements about the positions on the IIRO. Supporters nearly universally used the term "illegal alien" during policy debates to emphasize the illegal action and depersonalize the experience. In contrast, opponents used terms to personalize the experience of immigrants by referring to them as people and decoupling the action from the person or resident. Ultimately, these distinctions allowed both supporters and opponents to define the deserving and undeserving population.

Taking personal and public ownership of the debate framed residents' nativist viewpoints. Some residents urged the people of Carpentersville to draw on the collective and shared history of immigration to argue against the IIRO. For example, resident Horacio Minjares said, "The people who are proposing these ordinances are ignorant of their history."[37] However, while most residents were indeed descendants of immigrants, political actors distinguished between deserving and undeserving populations. Carpentersville's long-term, or native residents called their village "my town" and urged other residents and elected officials to "take back" their community from illegal immigrants. Thus, they argued that legal residents deserved to use their voice and political power to implement public policy, while illegal residents did not deserve similar rights.

These views were also clarified and vocalized by other organizations. The nationalist groups of the Minutemen of Chicago and Illinois, for instance, often used nativist language to shape the political rhetoric. In numerous village board meetings, they declared, "We must take back our country . . . illegal immigrants are a toxic threat to Americans." Yet, other groups countered these threats. A prime example is the Catholic Church. Local priests of St. Monica Church called for "dignity" and "respect" for every resident of the village, regardless of the status of residency. Similarly, the Illinois Coalition for Immigrant and Refugee Rights urged residents of Carpentersville to stop "demonizing" immigrants and urged for a peaceful discourse.[38]

Derogatory phrases, adversarial terms, and thoughts embody the nature of nativism. The nativist frame demonstrates how the politics of using phrases and terms allow actors to take advantage of characterizations of a deserving or undeserving population. Public opinion about policy debates is molded around these characterizations.

Summary

The fight for local control of immigration policy was centered on the demand of native residents to get relief from illegal immigrants—from their language, their crime, and their way of life. Carpentersville residents struggled to gain political power that would empower them to implement public policies to address their definitions of problems. An analysis of the framing of relief politics shows that the behavior of individual and group actors can be characterized in five frames: legal, communication, language, decline, and nativist. Such framing along these dimensions demarcated the battle lines between IIRO supporters and opponents in their quest for power. The adoption of the IIRO would diminish the threat to middle-class living. The failure of the IIRO would protect the rights and liberties of all residents.

FARMERS BRANCH

On January 22, 2007, a flurry of activity consumed the chamber of the Farmers Branch City Council. Observers of the policy debate packed into the city hall for the opportunity to witness and comment on the impending local immigration ordinance. Such a crowd was a rare event in Farmers Branch, largely because its civic affairs were generally pro forma. Yet, the emerging fight for local control of immigration policy ignited a furious passion among residents.

Tim O'Hare, former mayor and then a member of the city council, synthesized the city's legislative goals, "I think the goal we are trying to achieve is to keep illegals out of Farmers Branch and keep Farmers Branch from being an attractive place for illegal aliens to move."[39]

The politics of relief were expressed in this heated meeting of the city council. A newly edited Ordinance 2903 was presented for consideration. As the session began, a minister from the Farmers Branch Church of Christ opened the session with a prayer—asking God to bless the elected officials with leadership and wisdom. Shortly thereafter, a local radio show host, Mike Gallagher, presented the council with $10,075 that was raised by his listeners, who purchased t-shirts that said, "This is America. Please Speak English." The donation was for the establishment of a legal defense fund earmarked for any impending legal challenge to the ordinance. Next, 43 residents addressed the council about the adoption of Ordinance 2903. Frustrated, these residents spoke out about the decline of their community and the "Mexican invasion" of their neighborhoods. They wanted relief. Council members were equally upset. Mayor Pro Tem Ben Robinson cautioned, "Hyphenated Americans will cause the United States to collapse into anarchy like Iraq." The ordinance was unanimously passed, and a national fury ensued.[40]

The city's residents and elected officials did not shy away from the national attention. Mayor Tim O'Hare reflected:

> You have to remember when we first started talking about this it wasn't discussed in presidential debates, this wasn't discussed in senatorial elections, and everybody stayed away from it. And they stayed away from it because if you brought it up or said anything about it, everybody knew that the race card gets played. So Farmers Branch, along with a handful of other cities, but I think we were the one that was the most high profile, raised the awareness of the issue and shortly thereafter it's being discussed in presidential debates, it's being discussed in gubernatorial races across the country.[41]

Indeed, Farmers Branch charted its own course. Ordinances 2892, 2903, and 2952 were among the first ordinances in the nation to be adopted through local legislative processes and a direct vote of the electorate. Gerry Henigsman, executive vice president of a local apartment association, observed that the provision of a domicile—a place to call home—for illegal immigrants in the city was a key to the problem. He noted, "We don't mind if you spend your money here and shop, but we don't want you to live here ... and we're going to use living requirements to enforce that."[42] And that is exactly what the city intended to do.

Residents and politicians pursued relief from the problems of illegal immigrants in Farmers Branch. They wanted to control their own policy agenda and their own implementation of local immigration policies. The problem and solution streams joined the politics stream for the adoption of relief ordinances. The city's elected officials unanimously agreed about the attributes of the problem, and over two-thirds of residents also agreed. The policy design similarly enjoyed strong support among stakeholders. This raises an important question: What are the factors that led to policy adoption and why? Whether they supported or opposed the ordinances, residents sought to control their own destiny rather than rely on other state or federal governments to confront the issue. Thus, what determines whether residents seek the ability to set their own course and how?

Farmers Branch harnessed the political process to grapple with these questions. The politics of relief deal with the processes that allow individual and group actors to reconcile such questions. The outcome depends on the political arguments and arrangements among those who sought relief from the defined problem. The examination of these frames reveals the messy struggle for political power and the long journey toward relief.[43] Through the framing analysis, the roles of the individual actors, as displayed in Table 5.3, and the group actors, as displayed in Table 5.4, are examined.

Table 5.3. Politics Stream Matrix: Individual Actors in Farmers Branch

Who	Role	Ordinance Position	Relief Frame(s)	Quote
Tim O'Hare	Mayor, City of Farmers Branch	Support	Rule of law; suburban decline	"Our people have clearly spoken and we're going to recognize the will of the people."
Ben Robinson	Mayor Pro Tem, City of Farmers Branch	Support	Rule of law; suburban decline	"We are the federal government."
Bill Moses	Councilman, City of Farmers Branch	Support	Rule of law; intergovernmental relations	"I'm just sorry that the federal government has put us in this position."
Mike Gallagher	Host, 660AM, KSKY Radio	Support	Rule of law; intergovernmental relations; nativist	"We won't stop fighting the legal battles."
Bob Phelps	Mayor, City of Farmers Branch	Oppose	Rule of law; intergovernmental relations	"... Ordinance 2903 is bad for the city because it's costing the taxpayers hundreds of thousands of dollars."
Carlos Quintanilla	President, Accion America	Oppose	Rule of law; intergovernmental relations; nativist	"Si se puede!"
Elizabeth Villafranca	Chapter president, LULAC	Oppose	Rule of law; intergovernmental relations; nativist; suburban decline	"We are getting nothing positive out of [the ordinance] except for negative images of the city."
Stephanie Sandoval	Reporter, *The Dallas Morning News*	None	Transparency and good government	"It's an important story to tell ... there are many lessons."

Table 5.4. Politics Stream Matrix: Group Actors in Farmers Branch

Who	Role	IIRO Position	Relief Frame(s)	Quote
American Civil Liberties Union (ACLU)	Interest group	Oppose	Rule of law; intergovernmental relations;	"The ACLU doesn't stand down when the Constitution is on the table."
League of United Latin American Citizens (LULAC)	Interest group	Oppose	Rule of law; intergovernmental relations; nativist	"This is un-American, un-Texan and un-Christian, and we're going to take them to court, and we're going to win."
Mexican American Legal Defense and Educational Fund (MALDEF)	Interest group	Oppose	Rule of law; intergovernmental relations;	"No municipality has the authority to regulate immigration. The City of Farmers Branch's repeated attempts to do so are both impractical and unconstitutional."
Greater Dallas Catholic Churches	Interest group	Oppose	Nativist	"I wonder if Jesus and Mary would find a place in Farmers Branch? They probably wouldn't."
Let the Voters Decide	Pressure group	Oppose	Rule of law; intergovernmental relations; nativist; suburban decline	"Formed to oppose the controversial immigration ordinance."
Farmers Branch voters	Electorate	Support	Rule of law; intergovernmental relations; nativist; suburban decline	"68 percent of voters supported [Ordinance] 2903."
Farmers Branch Church of Christ	Interest group	Divided	Rule of law	"Our leaders in our city have sought our prayers. They know they need our wisdom."
Support Farmers Branch	Pressure group	Support	Suburban decline	"[the ordinance] was brilliantly simple."
Texas Minutemen	Pressure group	Support	Rule of law; nativist	"Illegal aliens are criminals. Arrest them send them home."

Rule of Law Frame

Politicians and residents alike sought relief by evoking the rule of law frame. Relief politics were commonly expressed in the form of the argument that illegal residency was a crime; thus, illegal immigrants were criminals and deserved deportation. Accordingly, supporters argued for the imperative to uphold the law. Ordinance 2903 empowered Farmers Branch to do just that.

Mayor Tim O'Hare was the central public figure to propagate the rule of law frame. He emphasized the rule of law as a mechanism to achieve relief from illegal immigration. He put forth, "People stand up for the rule of law but more than that it's the amount of money that people are paying for people who have broken our laws and continue to come into our country and break our laws that has most people concerned . . . now it is clearer than ever why this is important."[44] The mayor and his supporters argued that residents who abide by laws are fair, orderly, and above all, American. O'Hare further argued and convinced his fellow councilmen as well as constituents by conjuring up images of the constitution, rule of law, and the nation's republican history. He boldly claimed:

> Now, right or wrong, good or bad, laws in the United States matter. And the reason people want to come here is because they know that laws do matter. Because you're protected from oppression, protected from violence, protected from somebody ripping you off or the government forcing you to do what you don't want to do. And when we as a society say that laws don't matter for this group or that group, then that is the beginning of a crumbling of the constitutional republic that we have, and every nation in the history of the world, especially every great nation in the history of the world, has crumbed at some point and it usually is a result of crumbling from within.[45]

Such imagery of the historical legacy of the fight for self-governance in the United States reinforced O'Hare's political fight to obtain the rule of law in Farmers Branch. The delivery of this message not only resonated with the city's residents, but it also increased the popularity of the local legislative body, which ultimately bolstered electoral support for the ordinances.

However, elected political actors did not win the fight alone. Various non-profit organizations also impacted the politics of relief in Farmers Branch. These organizations included interest groups, churches, pressure groups, and legal groups. First, local business owner Elizabeth Villafranca started a Farmers Branch chapter of the League of United Latin American Citizens (LULAC). The daughter of immigrants and now a successful restaurateur, Villafranca grew concerned about the lack of human rights for residents. She argued that "[Ordinance 2903] goes after the most vulnerable people in our society . . . these people are so scared."[46] Her comments exemplified not only the emotional state of residents but also the practical and logistical worries that residents had in the period after the adoption of the ordinance. As a result, uncertainties of eviction were rampant. According to local politicians, this served as evidence that 2903 would have its desired effects to provide relief from illegal immigrants.

Second, two local churches quietly played a role in the political debate. The first church, the Farmers Branch Church of Christ, was composed of a congregation of influential local policymakers. Three councilmen and numerous city bureaucrats attended the church every Sunday. They sought the counsel of Pastor Eddy Ketchersid, who regularly prayed for wisdom and obedience for the city's decisionmakers. Many church members interpreted this to be a tacit endorsement of the ordinances. The second church, Mary Immaculate, the city's only Roman Catholic Church, urged caution throughout the debate. The church regularly hosted immigration policy forums. Reverend Bruce Bradley, the church's leader, said that he was obligated to meet the needs of his parishioners, noting that his church offers immigrants a sanctuary and protection. Likewise, the Roman Catholic Church in neighboring Dallas spoke up during a Mass on the World Day of Migrants and Refugees. On January 14, 2007, Dallas Bishop Charles Grahmann offered a provocative sermon at the Cathedral Santuario de Guadalupe. He preached, "You shall treat the alien who resides with you no differently than the natives born among you, for you too were once aliens." Bishop Grahmann continued his sermon, proclaiming:

> People have a right to migrate to sustain their lives and the lives of their families. A country has the right to regulate its borders—but it must do so with justice and mercy . . . [Immigrants arrive] to escape poverty and persecution, and we've often said that we need them to do jobs that others aren't willing to do, or not willing to do at the price being paid. So this migration becomes a reality, and to some, a threat.[47]

Indeed, relief politics were defined by the reconciliation of these realities and threats.

Third, pressure groups formed to influence relief politics. Let the Voters Decide was formed by a multiethnic group of volunteers to promote community involvement in the fight for local control of immigration policy. The group successfully lobbied businesses, politicians, and residents to force a direct vote on the adoption of Ordinance 2903. The city vote was held on May 12, 2007. While residents voted to adopt the ordinance, Let the Voters Decide continued to advance its agenda and received significant local, state, and national press attention. The development of a professional website only furthered their agenda and visibility.[48] In contrast, Support Farmers Branch was formed to support the adoption and implementation of Ordinance 2903. Tom Bohmier, the group's leader, voiced strong support for the city council, urging them to adopt the ordinance. Upon adoption of 2903, he said, "The City Council heard they should do this . . . people that aren't happy about it are sore losers."[49] Support Farmers Branch also helped to organize a legal defense fund for the city. In anticipation of legal challenges to the ordinances, the group organized the collection of donations to facilitate the city's defense. Pressure groups, such as Let the Voters Decide and Support Farmers Branch, employed similar means to achieve dissimilar outcomes. Both groups increased public participation and influenced key stakeholders; however, in the end, policy outcomes varied.

Fourth, legal groups became involved in the fight for local control of immigration policy. The American Civil Liberties Union (ACLU) led the national fight to curtail the implementation of such ordinances. In the Farmers Branch case, the organization argued that local policymakers and supporters had misinterpreted their jurisdiction of the policy domain. More importantly they failed to realize the ordinance's devastating social and economic impacts on their residents. According to Omar Jadwat, staff attorney at the ACLU Immigrants' Rights Project, "The politicians who support this ordinance and their advisors from national anti-immigrant organizations seem to regard this as some sort of game, even though the laws they have invented are terribly serious and have real consequences for the city and its residents. But it's time for them to realize that they've long since struck out."[50] Lisa Graybill, the legal director of the ACLU of Texas, also accused the city of overstepping its police powers. She said, "Farmers Branch has taken the curious approach of recreating their ordinance to be even more intrusive and offensive, to the point of subjecting everyone to an intrusive, Big Brother-like licensing regime. The city has lost sight not only of the law, but of common sense. . . ."[51] The arguments for relief were increasingly blurred as legal organizations became involved in the political debate.

Last, protesters also organized to oppose the local control of immigration policy. Community organizer Carlos Quintanilla founded Acción America as the main opposition group. According to Quintanilla, the group was created "in response to the absence of an organized defense of immigrants in Farmers Branch . . . becom[ing] a strong and booming voice for Hispanics taking the lead in efforts in Farmers Branch and Irving and other issues affecting Hispanics throughout the Dallas Metroplex."[52] During the vote of the city council, a march of several hundred people was organized to protest. The group demonstrated in front of the city hall and shouted, "O'Hare must go!" While a few supporters countered back, "America is for Americans," they were largely unorganized.

The rule of law frame demonstrates that definitions of relief influenced the outcome of the policy debate. Numerous actors and organizations were involved. Elected political actors, interest groups, churches, pressure groups, and legal groups impacted the politics of relief in Farmers Branch. These individuals and groups took advantage of the political process to reward fair and law-abiding citizens with relief from unfair and illegal residents in their community. They accomplished their goal through the adoption of local control of immigration policy.

Above all, the "Americanization" of the policy debate transformed the concept of relief into a benchmark for one's nationalism and pride for the country. In other words, a resident is American when she supports the ordinances. Mayor O'Hare strengthened this notion when he said, "And they know where we are and what we stand for. They know we are a patriotic town, they know we are a town who stands for the rule of law. They know we're trying to make a difference in the world, and that's attractive to a lot of people."[53] In the end, a resident's argument captured the mayor's sentiments quite simply. Bill O'Brien said, "I applaud Farmers Branch. Illegal means illegal, and it's unfair to create exceptions for illegal immigrants."[54]

Intergovernmental Relations Frame

The intergovernmental relations frame played a role in developing the case for relief to residents of Farmers Branch. The relationships among the three levels of government and their public powers raised numerous questions in the fight for local control of immigration policy. Which levels of government are responsible for legislating immigration policy? Who implements these policies, and whose responsibility is it to enforce the policies?

Speaking for the city council, Ben Robinson, mayor pro tem, declared without hesitation, "We are the federal government. We fund their activities."[55] Yet other elected officials disagreed. Texas state representatives Rafael Anchia and Roberto Alonzo urged the city's leadership to not seek local control of immigration policy and leave it to the federal government. Nonetheless, residents frequently rejoined, "We're going to send a message and set an example for the United States."[56] However, some other residents in nearby jurisdictions worried about the spillover effects; that is, illegal immigrants might flee Farmers Branch for other nearby jurisdictions without such ordinances. Ty Jones, a resident in neighboring Mesquite, argued, "I always thought that this was a national or state issue, not a local one. If each individual community does this, illegal immigrants will push themselves into other communities without these laws."[57]

Among the frames for relief, the intergovernmental relations frame resonated most deeply with residents of Farmers Branch. Many residents in the Metroplex interpreted Farmers Branch's actions positively. They even encouraged the city to proudly set an example for other cities with similar problems. Ronnie Smith said, "Farmers Branch showed tremendous courage and tenacity dealing with illegal immigrants. Every city should follow its example. . . ."[58] In particular, the comments of two residents in nearby Garland embodied the larger public sentiments among residents supporting the ordinances. Curtis Green argued, "If the actions taken by Farmers Branch are legally defensible, I would like Garland and other cities to follow the lead . . . taking action on a local basis would help emphasize the importance of legal immigration and the fact that illegal immigration won't be tolerated."[59] Cynthia Stock agreed. She went on to comment, "I strongly support the stand taken by Farmers Branch. If the laws already on the books were being enforced, that city would not have had to take such action . . . It's not right, and it's not fair to taxpayers and law-abiding citizens."[60]

In contrast, other public dialogue emphasized the national failure of society and the federal government to implement effective immigration policies. Other residents' minority opinions argued that the disparities among multiple localities with multiple laws would only worsen the problem. Beverly Elam proclaimed, "This is a federal issue, and we should demand that our federal government deal with it quickly. The laws should not differ from city to city or state to state."[61] Another resident noted, "Illegal immigration didn't begin yesterday, and it won't end tomorrow. Attempting to control it at the municipal level is probably more feel-good than effective. . . . The solution lies at the federal level and entails border enforcement and a guest worker program. Even with a comprehensive plan, it's going to take years."[62]

Relief politics sought to disentangle questions around the intergovernmental nature of immigration policy. Residents and stakeholders had numerous opinions on the issue, and constitutional frameworks did not motivate them. Instead, they argued that political actors needed to take action and create laws regardless of the structural arrangements among levels of government. According to residents, the system was broken, and Farmers Branch had a problem. Ordinance 2903 was their answer.

The Nativist Frame

Residents' nativist attitudes capitalized on the fears of their different neighbors to promote the illegal immigration ordinances. The nativist frame employs an approach to preserve the language and character of the native residents of Farmers Branch. Mayor Tim O'Hare set the tone for the public debates. He remarked, "To some people it is about race and I can't sit here and tell you that there's not a single person who voted for Ordinance 2903 that doesn't want to see brown people in their city. I'm sure there are. But it's not what I have heard." Latent phobia of immigrants—and their languages, customs, and lifestyles—reflected these attitudes and behaviors. Judy Trammell said, "I am not prejudiced against anyone, but I feel what Farmers Branch has done is very fair. We need people who will participate as citizens in our communities, not just as visitors, especially those who are sending funds back to Mexico. If they are benefiting from our great country, they need to speak the language and give back."

Yet, some residents urged caution. Glen Johnstone exclaimed, "Why not rename the city Xenophobes Branch? A city's inclusiveness and diversity give it character and strength. Local, state, and federal law enforcement should enforce the current immigration laws and stop illegal employment." Similarly, Eric Brandler said, "Accounting for both American principles and our historical heritage, we need to resist the urge to create an environment that makes all darker-skinned people criminal suspects." Residents in neighboring jurisdictions also worried about the unintended consequences of the Farmers Branch's policy decision. "Dealing with illegal immigrants by making English the official language of the city. Hmmm. I can't quite make the connection. To me, it reeks of Hispano-phobia. It's shocking and embarrassing. This white male hopes our City Council studies this Farmers Branch case carefully—it's a perfect example of what we do not want to do in Garland," said Nelson Prater.

The desire to label white, native residents as deserving or entitled also fueled the nativist backlash, which emerged as a central theme among nativists. Throughout the policy debate, residents were labeled as to whether they deserved or were entitled to access to public services. Residents sought to eliminate what they perceived to be free riders in the system; that is, individuals who consumed public resources without paying for them. Paying taxes became the litmus for one's deservingness. Local taxpayers were identified as the deserving population, while illegal immigrants were characterized as undeserving. Mayor Tim O'Hare was the chief proponent of this notion. He argued repeatedly, "There is no free lunch, although we do give a lot of free lunches inside our school districts, and with healthcare and everything else there is no free lunch."[63] Indeed, this resonated with his constituents.

Yet, the concept of who pays taxes became a nebulous issue because income, property, and sales taxes were conflated. Residents, regardless of legal status, pay either all, some, or none of these taxes. Proponents of the ordinances often commented that illegal immigrants did not pay taxes and thus did not deserve services. For instance, Johnny Bennett said, "This is not a discrimination issue. People are getting tired of illegal immigrants taking advantage of the system by receiving government benefits and not paying taxes." Mayor Tim O'Hare also echoed this sentiment. "I personally don't care if you come here from Mexico, Zimbabwe, Canada, Ireland or anywhere else, you and I in my view, shouldn't have to pay for someone else's children to get educated, or pay for them to get healthcare, shouldn't have to pay for someone to get free housing. It's just wrong." The problem with this argument centers on the public nature of the goods and services. Economists identify collective consumption goods, or public goods, which "all enjoy in common in the sense that each individual's consumption of such a good leads to no subtractions from any other individual's consumption of that good."[64] In other words, public goods are non-rivalrous and non-excludable.[65] Residents do not compete for the consumption of the good, and one's consumption of the good does not limit another one's consumption. Local roads, playgrounds, schools, and libraries, for example, are generally thought to be public goods. One of the ironies is that legal residents pay few taxes and enjoy many benefits, while illegal residents pay more taxes and may not benefit as much. The mere possibility of this irony debunks the deservingness argument.[66]

The Texas Minutemen fostered nativism in Farmers Branch. Its members affiliate with the anti-illegal immigrant group to focus on border patrol and surveillance of day labor centers. Clark Kirby directed the Minuteman Civil Defense Corps for the North Texas Chapter. He observed, "The illegal behavior is everywhere we go, and the police can't be everywhere, Immigration [Immigration and Customs Enforcement] can't be everywhere. Since the government is so hamstrung and paralyzed in enforcing our laws, the citizens have to pick up the slack."[67] Accordingly, his volunteers use spy tactics to survey immigrant workers and their employers. The Minutemen follow them around and use scare tactics to intimidate those who they perceive to be illegal immigrants. Some residents in Farmers Branch applauded their efforts, while others condemned them. A supporter commented, "What an excellent way to begin to solve the illegal problem—pull the rug out from under their feet!" Another resident noted, "The Minutemen are today's KKK. Shame on FB [Farmers Branch]."[68]

The use of incendiary language, litmus tests on public deservingness, and fringe nationalism capture the spirit of nativism. The nativist frame reveals the divisive nature of the politics of relief. Nativists used the political process to take advantage of a vulnerable population through vicious characterizations of an undeserving population. Then, public opinion was shaped in their favor to support the ordinances. Mayor O'Hare declared, "You can point to just about every facet of government—healthcare, education, taxes and say how illegal immigration has affected it."[69] Such declarations only served to conflate the policy debate.

Suburban Decline Frame

The socioeconomic decline of Farmers Branch was a focus of the politics of relief. Politicians and residents argued that illegal immigrants presented a social and economic threat to the suburban middle-class lifestyle that had been enjoyed for many decades. The demographic change of the population, from white to Hispanic, caused long-term residents to blame the change on illegal immigration. Symptoms of decline prevailed: dwindling population, decreasing income, increasing poverty, declining housing stock, shrinking property values, decaying infrastructure decay, and growing crime rates. One resident observed, "There was a great white flight in the area of Dallas and Forth Worth. This city is in transition, like many other inner cities in the country, and all of them seek the same thing: better schools, better jobs, better community, better health facilities . . . Is there an illegal alien issue in Farmers Branch? No. It's a city in transition."[70] Concerned residents and shrewd politicians took note of these transitions. They confronted suburban decline with an ordinance to push out an undesirable population on which they blamed their woes.

Local executive and legislative bodies responded to suburban decline. First, political actors used public rhetoric to address residents' concerns. For example, O'Hare said, "I'd say the top priority has been revitalizing the City, re-energizing the City, tearing down the old dilapidated things and putting up new things, just giving the City a facelift."[71] The public commitment to address the problem helped to establish the revitalization policy agenda. Next, the city council's first policy response was to create the Branch Revitalization Task Force. In May 2006, this group of seven residents was charged with assessing the city's needs and methods to revitalize the city so that it would be "more attractive for retail and residential development and redevelopment." Ed Bonneau was appointed chairman of the task force. His personal relationships provided him intimate access to the city's key policymakers. A multimillionaire and a resident of Farmers Branch for over five decades, Ed Bonneau's family was also a long-time member of the Church of Christ, where his son was the childhood best friend of the city's future mayor, Tim O'Hare. This relationship facilitated close contact and agenda setting between the task force and local political actors. Other task force members included residents from the private sector in real estate, banking, and development.[72]

Then, four months later in September, the second policy response was motivated by the task force's delivery of a report to the city council. In the report, the Task Force identified the problems with Farmers Branch as a result of the delayed immigration debate and its impacts on business. Specifically, they found:

From the standpoint of businesspersons and of members of the Task Force charged with promoting redevelopment, revitalization, and a positive city image . . . concerned that the City has been painted as divisive and unsafe, where property values and quality of schools are declining, and crime rates are increasing . . . business cannot afford the additional risk of being identified with a community or environment that connotes any hint of negative publicity.[73]

The Branch Redevelopment Task Force urged the mayor and council to act quickly and adopt the local ordinance to curtail illegal immigration. Doing so would improve the business climate, the public perception of the city, and provide redevelopment opportunities.

While many of the city's elected and appointed actors supported the policy response to suburban decline, a few key actors did not. On May 8, 2007, just prior to the referendum on 2903, Mayor Bob Phelps former Mayor David Blaire, and former City Manager Richard Escalante, released a public letter that announced their opposition to the ordinance. The mayor wrote, "We believe this is the worst ordinance ever considered by a Farmers Branch City Council. Continuing this course of action will create a financial and social crisis in our community that will take years to recover from."[74] In the aftermath of the adoption of 2903, Dallas area realtor Donna Harris said, "All I can say is WOW! What Farmers Branch doesn't see is all the work the illegal immigrants do in the Dallas area because their small little city is very old and built out. They don't have any areas of new developments. If they did, they would know it's the illegal immigrants who are building all the houses in our areas."[75]

Ultimately, the quest for relief is about the politics of suburban decline. These suburbs, like Farmers Branch, experienced symptoms of distress due to the uneven distribution of population and economic resources due to the fragmentation of local political systems.[76] The suburb's politicians and residents addressed such issues by identifying a population within their jurisdiction that may have been the cause of the socioeconomic decline. Illegal immigrants in Farmers Branch were blamed for these problems; therefore, local public policies were crafted to ameliorate the issues—thus relieving the distress. One journalist astutely observed that Farmers Branch "looks like a troubled community desperate to transform its image and reclaim its simple past, a time when all neighborhoods looked like each other."[77]

Summary

The politics of relief was a process of determining the distribution of power and decisionmaking in the fight for local control of immigration policy. Through the lens of thematic framing, we can glean the various dimensions of relief. The intergovernmental relations frame provided a rationale for local governmental jurisdictions since others had failed to implement a solution for the problem of illegal immigration. The rule of law framed illegal residency as a criminal issue. The nativist frame took advantage of residents' fears of others and latent xenophobia to advance relief in Farmers Branch. Framing suburban decline as a problem of demographic shifts and the arrival of illegal immigrants furthered the relief agenda. Political actors who successfully framed relief as a way to get rid of illegal immigrants were about to merge the problem and policy streams with politics. The identification of the problem of illegal immigration and the design of Ordinance 2903 as a policy response empowered actors to use their politics to set the agenda and lobby for the support to ultimately adopt the policy.

HAZLETON

On July 13, 2006, the national spotlight descended on the Hazleton City Council as it considered legislative action to take local control of immigration policy. After only two hours of debate, the controversial IIRA passed by a four-to-one vote. Fervently proud yet cautious, Mayor Lou Barletta left the council chamber wearing a bulletproof vest to speak to the observers outside. He defiantly remarked, "The illegal citizens, I would recommend they leave . . . What you see here tonight, really, is a city that wants to take back what America has given it." Meanwhile, in front of the city hall, many supporters and opponents gathered to voice their opinions, as riot police took notice. In one of the largest rallies in Hazleton's recent history, residents made clear their demands for relief from illegal immigration.

Barletta's remarks captured the crux of the politics of relief. On the quest for "relief," the mayor solidified support by "taking back" control of the city for his constituents. The fight for local control of immigration policy was centered on the need of a native population to gain relief from a foreign-born population. The need for relief was the result of problems that illegal immigrants and illegal immigration brought into the community. Accordingly, this relief arrived as public policies known as IIROs (or IIRAs). These laws reduced the loss of a middle-class lifestyle and the threat of suburban decline that low-income illegal immigrants posed to middle-income native residents, and so then the law became the vehicle to provide relief from these threats.[78]

Relief politics defined the struggle for power to gain local control of immigration policy in Hazleton. The problem and solution streams converged on the politics stream that determined the outcome of the debate.[79] The problem stream defined the public nature of the illegal immigration problem, and the solution stream produced the IIRA policy design. Policymakers defined a desired outcome to the city's problem: police the presence of illegal immigrants in Hazleton. The legal issues related to the policy solution, then, defined the politics of relief. Regardless of the outcome of the legal debate, the political debate was centered on how actors won control over their own local issues. Thus, what determines whether residents took control of their ability to set their own course and how?

The answers rest on the political discourse and legal arguments among those that seek relief. The politics of relief are a process by which actors secure power to influence the policy process. The struggle for political power and relief of the illegal immigration was expressed through the framing of relief issues.[80] Specifically, I examine the individual and group actors as displayed in Table 5.5.

The Judicial Frame

The political fight evolved into a judicial fight for local control of immigration policy in Hazleton. A key figure in judicial fight was Kris Kobach. An attorney, professor, and politician, Kobach authored the IIRA and provided counsel to the City of Hazleton.[81] Kobach developed a personal relationship with Barletta after he spoke out in support of Hazleton's right to enact such legislation. Barletta said, "It really only took one conversation to realize that he truly knew what he was talking about."[82] The mayor then entrusted Kobach with the city's legal affairs to defend the IIRA. Kobach continued to represent Hazleton and later described himself as "[the] lead counsel defending Hazleton, Pennsylvania, in its efforts to stop the employment of unauthorized aliens and the harboring of illegal aliens in apartments against a suit brought by the ACLU."[83]

Numerous individuals and organizations formed a coalition to bring legal action against the City of Hazleton. The group consisted of a consortium of attorneys and legal organizations, including 21 attorneys from private practice, the ACLU of Pennsylvania, the ACLU Foundation Immigrants' Rights Project, the Community Justice Project, and the Puerto Rican Legal Defense and Education Fund. On August 15, 2006, this consortium sent Mayor Barletta, the Hazleton City Solicitor, and city council a letter stating that the IIRA violated the Pennsylvania and United States constitutions as well as other civil rights. They asked the council to revoke the ordinance. When the city refused to stop the implementation of the act, a complaint was filed in the US District Court for the Middle District of Pennsylvania. During the fall of 2006, Judge James Munley issued a stipulation and order to restrain the implementation of Hazleton's IIRA. Munley wrote that immigrants would face "irreparable harm" if they were evicted from their residences. Furthermore, Munley opined that the "defendant offers only vague generalizations

Table 5.5. Politics Stream Matrix: Individual and Group Actors in Hazleton

Who	Role	Ordinance Position	Relief Frame(s)	Quote
Lou Barletta	Mayor, City of Hazleton	Support	Legal; intergovernmental relations; communication	"I saw a problem and I tried to do something about it."
Robert Ferdinand	Police Chief, City of Hazleton	Support	Legal	"A certain cold-bloodedness to it [crime] that we had never seen before."
Kris Kobach	Attorney	Support	Legal; intergovernmental relations	"There was no unmistakable act of Congress that bans local governments from adopting an IIRA."
Witold Walczak	Legal Director, ACLU of Pennsylvania	Oppose	Legal; intergovernmental relations	"This ordinance has the potential to cause real harm by costing people their jobs, their houses and requiring children to leave schools."
Omar Jadwat	Immigrants' Rights Project, ACLU	Oppose	Legal; intergovernmental relations	"We expect the government to make laws that will prevent discrimination, not require it."
James Munley	Judge, U.S. District Court	Oppose	Legal	"We find it in the public interest to protect residents' access to homes, education, jobs and businesses."
Theodore McKee	Judge, U.S. Court of Appeals	Oppose	Legal	"[Hazleton] has attempted to usurp authority the Constitution has placed beyond the vicissitudes of local governments."

about the crime allegedly caused by illegal immigrants but has nothing concrete to back up these claims . . . We find it in the public interest to protect residents' access to homes, education, jobs and businesses."[84] The plaintiffs and defendants immediately replied. ACLU attorney Witold Walczak said, "I think what's important is the judge recognized that this ordinance has the potential to cause real harm by costing people their jobs, their houses and requiring children to leave schools."[85] Mayor Barletta countered, "I'm not discouraged. They may have delayed the enforcement for now, but this too shall pass. We've only begun to fight."[86] Hence, the legal fight began.

In March of 2007, a two-week trial began in federal court. Briefly, the plaintiffs argued that Hazleton's IIRA was intended to scapegoat immigrants for the city's real problems of economic decline, crime, and neighborhood decay. Arguments were presented that the act violated the Supremacy Clause of the Constitution as well as due process and equal protection rights—all while usurping federal power. The defendants' arguments were aptly captured by Kobach's view: "There was no unmistakable act of Congress that bans local governments from adopting an IIRA."[87] Then, on July 26, 2007, Judge Munley found Hazleton's law unconstitutional, and he prohibited its enforcement.

The City of Hazleton appealed the ruling to the US District Court for the Middle District of Pennsylvania. On October 30, 2008, the plaintiffs and defendants presented their oral arguments. Then, on September 9, 2010, the court unanimously upheld the district court's rulings and found the ordinances unconstitutional. Judge McKee, writing on behalf of the court, concluded that Hazleton "has attempted to usurp authority the Constitution has placed beyond the vicissitudes of local governments." He also wrote that the local policies should not be preempted by federal policies. "It is of course not our job to sit in judgment of whether state and local frustration about federal immigration policy is warranted. We are, however, required to intervene when states and localities directly undermine the federal objectives embodied in statutes enacted by Congress."[88] Furthermore, the Hazleton IIRA "creates the exact situation that Congress feared: a system under which employers might quite rationally choose to err on the side of discriminating against job applicants who they perceive to be foreign."[89] The plaintiffs agreed. An attorney for the ACLU commented, "This is a major defeat for the misguided, divisive and expensive anti-immigrant strategy that Hazleton has tried to export to the rest of the country."[90]

However, the defendants vowed to continue the fight. In a press conference after the ruling, Barletta said, "I've never wavered in my belief that Hazleton has the right to pass the Illegal Immigration Relief Act and firmly believe our case will be vindicated in the higher court."[91] He continued to forcefully declare, "This ruling is a loss for Hazleton and its legal residents. It is also a blow to the rights of the legal immigrants who choose to call Hazleton their home." Attorney Kris Kobach accused the judges' ruling as "extreme" and "flimsy," noting that the decision "places the Third Circuit on the extreme end of these issues."[92] By framing the judicial fight in political terms, the plaintiffs and defendants aimed to capture the public's demand for relief, or justice.[93]

Residents worried about the role of the judiciary in the fight for local control of immigration policy. Some residents were upset that judges would take on an activist role, and others were simply apathetic about the entire fight. Others were concerned about the legal costs of the judicial fight. For example, Rodney McAfee, a resident of Hazleton, expressed his concern, "We're citizens. What are we supposed to do? It's not right. With these judges, all you need is a swipe of the pen and a smack of the gavel to thwart the will of the people."[94] Other residents expressed disillusionment with the judicial process. Resident Yesenia Hernandez expressed, "I don't think [overturning the law] will necessarily calm things down. Not even the US government can stop illegal immigration. I just don't think this will ever be resolved."[95] Still others expressed concern about the costly legal battle of appealing the IIRA. Barletta said, "They [ACLU] want the court to award them over $2 million from the good people of Hazleton to pay their legal fees."[96] In response to the threat of hefty legal bills, he organized an Internet-based group, Small Town Defenders. The group raised over $500,000 for the legal appeal. Donors could submit a contribution online and then sign a petition to fight for the IIRA. The group encouraged residents to "take a stand and join the fight for Hazleton. If they stop Hazleton, they may stop your community next. Become a Small Town Defender."[97] In sum, by 2011, the city faced nearly $3 million in legal fees and was confronted with the reality that fees might double as appeals continued.[98]

The judicial frame shows that the outcomes of legal challenges impacted the politics of relief. The primary question that faced the courts focused on whose public interest would be served: citizens or illegal immigrants in Hazleton. Indeed, both the plaintiffs and defendants argued on behalf of the public interest. They fought for the common interests of people from Hazleton, although they had different definitions of the "public." The plaintiffs viewed the public as the entire population of Hazleton—native residents and immigrants. In other words, all people living in Hazleton who called Hazleton home constituted the public. Their collective interests represented the public interest. The defendants viewed the public more narrowly—the citizens of Hazleton. Legal residency was a litmus test for the public interest. This legal disagreement evolved from divergent political definitions of the public interest. They were motivated by whether relief was a desired outcome. Throughout the judicial fight, Barletta remained committed to this outcome.

He commented, "We have committed the city to continue this fight and will continue to raise money nationally. I'm confident the people of this country will back the city in that fight."[99]

The Legal Frame

Relief politics in Hazleton were centered directly on questions of the law. Political discourse about the law and order shaped the legal frame. Political actors and legal organizations contributed to this discourse. The ACLU played a key role in fighting Hazleton's IIRA. The organization served as the lead counsel for the plaintiffs in the federal lawsuit. The attorneys defined the problem and shaped the politics of relief around questions of the law. The final goal was to overturn the laws. Anthony Romero, executive director of the ACLU said, "I hope to stop the whole anti-immigrant movement dead in its track."[100]

Partnering with other legal organizations and local firms, the plaintiffs' legal team laid out four arguments on the unconstitutionality of the law. First, they argued that the IIRA violated the Supremacy Clause in the constitution by infringing on the federal government's authority over immigration policy. The act's definition of an immigrant was inconsistent with federal law. It also compelled local officials, landlords, and business owners to determine the legal status of residency in the United States. Second, the IIRA violated landlord and employer rights to due process. It required them to seek proof of residency status from all tenants and employees to avoid fines and losing a business license. At the same time, it created an incentive to deny goods or services to legal residents as a precaution to avoid violating the IIRA. Thus, it made compliance quite difficult, if not impossible. Third, the law violated the equal rights protection of Hazleton's residents and placed a "unique burden" on them. They would be required to provide proof of residency status to obtain a job and secure housing. There was no mechanism to determine the definition of an illegal alien, and there was no process to contest the definition, which violated one's equal protection under the law. In consequence, the IIRA subjected residents to unwarranted discrimination. Residents with foreign last names, foreign accents, or foreign physical appearance faced additional discrimination. Fourth, the act violated First Amendment rights of free speech. Residents with limited proficiency in English were unable to communicate with their own local government that represented them. In contrast, the defendants argued that the city had an inherent right to protect the welfare of their residents. In the absence of federal action, the City of Hazleton argued that it had the police power to enact and implement the IIRA.

The politics of relief were subject to legal interpretations of constitutional rights. Omar Jadwat argued, "We expect the government to make laws that will prevent discrimination, not require it. Hazleton's ordinances clearly violate federal law, but more than that, they violate America's tradition of fairness and democracy."[101] Hazleton's attorney Kris Kobach disagreed and said, "We have a perfect rationale to enact [the IIRA] . . . to protect our citizens."[102] Such arguments appealed to large audiences for and against relief. They provided an easy understanding of the political positions for both sides and armed them with talking points in the debate.

The Intergovernmental Frame

The dynamic relationships between the levels of government played a role in making the case for relief. Political actors in Hazleton asked questions about the nature of immigration policy and its relationship to intergovernmental affairs. Who legislates immigration policy? Who enforces immigration law? Policymakers' answers provided residents a stronger case for relief.

At the heart of the issue was the argument about whether immigration policy was a local or federal policy area. Hazleton put forth that its IIRA was a local matter rather than a federal one because its law sought to penalize the landlord and the business—not the illegal immigrant. Barletta succinctly noted, "We believe we're not interfering with immigration law. We're not penalizing the illegal immigrant. We're penalizing the businesses who hire them and the landlords that rent to them."[103] Indeed, the failure of the federal government to carry out immigration policy was a common issue reported. For instance, in a nationally televised interview on *60 Minutes*, Barletta argued, "Obviously if the federal government was doing something about it you wouldn't be here today. And I wouldn't be talking about it."[104] Interviewer Steve Kroft continued to ask Barletta about the incidence of the problem. Barletta went on to say, "I mean, we're over 2,000 miles from the nearest Mexican border. So, if cities like Hazleton, Pennsylvania, that sits on top of a mountain is having an illegal immigration problem, I can only imagine what it's like elsewhere in the United States."[105] In other words, Hazleton's immigration problem was localized, and as a result, policymakers argued for a local policy response.

Others worried that local immigration policy might become quite fragmented. While some municipalities could welcome all people, others could strictly enforce laws. Similarly, states also may or may not have immigration laws. Federal immigration policies would thus transcend municipal and state policies and likely add to the confusion. This would result in a highly uneven landscape of immigration policy. The pro bono counsel for the plaintiffs, Thomas G. Wilkinson, Jr., argued, "It is the responsibility of the federal government to regulate this very visible and volatile area of the law. To regulate such issues inconsistently and haphazardly on a local basis would be highly inappropriate."[106] Witold Walczak, the legal director of the American Civil Liberties Union of Pennsylvania, agreed with Wilkinson. He added, "Immigration reform is an important issue, but if every little town like Hazleton across the 50 states makes up their own rules about immigration, we're going to be left with an even bigger mess. Clearly we can't have every community setting foreign policy."[107] An assortment of policies at three levels of government raised more questions than answers about how to effectively provide relief from illegal immigration.

The enforcement of the IIRA also became an issue of intergovernmental politics. Barletta said that Hazleton would hire an additional housing officer, but even that might present problems. Barletta noted, "We've gone to ICE [Immigration and Customs Enforcement]. I would think that [it] would want to play that role."[108] However, Tsiwen Law of the Pennsylvania Bar Association conjectured, "If you're asking a city clerk or a landlord to review the status of people under 40 different types of visas, it's a little ridiculous. Even immigration lawyers themselves have problems."[109] This was not a problem that was unique to Hazleton. Nationally, other municipalities grappled with similar enforcement issues. In Riverside, California, for example, a landlord asked, "I don't know who's illegal and who isn't. I'm not Homeland Security."[110] Another business owner asked, "They're making us the immigration agents. How are we, as laymen, supposed to know?"[111]

In sum, local immigration policy creates another layer of complexity in an already fragmented policy environment. For Barletta and the City of Hazleton, this environment is simply the consequence of a lack of federal guidance and implementation. For them, the only way to create effective policy is to create local policy. In contrast, for the plaintiffs, this environment further blurs the intergovernmental relationships between localities, states, and the federal government, making it more difficult to govern and implement effective policy. Witold Walczak summarizes, "This is a complex process and even immigration judges get it wrong frequently. How is this borough government going to determine who's legal?"[112]

The Communication Frame

A variety of forms of political communication expressed relief politics. Actors harnessed electronic media to communicate political messages. The debate was influenced by the prevalence of news coverage on germane issues on television and the Internet. The message of relief was disseminated through these communication channels to reach a national audience.

Mayor Barletta never shied away from the television limelight. During the 2000s, Barletta was virtually the sole public supporter of the IIRA, and he

seemed to relish the opportunity. Without a grassroots organizational structure in Hazleton, few other civic leaders, businesses, or organizations spoke
out in support or opposition to the IIRA. Multiple venues gave him the opportunity to spread his message. In fact, as word spread throughout the nation
about his administration's attempt to gain local control of immigration policy,
even more interest developed in the Hazleton story as the size of the audience increased. In November 2006, Barletta appeared on *60 Minutes* and was
interviewed by Steve Kroft in a segment entitled "Welcome to Hazleton."
Mayor Barletta also appeared numerous times on the CNN show *Lou Dobbs
Tonight* to campaign for Hazleton's IIRA. In 2008, he told Lou Dobbs, "The
ACLU, who is defending the illegal aliens who are suing the city, the plaintiffs are many of them are illegal aliens, are working pro bono for the illegal
aliens. . . . Something is wrong there that a mayor that wants to stand up for
the rule of law is drug through the courts and other mayors are defying the
laws."[113] These interviews nationalized the Hazleton's local fight and further
empowered Mayor Barletta and his supporters. "I realize we're not fighting
for Hazleton anymore. We're fighting for the whole country."[114] He successfully made the fight about an issue that was larger than his community so that
he could carry the fight to a larger platform.

However, not everyone was pleased to see Hazleton in the national headlines, let alone to see Mayor Barletta as the spokesperson of the city. A
Hazleton resident said, "All the bad is focused on us. They never focus on
the good we do."[115] Moreover, Witold Walczak of the ACLU said Barletta
was "an opportunistic mayor [who used the ordinance] to become a national
media star."[116] A minority of residents in Hazleton commonly reported, "Lou
Barletta cares about one person: Lou Barletta."[117] Mayor Barletta long had
ambitions for seeking higher political office. He ran for US Congress in Pennsylvania's 11th congressional district. He lost to incumbent Paul Kanjorski in
2002 and 2008. Then, in 2010, he won the seat.

Despite the mayor's ambitions and his critics, he remained committed to
fighting for local control of immigration policy. Barletta said, "I want the rest
of Hazleton to know I will continue to fight this, whatever position I am in
. . . [I am] confident whoever replaces me will be just as determined."[118] So
he employed a strategy to address his harshest critics. He changed the focus
of the debate from himself to outsiders in Washington and New York med-
dling in Hazleton's affairs. He argued that national organizations and media
outlets had descended upon Hazleton without any context or understanding
of the history of the community. As a lifelong resident and mayor, he was positioned to fight for the place he knew best. For example, Barletta frequently
challenged the ACLU. He charged, "I'm sure the ACLU hopes this little city
runs out of money. But this little city has a big heart."[119]

The Internet served as a public forum to discuss and debate the case of Hazleton. Small Town Defenders was the most popular online portal for supporters of Hazleton. The site actively spread the message nationally and cultivated support through a fundraising effort. The group was endorsed by the city's elected officials and included a personal message from the mayor. It also cataloged national news stories about Hazleton. Likewise, the FIRE (Federal Immigration Reform and Enforcement) Coalition maintained a vibrant presence online and hosted discussion boards. The organization's members organized rallies in support of Hazleton's IIRA. Specifically, FIRE describes its mission as a group that "represents federal, state, and local interests in stopping the flood of illegal immigration and promoting reasonable policies for limited, controlled legal immigration. FIRE Coalition's efforts extend beyond federal matters to include state and local concerns as well."[120] Groups like FIRE were motivated by a mission to empower localities to take control of local immigration policy. Their presence was wide, and many other groups formed, drawing on these examples.

Various forms of communication shaped the politics of relief in the immigration debate in Hazleton. Continual news cycles disseminated political messages in real time, thus allowing political actors to regularly reframe the message of relief. The nationalization of the issue only piqued interest in the case and made this political debate part of the public dialogue. It spanned from Hazleton to the federal courts in Scranton and Philadelphia and from the nation's capital to the West Coast. These messages were not bound by geography. The airwaves and cables carried them nationally and raised awareness on the issue. As a result, the issue was further localized for residents everywhere.

Summary

Relief politics provided an outlet for communication about problems in Hazleton. Whether residents would achieve relief was dependent on legal questions. The framing of legal interpretations of the law, the organization of intergovernmental relations, and the communication of messages shaped the political process. Two appeals in the judiciary demonstrated to residents and the nation that the city remains committed to the fight for local control of immigration policy. Even before the implementation of the IIRA, the law began to have some of its *intended* consequences. The proportion of the Hispanic population declined. Despite the lack of concrete data, Mayor Barletta estimated that as many as 5,000 Latinos left Hazleton. He said, "Some [left] in the middle of the night . . . you would suspect they were illegals that left so quickly."[121] One longtime resident observed, "The drug dealers are starting to leave town. [Streets are] better empty than full of drug dealers and murderers and thieves."[122] However, other residents worried about the impacts of the population loss and the stalled IIRA. For example, Elvis Soto, a legal immigrant from the Dominican Republic, said, "Before, it was a nice place. . . . Now, we have a war against us. I am legal but I feel the pressure also."[123] Similarly, Isabel Rubio, a small business owner, is a legal immigrant and has resided in Hazleton for over two decades. She said, "I am in a lot of stress right now. . . . Everyday, we hope to have a good day."[124] Despite any changes in the city and residents' opinions since the fight for local control of immigration policy began, Mayor Barletta vowed to continue to the appeal in court. "We'll fight this to the highest court."[125] Indeed, the fight continues.[126]

CROSSROADS

Carpentersville, Farmers Branch, and Hazleton are at a crossroads. Political leaders and citizens have a choice in determining which path to choose for the future.

The Carpentersville IIRO failed to be adopted and implemented. The political stream failed to bring the problem and policy streams together. As Kingdon aptly notes, "The political stream flows along according to its own dynamics and its own rules."[127] The dynamics and rules in Carpentersville mandated that residents and political actors harness the practice of politics to determine the winners and losers in this fight. Opponents of the IIRO won. Supporters of the IIRO lost. They did not gain the ability to implement local immigration policy. Bill Sarto's and Linda Ramirez-Sliwinski's goals to block the IIRO were achieved. Paul Humpfer's and Judy Sigwalt's policy goals to adopt the IIRO were ultimately not successful.

In Farmers Branch, supporters of 2903 won the fight for local control of immigration policy. Opponents of 2903 lost. Mayor Tim O'Hare's goals to adopt 2903 were achieved with complete support of the city council and 68 percent of voting residents. Former Mayors Bob Phelps and David Blaire, supported by numerous interest and pressure groups, were unsuccessful in their bid to block adoption of 2903. According to Blair, "This has been tremendously divisive . . . [it] wasn't vetted by the community before they took action and it was done very quickly."[128] On the other hand, Mayor Tim O'Hare still holds, "I believe the things we passed will achieve that goal."[129]

In Hazleton, the law was adopted but not implemented. Opponents of the IIRO lost. Supporters of the IIRO won. They gained the ability to adopt local immigration policy. Mayor Lou Barletta's goals were achieved. However, Barletta's goals were not fully realized because the IIRO was immediately put on hold when the US District Court issued a restraining order to halt the law's implementation.

According to the courts, the City of Hazleton "attempted to usurp authority that the Constitution has placed beyond the vicissitudes of local governments" and "could not possibly be in greater conflict with Congress's intent."[130] Mayor Barletta disagreed and promised to appeal, while the ACLU's Omar Jadwat said the court's decision is "a major defeat for the misguided, divisive and expensive anti-immigrant strategy that Hazleton has tried to export to the rest of the country."[131] Even though the city faced a conundrum as to whether to appeal as hefty legal fees accrued, Barletta ensured that the fight would continue.

In Carpentersville, Farmers Branch, and Hazleton, the roads they have traveled represent opportunities to learn from the past and move forward toward a greater public good. The road to suburban growth will lead to a renewal, or even rejuvenation. In contrast, the road to suburban decline will lead to further decline, or even decay, in these suburban communities. The failure to place suburban decline on the public agenda to confront declining population and housing issues increases the likelihood of more decline. Finally, the road that leads to the status quo results when there is no public or private action. The cities may experience suburban decline or suburban growth, or the status quo or current conditions may remain the same.

There are reasons for hope and positive change, as well as concern, in all three towns. In Carpentersville, there is some evidence that the community may have eased the path toward suburban growth. Indeed, the political debate was not without electoral consequences. Through the end of his term in 2009, Sarto continued to argue, "Now it really is time to move past this foolishness . . . [n]o one town is going to solve this issue. *The Federal Government, Congress and the White House are the ONLY ones who can come up with a real national solution!*"[132] The political struggles over the question of local versus federal jurisdiction led to an important change in the executive administration of the village. Bill Sarto dramatically lost his bid for reelection as Village President.[133] Trustee Ed Ritter was elected Village President. Likewise, Sarto's ally Linda Ramirez-Sliwinski lost her reelection bid for Village Trustee.

As the two lone politicians in Carpentersville who led the opposition to the IIRO, their political struggles may very well have paved the road to the village's path to suburban renewal. Bill Sarto's and Linda Ramirez-Sliwinski's efforts led to the board tabling the IIRO vote indefinitely. This decision, coupled with the 2009 election results, presented noteworthy changes and a window of opportunity for Carpentersville. Newly elected political leaders arrived with new priorities. Ed Ritter, who was elected to succeed Sarto as village president, attempted to maintain a neutral position during the IIRO debate. Brad McFeagan, one of the youngest trustees elected to the board of trustees, represented "new blood and a fresh perspective" on village issues.[134] The board expressed a common desire to move forward with new business.

In Farmers Branch, the 1989 Comprehensive Plan summarized, "It is clear to the citizens of Farmers Branch that change is a fact of life in all of the communities in the Dallas Metroplex. . . . As Farmers Branch faces the future, it has two choices: it can wait and let the future happen, or it can choose its future and then make that desired future happen. Farmers Branch has chosen the latter course." [135] Mayor Tim O'Hare said, "We have shown people that you can change your fate, and it doesn't have to keep on going downhill. No doubt in my mind, we have started heading upward. Is there a long way to go? Absolutely, there is a long way to go."[136] Upon reflection of his term in office, Mayor Tim O'Hare predicted:

> I think because of our location, our central location in the Metroplex, I think you'll see Farmers Branch explode and boom with all of the freeways that we have around us, with the airports that we are close to, with our proximity to downtown, I truly believe you will see Farmers Branch just explode and it will be a totally different place in 20 years than it is today. And I think it will be for the better.[137]

Ultimately, prior to his departure as mayor, O'Hare said, "No doubt in my mind that this was the way to go. No regrets whatsoever."[138]

Restraining orders remained in effect as the city appeals the case. On March 21, 2012, a panel of three US Court of Appeals judges for the Fifth Circuit agreed with the lower District Court and ruled that the IIRO usurped federal laws. Mayor Bill Glancy directed the city's attorneys to ask for a rehearing of the full 18 members of the Fifth Circuit. Lisa Graybill, legal director of the ACLU of Texas, said, "Every court in the country that has reviewed these local anti-immigrant housing ordinances has put a stop to them."[139] However, public commitment to the ordinance was steadfast, and the majority of residents supported the city's legal course of action. The fact that the city has spent nearly $5 million on legal fees clearly demonstrates policymakers' commitment to fighting for the ordinance. The mayor remarked, "No one likes to spend money on this, and in reality, the only one who wins are the lawyers."[140]

In Hazleton, the city boasts, "You'll see that our downtown is in the midst of a vibrant revitalization. Old buildings are being renovated. New buildings are being constructed. And new businesses are springing up all over."[141] Such changes are slow to arrive and costly to sustain. In any event, while far from a recovery, this does show some political support for a city renewal.

However, on every page of the city's official website, there is a banner asking for support to fight illegal immigration. Of nearly $500,000 raised for the legal defense costs, merely $10,000 remains. Lou Barletta certainly left his mark on the city—a ferocious drive to eliminate illegal immigrants from Hazleton—at any cost.

Mayor Joe Yanuzzi, elected in 2011 after Lou Barletta's departure to the US Congress, delivered his first State of the City address; he spoke about concerns about Hazleton's future. He said,

> Citizens must do their fair share. They must assist in the cleaning up of our city. They must assist in policing our city. They must report code violations as soon as they see them. We can't give the criminals a chance to settle in. We must make it uncomfortable for them. We outnumber the bad guys. . . . Together, we can stop the decline of our community and rebuild a great city, a Hazleton we can be proud of.[142]

The new mayor urged residents to get involved and have an active stake in the renewal of Hazleton. His remarks subtly refer to the problem population in Hazleton. The "bad guys" commit crime and violate the city's code. The message is clear that by making them uncomfortable, they will be forced to leave the city. While he does acknowledge the city's decline, the political message and agenda still appear to be focused at the core on the problem of illegal immigration.

Moving forward, there are important, if not enduring, questions that face the residents of Carpentersville, Farmers Branch, and Hazleton. How will these suburban communities confront suburban decline? How will they confront immigration? In his farewell address, Village President Sarto observed,

> Carpentersville is not an easy place to govern. There are some strong-willed individuals who have a difficult time with change. Some I would say are stuck in the 1950s. They refuse to move into the new millennium. Some are short sighted and stubborn and will never accept the changes that have come to the Village over the past 30 years.[143]

The future is far from certain. These towns stand at crossroads. The path depends on the willingness to confront these issues in a fair and just manner for all residents. This will depend on residents' and political actors' willingness to accept the new demographic realities of suburban diversity. Without a political agenda and renewal policies to address suburban decline, population loss, the decline of the housing stock, and social welfare, concerns will only worsen. Other policy debates on other fringe issues may dominate future political agendas. This might result in the avoidance of public responses to suburban decline. Further disguising the problem of suburban decline is a perilous road. The lack of a political agenda to renew these communities will result in the loss of population and the flight of jobs. If the agenda remains dominated by illegal immigration, few other issues will be resolved.

In Carpentersville, Farmers Branch, and Hazleton, socioeconomic conditions, like demographic change and suburban decline, led the political system to produce demands and supports for a call to public action. Individual and group actors competed in the political system to develop an output, or a policy response, to confront the problem of illegal immigration. The system's output interacts with the outside environment, which may or may not yield a change in the environment. In the case of the IIRO, it failed to become an output in Carpentersville; it emerged as an output in Farmers Branch, and the environment interacted as a referendum vote; and in Hazleton, the IIRO was adopted and the environmental interaction resulted in the decline of the Latino population. Ultimately, the policy may feed back to the beginning of the system.

NOTES

1. *Villas at Parkside Partners et al. v. City of Farmers Branch* 675 F.3d 802 at 22 (5th Cir. 2012).

2. Associated Press, "Court Upholds Ban on Texas Immigrant Housing Law," March 22, 2012.

3. Kingdon, *Agendas, Alternatives, and Public Policies,* 162.

4. Karen S. Johnson-Cartee, *News Narratives and News Framing: Constructing Political Reality* (Lanham, MD: Rowman & Littlefield, 2005).

5. See Appendix 2 for an explanation of methodologies. Note that many key informants requested anonymity; therefore, I refer to the data generally as "interviews."

6. The large majority of the protesters voiced opposition to the IIRO; however, a minority of attendees voiced support for the IIRO. Residents not only from Carpentersville but the entire region of Chicago attended.

7. Larrisa Chinwah, "Protest Doesn't Faze Trustees," *Daily Herald,* October 5, 2006.

8. Chinwah, "Village's Debate Begins," 1.

9. Chinwah, "A Question of Too Much Law," 1.

10. Carpentersville Village Board of Trustees meeting, June 19, 2007.

11. Ibid.

12. On December 4, 2007, the Village Board of Trustees voted 5-1 to participate in the federal 287 (g) program.

13. George Houde, "Trustees Prodding D.C. on Immigration," *Chicago Tribune,* November 23, 2006.

14. Carpentersville Village Board of Trustees meeting, June 19, 2007.

15. Ibid.

16. Carpentersville Village Board of Trustees meeting, September 5, 2006.

17. Chinwah, "A Question of Too Much Law," 1.

18. See Grant Crowell, "The Worst of Carpentersville," accessed May 1, 2009, www.youtube.com/user/grantast.

19. Ibid.

20. Ibid.

21. Erwin A. Blackstone, Michael Bognanno, and Simon Hakim, *Innovations in E-government: The Thoughts of Governors and Mayors* (Lanham, MD: Rowman & Littlefield, 2005): 10.

22. Richard Davis, *Typing Politics: The Role of Blogs in American Politics* (New York: Oxford University Press, 2009): 13.

23. David D. Perlmutter, *Blogwars* (New York: Oxford University Press, 2008): 205.

24. Richard Davis, *Typing Politics: The Role of Blogs in American Politics* (New York: Oxford University Press, 2009): 12.

25. Some websites are no longer available; cached websites are accessible.

26. Personal blog of Bill Sarto, accessed November 28, 2008, http://billsarto.com.

27. Carpentersville Action Network: A Blog about Happenings in the Village of Carpentersville, "Daily Herald, Chinwah need some soul-searching," June 7, 2007.

28. Anonymous personal interview, May 8, 2009.

29. Amílcar Antonio Barreto, *The Politics of Language in Puerto Rico* (Gainesville: University Press of Florida, 2001).

30. Carpentersville Village Board of Trustees meeting, April 17, 2007.

31. Ibid.

32. Carpentersville Village Board of Trustees meeting, June 5, 2007.

33. Chinwah, "Protest Doesn't Faze Trustees," 16.

34. Ibid.

35. Carpentersville Village Board of Trustees meeting, September 5, 2006.

36. Newton, *Illegal, Alien, or Immigrant*, ix.

37. Chinwah, "Village's Debate Begins," 1.

38. "Carpentersville," Illinois Coalition for Immigrant and Refugee Rights, accessed November 28, 2008, http://icirr.org.

39. Branch Bulletin, "Tim O'Hare: The Interview," 1. Tim O'Hare's most recent office was Mayor of the City of Farmers Branch. Previously, he served on the City Council.

40. City Council meeting, City of Farmers Branch, January 22, 2007.

41. Branch Bulletin, "Tim O'Hare: The Interview," 1.

42. Stephanie Sandoval, "Groups Decry FB Law, Apartment Association, Others Weigh Action; Some Migrants Fearful," *Dallas Morning News*, November 15, 2006.

43. Johnson-Cartee, *News Narratives and News Framing*, 1-42.

44. Branch Bulletin, "Tim O'Hare: The Interview," 1.

45. Ibid.

46. Robert Wilonsky, "Farmers Branch: It's Scary," *Dallas Observer*, accessed December 14, 2006, http://blogs.dallasobserver.com/unfairpark/2006/11/farmers_branch_its_scary.php.

47. Roman Catholic Diocese of Dallas, Texas, accessed November 25, 2009, http://religionblog.dallasnews.com/archives/2007/01/no-room-at-the-farmers-branch.html

48. Let The Voters Decide, accessed November 25, 2009, http://www.voters decide.org.

49. Stephanie Sandoval, "Foes of Farmers Branch Law Delay Petition," *Dallas Morning News*, December 12, 2006.

50. Press Release, ACLU, September 22, 2008, accessed November 15, 2011, www.aclu.org/immigrants-rights/farmers-branch-texas-anti-immigrant-ordinance-blocked-while-challenge-continues.

51. Ibid.

52. Acción America, accessed November 25, 2009, http://accionamerica.com.

53. Branch Bulletin, "Tim O'Hare: The Interview," 1.

54. Bill O'Brien, "Editorials," *Dallas Morning News*, November 18, 2006.

55. City Council meeting, City of Farmers Branch, January 22, 2007.

56. Ibid.

57. Ty Jones, "Editorials," *Dallas Morning News*, November 18, 2006.

58. Ronnie Smith, "Editorials," *Dallas Morning News*, November 18, 2006.

59. Curtis Green, "Editorials," *Dallas Morning News*, November 18, 2006.

60. Cynthia Stock, "Editorials," *Dallas Morning News*, November 18, 2006.

61. Beverly Elam, "Editorials," *Dallas Morning News*, November 18, 2006.

62. Anonymous personal interview, April 25, 2007.

63. Branch Bulletin, "Tim O'Hare: The Interview," 1.

64. Paul A. Samuelson, "The Pure Theory of Public Expenditure," *Review of Economics and Statistics* 36, no. 4 (1954): 387-389.

65. Weimer and Vining, *Policy Analysis*, 72.

66. It should be noted that laws on public benefits for immigrants vary widely. The Personal Responsibility and Work Opportunity Act of 1996 prohibits illegal immigrants from receiving federal welfare benefits. In 1982, the US Supreme Court ruled in *Plyer v. Doe* (457 US 202) that it was unconstitutional to deny illegal immigrants primary and secondary education.

67. Megan Feldman, "The Hunted," *Dallas Observer*, accessed December 14, 2006, www.dallasobserver.com/2006-12-14/news/the-hunted.

68. Anonymous personal interview, April 25, 2007.

69. Branch Bulletin, "Tim O'Hare: The Interview," 1.

70. City Council meeting, City of Farmers Branch, January 22, 2007.

71. Branch Bulletin, "Tim O'Hare: The Interview," 1.

72. Members included: Gene Bledsoe, Real Estate and Marketing; Jeff Brand, Development; Ben Cunningham, Banking; Pat Haggerty, Commercial Real Estate; RL Lemke, Development; Tim Scott, Marketing; and Ed Bonneau, Chair.

73. Public Memo, Branch Redevelopment Task Force, City of Farmers Branch, Texas, September 26, 2006.

74. Public Letter, City of Farmers Branch, Texas, May 8, 2007.

75. Donna Harris, *Dallas Real Estate Blog*, accessed November 15, 2006, http://dallasrealestateagent.blogspot.com.

76. Lowell W. Culver, "The Politics of Suburban Distress," *Journal of Urban Affairs* 4, no. 1 (1982): 1-18.

77. Craig Hanley, "Scenes from the Class Struggle in Farmers Branch," *D Magazine*, May 2007.

78. Pierre Bourdieu, *Distinction: A Social Critique of the Judgement of Taste* (Cambridge, MA: Harvard University Press, 1984): 97-168.

79. Kingdon, *Agendas, Alternatives, and Public Policies*, 162.

80. Johnson-Cartee, *News Narratives and News Framing*, 1-42.

81. An attorney by training, he worked as a White House Fellow in the first George W. Bush Administration, and later under Attorney General John Ashcroft. He holds the position of Daniel L. Brenner Professor of Law at University of Missouri–Kansas City. In 2010, he was elected Secretary of State of Kansas.

82. "Kan. lawyer is architect of many immigration laws," *Associate Press*, May 10, 2010.

83. Kris Kobach Official Website, accessed January 30, 2012, www.kriskobach .org/site/Html/expanded.html.

84. See *Lozano et al. v. City of Hazleton*, 496 F.Supp.2d 477, 484 (M.D. Pa. 2007).

85. Kent Jackson and L.A. Tarone, "Judge Blocks Illegals Law," *Hazleton Standard-Speaker*, November 1, 2006.

86. Ibid.

87. Julia Preston, "Court Rejects a City's Efforts to Restrict Immigrants," *The New York Times*, September 9, 2010.

88. See *Lozano* 496 F.Supp.2d 477, 484.

89. Ibid.

90. ACLU Press Release, "Hazleton, PA Anti-Immigrant Law Is Unconstitutional, Federal Appeals Court Rules," New York, September 9, 2010.

91. Kent Jackson, "Barletta Confident of Appeal Win," *Hazleton Standard Speaker*, September 9, 2008.

92. Julia Preston, "Court Rejects a City's Efforts to Restrict Immigrants," *The New York Times*, September 9, 2010.

93. The US Supreme Court remanded the case to the US Court of Appeals for the Third Circuit on June 5, 2011.

94. Michael Matza, "Chatter But No Sense of Closure," *The Philadelphia Inquirer*, July 27, 2007.

95. Ibid.

96. *Lou Dobbs Tonight*, "No Amnesty for Illegal Aliens," *CNN* Transcript, accessed September 10, 2008, http://transcripts.cnn.com/transcripts/0809/10/ldt.01. html.

97. See Small Town Defenders Petition and Donation Website, accessed November 1, 2011, www.smalltowndefenders.com.

98. Gebe Martinez, *Unconstitutional and Costly: The High Price of Local Immigration Enforcement*, Center for American Progress, January 24, 2011, accessed on January 30, 2012, www.americanprogress.org/issues/2011/01/unconstitutional_and_ costly.html.

99. Kent Jackson, "Barletta Confident of Appeal Win," *Hazleton Standard Speaker*, September 9, 2008.

100. Michael Vitez, "Is a City America's Gatekeeper?" *The Philadelphia Inquirer*, March 13, 2007.

101. "Coalition Returns to Court," ACLU Press Release, 1.

102. See *Lozano* 496 F.Supp.2d 477, 484.

103. Gaiutra Bahadur, "In Riverside, All Sides Are Now Taking Office," *The Philadelphia Inquirer*, August 6, 2006.

104. Daniel Schorn, "Welcome to Hazleton," *60 Minutes*, November 19, 2006.

105. Ibid.

106. "Coalition Returns to Court," ACLU Press Release, 1.

107. Ibid.

108. Bahadur, "In Riverside, All Sides," 1.

109. Ibid.

110. Ibid.

111. Ibid.

112. Simonich, "Hazleton Ordinance Aimed," 1.

113. "No Amnesty for Illegal Aliens," *CNN*, 1.

114. Michael Vitez, "Is A City America's Gatekeeper?" 1.

115. Michael Matza, "Chatter But No Sense of Closure," *The Philadelphia Inquirer*, July 27, 2007.

116. Amy Worden, "Ruling Awaited in Hazleton Immigration Case," *The Philadelphia Inquirer*, March 23, 2007.

117. Anonymous personal interview, June 8, 2007.

118. Kent Jackson, "Barletta Confident of Appeal Win," *Hazleton Standard Speaker*, September 9, 2008.

119. Matza, "Chatter But No Sense of Closure," 1.

120. See Federal Immigration Reform and Enforcement (FIRE), accessed November 1, 2011, www.firecoalition.com/about.

121. Ellen Barry, "City's Immigration Law Turns Back Clock," *Los Angeles Times*, November 9, 2006.

122. Ibid.

123. Michael Rubinkam, "Tough Immigration Law Hits Pennsylvania Town," *Associated Press,* November 1, 2006.

124. Ibid.

125. Simonich, "Hazleton Ordinance Aimed," 1.

126. On June 6, 2011, the US Supreme Court remanded the US Court of Appeals for the Third Circuit in Philadelphia. "It's a do-over in the Third Circuit. We re-brief it, re-argue it and have a helpful Supreme Court decision in our hip pocket," said Hazleton's counsel Kris Kobach. See Kent Jackson, "Supreme Court Gives Hazleton's Ordinance a Second Chance," *Standard-Speaker*, June 7, 2011.

127. Kingdon, *Agendas, Alternatives, and Public Policies*, 162.

128. Thomas Korosec, "Farmers Branch Voting on Leases to Immigrants," *Houston Chronicle*, April 30, 2007.

129. Branch Bulletin, "Tim O'Hare: The Interview," 1.

130. See *Lozano* 496 F.Supp.2d 477, 484.

131. "Coalition Returns to Court," ACLU Press Release, 1.

132. "A Personal Agenda Shown by Some," Personal blog of Bill Sarto, accessed November 28, 2008, http://billsarto.com.

133. Sarto received 16 percent of the vote, or 339 votes. Krenz received 34 percent of the vote. Ritter received 48 percent of the vote, 993 votes. Fifteen percent of registered voters cast ballots.

134. Anonymous personal interview, May 7, 2009.

135. 1989 Comprehensive Plan, City of Farmers Branch, Texas.

136. Branch Bulletin, "Tim O'Hare: The Interview," 1.

137. Ibid.

138. Ibid.

139. Press Release, ACLU, September 22, 2008, accessed November 15, 2011, www.aclu.org/immigrants-rights/farmers-branch-texas-anti-immigrant-ordinance-blocked-while-challenge-continues.

140. Dianne Solís, "Farmers Branch to Appeal Ruling Against Illegal Immigrant Rental Ban," *Dallas Morning News*, April 25, 2012.

141. See City of Hazleton Website, accessed January 30, 2012, www.hazletoncity.org/public/comm.-econ.-dev./come-home-to-downtown-hazleton.html.

142. Joe Yanuzzi, "State of the City," Hazleton, Pennsylvania, January 25, 2012.

143. "Thank You," Personal blog of Bill Sarto, accessed November 28, 2008, http://billsarto.com.

Chapter Six

Public Policy and Planning for the Multiethnic Metropolis

Is a city America's gatekeeper?[1]

—*Michael Vitez, The Philadelphia Inquirer*

In 2007, *The Philadelphia Inquirer* ran a front-page article that asked whether a city could act as the nation's "gatekeeper." This was the critical question that residents were faced with in Carpentersville, Farmers Branch, and Hazleton. A gatekeeper guards an entrance and controls access. Not all people had a right to enter these cities—by policy design. Policymakers fought to make IIROs control the entrance to these cities, guarding the city from illegal immigrants.

This vignette raises important questions about who has a right to the city.[2] Henri Lefebvre, the French Marxist philosopher, is largely credited with the development of the right to the city framework. He theorized that the city is a geographic place of conflict. Lefebvre was primarily concerned about "the problems of the city and urban society." Observing that problems arose as cities grew increasingly urban and as industrialization concentrated capital in the core, he argued that there were inherent tensions as laborers produced capital yet received few economic returns. To Lefebvre, the "right to the city" was a collection of rights "to freedom, to individualization in socialization, to habitat and to inhabit. The right to the oeuvre, to participation and appropriation."[3] As residents are part of the process of urbanization, he argues that they, too, have rights to housing and control over public spaces. Thus, policymakers should consider if immigrants have a right to the city—and the suburb.[4]

As these laws seek to restrict who can use the space of the city, the social dimensions of the IIROs are spatialized. If there are inherent rights to public

145

space, are IIROs justified? According to Susan Fainstein, the "just city" is democratic, diverse, and equitable.[5] In practice, IIROs segregate or exclude residents spatially. This spatial process, then, raises numerous questions for the just city.[6] Questions about housing and civil rights abound. Questions about the democratic nature of local governance abound. Questions about equal access to the city's public spaces and local services abound. The answers to these questions show that the degree to which new immigrants can formulate a cohesive voice, the more "just" the city's. Yet without representation, the fight for equal housing, fair labor practices, and access to services is limited at best. Community organization can empower the voiceless to challenge the local responses to take control of immigration policy. But without political participation, voices are not heard.

In this chapter, I consider policy alternatives and planning options for the multiethnic metropolis. Where does the fight for local control of immigration policy go for these communities? I begin with a cross-case analysis of the politics of relief in Carpentersville, Farmers Branch, and Hazleton. Next, I reflect on the challenges of the suburban backlash to the multiethnic metropolis. Then, I present policy and planning implications for federal, state, and local governments. I conclude with some thoughts on how twenty-first century realities will shape the debate moving forward.

DIMENSIONS OF RELIEF

There are a number of common themes and distinct features of relief among the three cases. Table 6.1 shows a matrix of the politics of relief on dimensions of problems, solutions, and politics. The following discussion compares and contrasts these cases.

Problems

In all cases, the cities were faced with demographic change. The native population was white and older, while the foreign-born population was Latino and younger. In Carpentersville and Farmers Branch, the transition was gradual over a period of four decades. In Hazleton, the transition occurred in the period of a decade. Social and economic changes accompanied these demographic changes. Residents identified similar problems, such as the quality of the housing stock, the prevalence of crime, the stretching of public services, and the growth of Spanish language speakers. The causes of these problems were defined as demographic change and suburban decline.

These problems coalesced around similar triggering events. Each city experienced acts of violent crime, which focused public attention to the problem

Table 6.1. Matrix of Relief in Carpentersville, Farmers Branch, and Hazleton

Stream	Dimensions	Carpentersville	Farmers Branch	Hazleton
Problem	Population	Gradual transition to half Latino in four decades	Gradual transition to half Latino in four decades	Quick transition to one-third Latino in one decade
	Issues	Housing; crime; services; language	Housing; crime; services; language	Housing; employment; crime; services; language
	Trigger event	Violence; gangs	Murder; gangs	Murder; drugs; gangs
Solution	Law	IIRO	IIRO	IIRA
	Source	Copied from Hazleton	Copied from Hazleton	New city law
	Elements	Housing; business; language	Housing; language	Housing; business; language
Politics	Institutional	Strong mayor; divided council	Strong mayor; unanimous council	Strong mayor; unanimous council
	Support	Strong grassroots	Strong grassroots	No grassroots
	Debate	Strong debate; IIRO tabled	Strong debate; referendum to adopt	Few debates; adopted

of illegal immigration. Gang violence was rampant in Carpentersville. Murders claimed innocent residents in Farmers Branch and Hazleton. Drug trafficking was common. Residents of these three cities attributed these crimes to the presence and growth of illegal immigrants. Policymakers argued that without reform of national immigration policy, their jurisdictions would be forced to carry the burden of adopting and implementing immigration policy for the safety and welfare of their residents.

Solutions

In the mid-2000s, Carpentersville, Farmers Branch, and Hazleton considered similar ordinances as solutions to similar problems. Farmers Branch and Carpentersville turned to Hazleton to develop their IIROs. All of the ordinances had provisions to confront housing and languages problems. Farmers Branch and Hazleton considered an employment provision, but they did not include it in the final ordinance. Among residents, there was a consensus that the government needed to crack down on illegal immigration. Yet, among the opponents, there was also consensus that the ordinances were unconstitutional. The ACLU played an important role in the public narrative about the constitutionality of such laws. The ACLU argued that IIROs violated the Supremacy Clause, due process, equal rights protection, and free speech. The organization supported the plaintiffs in Farmers Branch and Hazleton. While both cities developed nearly identical ordinances to improve the likelihood of judicial scrutiny, the ACLU's legal team was successful in the trial and appellate courts. These successful judicial challenges had a large enough impact to persuade Carpentersville against the adoption of an IIRO.

Politics

The political stream was composed of three dimensions. The institutional strength of the local political executive played a role in shaping the politics of relief. The level of support among grassroots organizations influenced local institutions. The characteristics of the political debates determined the outcomes of the policies.

The institution of the local political executive and the relationship to the legislative body built the foundation of support for the politics of relief. In Carpentersville, Bill Sarto defeated Paul Humpfer for the nonpartisan position of village president. Humpfer, a village trustee, and fellow trustee Judy Sigwalt coauthored the village's IIRO. With the support of one other village trustee, Sarto led the public charge against the ordinance. The remaining three trustees on the board refused to bring the ordinance to a vote, thus effectively defeating the IIRO. In their bids for reelection, IIRO opponents Sarto and Ramirez-Sliwinski were defeated.

In Farmers Branch, Mayor Bob Phelps opposed Tim O'Hare's IIRO proposal. Residents of Farmers Branch voted heavily in favor of the ordinance in a referendum vote. After the retirement of Mayor Phelps, Tim O'Hare was elected mayor based on his platform of cracking down on illegal immigration. The city council unanimously supported O'Hare and the IIRO. After nearly a four-year fight that consumed his first term, Tim O'Hare did not seek reelection.

In Hazleton, Mayor Lou Barletta was a strong voice for the IIRO both locally and nationally. With the support of all city council members but one, the IIRO was adopted. Barletta was later elected to the US House of Representatives on the platform of immigration reform. Thus, it is clear that strong executives set the policy agenda and emerged as strong but divisive figures in the fight for local control of immigration policy. In each city, there were clear electoral consequences based on one's support or opposition to the IIRO. Executives retired, lost elections, and moved on to higher office.

Finally, the impact of the Hazleton case on other cities cannot be understated. Even though Hazleton policymakers were inspired by the San Bernardino, California experience, Mayor Lou Barletta crafted his politics of relief so that the city would become a microcosm of national immigration policy. In fact, that is exactly what happened. Not only did Carpentersville and Farmers Branch model Hazleton's IIRO, hundreds of other municipalities and states have mimicked the Hazleton ordinance.[7] During the debate, others warned about this impact. For example, a letter from a group of attorneys and legal organizations warned Hazleton Mayor Barletta that other local governments would model their own ordinances on Hazleton's IIRO. It read, "This ordinance, if allowed to stand, will take Hazleton, and the towns that enact laws mimicking it, back to the worst days of America where certain kinds of people could not by law own property, run businesses nor live in certain places."[8] Foster Maer, staff attorney for the Puerto Rican Legal Defense and Education Fund that assisted the plaintiffs, noted that the legal fight in Hazleton was the first local attempt to regulate housing and employment for illegal immigrants to be appealed. Maer said, "Both implicitly and explicitly, many communities are saying 'Wait until we hear what the courts are saying so we don't get into the same bind as Hazleton.'"[9]

THE SUBURBAN BACKLASH

In the original complaint on August 15, 2006, the plaintiffs argued, "Blaming many of its ills, including crime, failing schools, rising tax rates, and decaying neighborhoods, Hazleton passed the Ordinance with the express goal to drive what it calls 'illegal aliens' out of town."[10] Suburbanites turned to immigrants—legal or illegal—in search of a reason for the decline of their communities. In Carpentersville, residents "had enough." They were ready to place blame on their city's Latino population. Additionally, in Farmers Branch, white residents grew weary of the influx of Spanish-speaking residents and the city's social problems. In short, white residents experienced a backlash to the simultaneous arrival of immigrants and suburban decline.

There is a long history of the suburban backlash, and it is well documented in a burgeoning body of literature.[11] Historian David Freund, in his study of suburban Detroit, best characterizes the backlash:

> By the 1960s, most whites were property owners, concentrated in all-white communities that were separated from—and in the case of suburbs, viewed as *sanctuaries* from—urban, minority communities. Most whites were convinced that the spatial and socioeconomic segregation of the metropolis was purely the result of free market forces. Seen in this context, northern white "backlash" against the civil rights movement and a new federal commitment to racial equality hardly seems new.[12]

Thus, suburbs offered protection from black residents and later Latino residents. More importantly, the institutional boundaries of local suburban government became the sanctuaries for these residents. So the backlash challenges residents' rights to equal public services, civil rights, and finally, democratic values of justice. The politics of the backlash supported direct democratic initiative rather than judicial process. It appears that, if left to a ballot initiative, the ordinances would become law. Voting residents made their voices clear in support of IIROs. By resorting to ballot initiatives, politicians appealed to democratic values. Yet, they ran the risk of governing by the tyranny of the majority.[13] Either way, the courts will have the final verdict in these cases until the US Congress takes up the issue.

In the end, the backlash was about larger issues. The need for relief was a backlash to the demographic change, globalization, suburban decline—all of which were embodied in the lawsuits that challenged the IIROs. Specifically, residents had mixed reactions to the outcomes of the lawsuits. For instance, Farmers Branch resident William Averitt commented, "The federal government has done nothing, the city has done something, now the federal government is going to squash it."[14] B. J. Clark questioned, "What's the use of having an election if a judge is going to overrule it?[15] Other residents disagreed. Farmers Branch resident Larry Kenward claimed, "It's always good to have a vote . . . even though it didn't come out the way I wanted. The city has no business enforcing federal law like that, other than cooperating with the feds."[16] And, "I think we should live and let live, and those that are already here should be given some means of becoming legal," said resident Geneva Ables.[17]

Perhaps the plethora of lawsuits further empowered policymakers and supporters of the IIRO to work even harder in the fight. "The American people are tired of judges legislating from the bench," Mayor Time O'Hare said. "We will finally have our opportunity to have this matter heard at the appellate court level where we fully expect to prevail . . . This decision is not unexpected but welcomed because it allows us to get closer to this ordinance becoming reality."[18]

Ultimately, we return to the question about whether a city is America's gatekeeper. The backlash was fueled by the local failure to act as a gatekeeper for these governments. The notion of American identity and the social construction of reality further added to the backlash as the definitions grew increasingly blurry.[19] Native-born residents defined identity by birthplace status, whereas foreign-born residents defined identity by economic position. A discursive construction as to who belongs in the United States and who has an inherent right to the city shaped the outcome of the debate.[20]

POLICY AND PLANNING IMPLICATIONS

The nation's immigration laws consist of a myriad of complex intergovernmental policies and regulations. During the twentieth century, immigration policy morphed from a centralized and federal policy domain to a decentralized and fragmented policy domain. Legislative action is needed to solve the many problems that have developed in consequence. The judiciary cannot ameliorate the problems. This environment raises numerous implications for policy and planning. I reflect on the federal, state, and local implications in turn.

Federal

The US Congress must adopt new policies to reform the nation's complex web of immigration laws and regulations. Should state and local governments control immigration policy? How are the rights of immigrants protected? The answers to these questions will depend on views on devolution, and more broadly, federalism. In any event, local control of immigration policy must be curtailed. Congress must decide what the role of government is and how the intergovernmental relations will be navigated. Principles of federalism provide a framework to redesign immigration policy. State and local interests must be balanced with federal interests. The arguments in support of or in opposition against the devolution of immigration policy rest on the varied concepts of federalism.[21]

Dual federalism, cooperative federalism, and new federalism are three models of federalism that inform this debate. Dual federalism holds that the system of government is based on federal and state governments that simultaneously govern in sovereign branches.[22] Drawing on the notion that the power of the national government is limited, states and the federal government have their independent domains of authority. Cooperative federalism holds that the system of government shares power and policy authority between states and the federal government.[23] These governments cooperate in the implementation of public programs and regulations. New federalism holds that the system of government devolves power from the federal to state governments, empowering state governments to govern individually using federal resources.[24] In terms of immigration policy, the concept of federalism that prevails may very well determine the outcome of the local fight for immigration policy.[25] The dual federalist viewpoint would support the state control of immigration policy on the basis of state police power within state borders. State laws in Arizona and Alabama support this view.[26] The cooperative federalist and new federalist viewpoints would support state implementation of federal programs, such as the Immigration and Nationality Act Section 287 (g), in which state and local police departments enter into an agreement with the federal government to enforce immigration laws.

These frameworks on federalism will need to guide national policymakers in the adoption of federal reform of immigration policy if we are serious about confronting this issue. To effectively address the problems in the system, immigration reform should be comprehensive. It should deal with the external and internal flows of population migration. The nation's need to protect the homeland through border patrol needs to be balanced with a human approach to dealing with some 12 million illegal immigrants. In general, policymakers have converged on two approaches. Some argue the public policies should focus on eliminating the illegal immigrants who live in the country and prevent others from entering. Others argue that there should be a pathway toward citizenship or residency for illegal immigrants already living in the country. State and local participation in federal programs, such as Secure Communities and 287 (g), will focus the agenda on the limitation of illegal immigration through a cooperative federalist arrangement. Other state and local governments will choose to focus the agenda on building human capital as they opt out of these federal programs. Of course, as political leadership changes, these decisions may ebb and flow.

The federal government might also consider building social capital among the nation's youth. The DREAM (Development, Relief, and Education for

Alien Minors) Act is one example of a Congressional legislative attempt to do just that. The law would grant permanent residency to individuals "of good moral character" who complete high school.[27] A decade later and numerous revisions, the law is at standstill. In 2012, President Obama announced that the administration would no longer deport young illegal immigrants, as proposed by the DREAM Act. This is sensible immigration reform. It builds stronger communities and develops human capital in the nation's labor force during an uncertain economic era. Education is one of the best vehicles to accomplish these goals and ultimately one of the best ways to integrate society.

Ultimately, the national system is too fragmented and outdated. Reform needs to take into account the new social and economic realities of the twenty-first century. Decisions must be made whether or not federal policymakers move forward with either approach. Until then, municipalities are faced with a Catch-22: the courts have ruled that local government cannot control immigration policy, but the federal government has yet to reform national immigration policy. Thus, the indecision reinforces the local challenges that cities and suburbs are faced with on a daily basis.

State

States should consider developing social and economic services to facilitate the needs of new immigrants. Since these residents sometimes have different needs than others, supporting them is paramount. Language barriers should be minimized. Offering public services in dual languages while simultaneously supporting English language education programs will allow new immigrants to make seamless transitions. State welfare policies should assist new immigrants in obtaining job training, access to mass transit, and childcare services so that economic opportunities can be fully realized. Tuition assistance and state aid should be awarded to advance socioeconomic mobility. At the same time, states need to support local governments and nonprofit groups that serve these communities on the frontlines. Above all, it is essential that states avoid residency verification for eligibility. Such a policy will only further alienate new immigrants and ultimately hold back progress. As many states attribute much of their population growth to immigrants, it will become increasingly important to meet the needs of new immigrants to remain competitive.

States need to pursue smart growth strategies that limit development on the metropolitan fringe and refocus public investment in existing communities near the urban core.[28] With guidance by the state, this development practice concentrates population, housing, and economic activities around urban centers. By doing so, it alleviates the long-term social, economic, and environmental impacts of sprawl. Inner-ring suburbs stand to benefit from smart growth policies and planning. For example, the state of Maryland developed a statewide smart growth initiative that focused public funding for new infrastructure to areas that were located near the metropolitan core, thus creating disincentives for new sprawl.[29] The result is urban and suburban revitalization. Declining communities such as Carpentersville, Farmers Branch, and Hazleton would be the targets for renewal rather than the targets of decline. Today immigrants call these places home. With policy intervention, they have the potential to be vibrant, healthy communities.

Last, states must plan for population diversity. Cities and suburbs are the states' living laboratories of diversity. Disparate groups of people from a multitude of races, ethnicities, cultures, and countries share metropolitan space. Effective planning needs to enable the public sphere to navigate socioeconomic conflicts that arise from diversity. Wood and Landry identify this need as an important issue to reconcile. They argue that "dealing with and valuing diversity, difference and the desire for distinctiveness is the central dilemma of our age. Acknowledging and living at ease with the landscape of diversity is different from focusing on differences. The challenge is to create a coherent narrative for diversity and how it can answer the problems of our age."[30] Planners need to create a narrative that educates and harnesses support for it in the community. Indeed, this is a great challenge, but it is a challenge that must be overcome.

Local

Just as local governments attempted to use public policy to restrict and penalize immigrants, other local governments have done the opposite. In the 2000s, several dozen big cities adopted the practice of not enforcing federal immigration policies. In these instances, cities commonly do not use local resources to enforce federal immigration law, nor do they participate in federal programs. Similarly, they do not direct police and public services to inquire about residency status. Some cities, such as San Francisco and Philadelphia, declared their jurisdiction as sanctuary cities. For example, Mayor Michael Nutter of Philadelphia declared an executive order to (1) provide access to all city services, (2) disallow the inquiry regarding immigration status by any city employee, and (3) abide by an oath to not disclose immigration status.[31] The actions of these jurisdictions demonstrate a compassionate understanding for the needs of immigrants; however, the sanctuary city movement provides further evidence of the nation's broken system.

However, inclusionary cities still do provide a sharp contrast from exclusionary suburbs. There are noteworthy efforts that inclusionary communities have responded to the arrival of immigrants. Goździak and Bump, for example, demonstrate important policy responses to the integration of immigrants in society.[32] Inclusionary programs seek to teach English, plan for multicultural health care services, develop skilled training and higher education opportunities, implement economic development opportunities, create homeownership opportunities, and ensure safety for all residents. Exclusionary communities would be well served to think about these efforts, too. The difference between these communities is that inclusionary communities aim to welcome new residents—regardless of their residency status. They value the diversity of cultures, peoples, and perspectives. Consider the case of Wheaton, Maryland and Herndon, Virginia. As suburbs of Washington, DC, they are the new gateways for immigrant settlement. Journalist Doug Saunders calls them "arrival cities," places where new immigrants move to and develop new communities.[33] Herndon was transformed in the 1990s as the Hispanic population boomed, particularly migrant day laborers. The city cracked down on the population and pushed them out. The economy later suffered. Whereas Herndon shunned immigrants, Wheaton welcomed them. Immigrants revitalized an aging downtown in this inner-ring suburb. New shops, new restaurants, and cultural activities attracted residents from around the region to spend time in Wheaton. In the long run, social capital developed in these immigrant communities.

The support of nonprofit organizations and community groups provides a welcoming environment to new immigrants.[34] Establishing a sense of community and building roots is an important part of integration. Community development corporations might also inject the support that localities need to successfully build human capital as new immigrants settle into established places like Carpentersville, Farmers Branch, and Hazleton. Local governments should harness these groups to foster education, economic opportunities, and improve public services. Some examples from these cases offer insight. In the Dallas-Fort Worth Metroplex, the DFW International Community Alliance seeks to promote understanding and cultural sensitivity in regions of diversity.[35] Such groups welcome new immigrants and build local networks to integrate residents into the community. Similarly, strategic partnerships with local governments and the private sector might help to provide economic opportunities for new residents. For example, Hazleton's CAN DO is a nonprofit economic development corporation focused on the improvement of the quality of life through the creation of employment opportunities.[36] While CAN DO has focused on attracting business to Hazleton, the group has the infrastructure to serve as an informational clearinghouse for new job opportunities for residents. Local public services can also be retooled to support the needs of new immigrants. Teaching English as a second language, incorporating cultural understanding into school curricula, and providing local job training and related services integrates new residents. Local government cannot provide all of these resources. However, it is critical to build a healthy local network of groups to balance the needs of new immigrants and native residents.

Last, this case offers some valuable implications for urban planners. The collection and analysis of statistical data is an important function of planning. Whether it is demographic, housing, employment, or crime data, the availability of these data—and an analytical interpretation of them—provides statistical evidence of social and economic trends in the city. This creates an independent voice on the problem definition of issues facing a community. For example, objective rational planning diffuses rhetorical claims about the causes of public problems or the characteristics of the population. So, with the appropriate information, planners can inform public managers and policymakers about the consequences of decisions. Good planning educates everyone. The planning profession should value the distribution of information and collaboration with residents and community organizations.[37]

The process of immigration is a local experience. Yes, federal and state laws influence flows of population migration, but ultimately, on a daily basis, the impacts on the lives of immigrants and native residents are local. Jobs are local. Schools are local. Churches are local. Playgrounds are local. Hospitals are local. Civic engagement is local. The local nature of our lives suggests that the people that we interact with are members of our communities, too. If immigrants call the same communities home as other native residents, then the public responses need to consider the local experience. Therefore, local communities must be part of the solution. Intergovernmental responses need to be crafted in such a way that acknowledges these local experiences. The people who know their communities the best should have a seat at the table and a voice in the process of reforming the nation's immigration system. Of course, the nation's laws must protect the most vulnerable people in society, and inclusionary local laws help augment the positive experiences of new immigrants.

In summary, federal, state, and local governments have a role in supporting new immigrants. These policies and planning tools are not without controversy. There will be political debate and challenges to the policy and planning responses. Yet, if society is serious about helping the most vulnerable residents, this role needs to be embraced. The nation's history shows that immigrants arrive in waves—and the latest wave can be characterized by the same nativist challenges that immigrants experienced previously. Now, the demographic realities and global dimensions of population migration make it difficult to not accept these new forms of diversity. Public policy and planning can be effectively utilized to make this experience positive and build an even stronger democracy.

TWENTY-FIRST-CENTURY METROPOLITAN REALITIES

It is worth contemplating the role of globalization and city. As the United States began the twentieth century, immigrants supported the nation's economy and urban development. The process of urbanization fueled the nation's globalization.[38] Cities were home to millions of new immigrants. Manufacturing industries created many jobs, and the results produced generations of middle-class families. The American Dream was realized.[39]

After the Second World War, the landscape shifted dramatically. Cities declined as suburbs boomed. Manufacturing declined as a new service economy grew. New immigrants arrived from Latin America and Asia, and they bypassed central cities to settle in the suburbs. By the arrival of the twenty-first century, new metropolitan realities were reshaping the city in numerous ways.[40] Central cities witnessed some revitalization, yet poverty remained heavily concentrated in the urban core. The urban crisis transformed into the suburban crisis as suburbs remained segregated, low-density suburban development persisted, and uncontrolled sprawl showed no signs of subsiding. Suburbia diversified in a marked fashion along racial, ethnic, class, and foreign-born dimensions. In essence, suburbs exhibited many of the same characteristics as central cities. They could no longer be ignored.

Today, we live in a globalized and metropolitanized society.[41] Thomas Freidman keenly observes, "The world is now flat."[42] As the fight for local control of immigration policy showed, some suburbanites did not fully realize the extent of the global "flat" dimensions of the nation's cities and suburbs. This is a reality. There are at least three implications of a "flat" world. First, the twenty-first-century demography is increasingly more diverse than ever before. New immigrant settlement patterns demonstrate a mosaic of racial and ethnic clusters.[43] Second, suburban decline is a reality. As long as new development occurs on the metropolitan fringe and investment follows that development, older and inner-ring suburbs will stagnate and decline without intervention.[44] If anything, the process of decline will continue as the lifecycle of neighborhoods continues, fueling a native backlash to the realities. Third, there is a national imperative to reform immigration policy. Without action, this political fight will only fracture more local governments. These realities will continue to shape the national dialogue and the national political conflict over comprehensive immigration reform in the United States.

It is clear that this debate will to continue to unfold for quite some time. The US Supreme Court's ruling in *Arizona v. United States* makes this evident. The Court struck down three of the four provisions of the state's controversial law, S.B. 1070—a predecessor to the IIRO—on the grounds that the state law preempts federal laws. The state may *not* require individuals to carry registration documentation, to permit police to arrest upon suspicion of residency status, and to criminalize job searches of illegal immigrants. However, police may investigate the residency status of any detained individual. Legal opinions continue to evolve and perspectives vary across the country.

Finally, as the nation's cities and suburbs grapple with these issues, the nation's future remains uncomfortably uncertain for many Americans. Debates about immigration policy raise questions about the United States' role in the world. Will the country fully accept the "flattening" of its society in a global context? Fareed Zakaria raises a candidly relevant question. Is the twenty-first century the "post-American" century?[45] Only time will tell.

NOTES

1. Michael Vitez, "Is a city America's gatekeeper?" *The Philadelphia Inquirer*, March 13, 2007.

2. A large body of literature in human geography considers this question. While I introduce the concept for illustrative purposes, this is not an exhaustive inquiry into the right to the city. See Henri Lefebvre, *The Production of Space* (Oxford, UK: Blackwell, 1991 [1974]).

3. Lefebvre, *The Production of Space*, 174.

4. The question of who has a right to the city (both native residents and immigrants) is examined generally by geographers and critical social theorists. Some noteworthy examples include Don Mitchell, *The Right to the City: Social Justice and the Fight for Public Space* (New York: Guilford Press, 2003); Mark Purcell, "Citizenship and the Right to the Global City: Reimagining the Capitalist World Order," *International Journal of Urban and Regional Research* 27, no. 3 (2003): 564-590; Clara Irazábal, ed., *Ordinary Places, Extraordinary Events: Citizenship, Democracy and Public Space in Latin America* (New York: Routledge, 2008).

5. Susan Fainstein, *The Just City* (Ithaca, NY: Cornell University Press, 2011).

6. This framework can also be extended to the suburb. See Genevieve Carpio, Clara Irazábal, and Laura Pulido, "Right to the Suburb? Rethinking Lefebvre and Immigrant Activism," *Journal of Urban Affairs* 33, no. 2 (2011): 185-208.

7. Lina Newton, "Policy Innovation or Vertical Integration? A View of Immigration Federalism from the States," *Law & Policy* 34, no. 2 (2012): 113-137.

8. Foster Maer, et al., Public Letter to Mayor Lou Barletta, Hazleton, Pennsylvania, August 15, 2006.

9. Kent Jackson, "Barletta Confident of Appeal Win," *Hazleton Standard Speaker*, September 9, 2009.

10. See US District Court for the Middle District of Pennsylvania, Complaint, *Lozano et al. v. City of Hazleton*, August 15, 2006.

11. See Kenneth D. Durr, *Behind the Backlash: White Working-Class Politics in Baltimore, 1940-1980* (Chapel Hill: The University of North Carolina Press, 2003); Ronald P. Formisano, *Boston Against Busing: Race, Class, and Ethnicity in the 1960s*

and 1970s, 2nd ed. (Chapel Hill: The University of North Carolina Press, 2004); Lisa McGirr, *Suburban Warriors: The Origins of the New American Right* (Princeton, NJ: Princeton University Press, 2001); Matthew D. Lassiter, *The Silent Majority: Suburban Politics in the Sunbelt South* (Princeton, NJ: Princeton University Press, 2007); Robert O. Self, *American Babylon: Race and the Struggle for Postwar Oakland* (Princeton, NJ: Princeton University Press, 2004).

12. See, emphasis added, David M. Freund, *Colored Property: State Policy and White Racial Politics in Suburban America* (Chicago: University of Chicago Press, 2007): 385.

13. John Stuart Mill, *On Liberty* (London: Longman, Roberts & Green, 1869).

14. Stephanie Sandoval, "Order to Halt Rental Ban Frustrates FB Residents," *Dallas Morning News*, May 26, 2007.

15. Ibid.

16. Ibid.

17. Ibid.

18. Dianne Solís, "Judge Rules Farmers Branch Rental Ban is Unconstitutional," *Dallas Morning News*, March 25, 2010.

19. Peter L. Berger and Thomas Luckmann, *The Social Construction of Reality: A Treatise in the Sociology of Knowledge* (Garden City, NY: Anchor Books, 1966).

20. Frank Fischer, *Reframing Public Policy: Discursive Politics and Deliberative Practices* (New York: Oxford University Press, 2003).

21. There is a large body of literature on federalism. See generally Stanley Elkins and Eric McKitrick, *The Age of Federalism: The Early American Republic, 1788-1800* (New York: Oxford University Press, 1995); Robert F. Nagel, *The Implosion of American Federalism* (New York: Oxford University Press, 2002); Larry N. Gerston, *American Federalism: A Concise Introduction* (Armonk, NY: M.E. Sharpe, 2007).

22. Edward Samuel Corwin, Harold William Chase, and Craig R. Ducat, *Edward Corwin's The Constitution and What It Means Today, 14th Ed.* (Princeton, NJ: Princeton University Press, 1978).

23. See generally Theodore J. Lowi, *The End of the Republican Era* (Norman: University of Oklahoma Press, 1995).

24. Timothy Conlan, *From New Federalism to Devolution: Twenty-Five Years of Intergovernmental Reform, Rev. Ed.* (Washington, DC: Brookings Institution Press, 1998).

25. Garrett Kennedy, "Illegal Is Not Simply Illegal: The Broad Ramifications of a Pennsylvania Town's Attempt at Immigration Control, and The Inherent Problems of Racial Discrimination," *University of Pennsylvania Journal of Business and Employment Law* 10, no. 4 (2008): 1029-1058.

26. See Arizona S.B. 1070 *Support Our Law Enforcement and Safe Neighborhoods Act*; see also Alabama H.B. 56 *Hammon-Beason Alabama Taxpayer and Citizen Protection Act*.

27. Development, Relief, and Education for Alien Minors Act of 2001, S. 1291, 107th Cong. (2001).

28. There is a large body of literature on smart growth. See generally Scott Bollens, "State Growth Management," *Journal of the American Planning Association*

58, no. 4 (1992): 454-478; Andres Duany, Jeff Speck, and Mike Lydon, *The Smart Growth Manual* (New York: McGraw-Hill Professional, 2009); Gregory D. Squires, ed., *Urban Sprawl: Causes, Consequences, and Policy Responses* (Washington, DC: Urban Institute Press, 2002); Karen Danielsen, Robert Lang, and William Fulton, "Retracting Suburbia: Smart Growth and the Future of Housing," *Housing Policy Debate* 10, no. 3 (1999): 513-540; Myron Orfield, *Metropolitics: A Regional Agenda for Community and Stability* (Washington, DC: Brookings Institution Press, 1997).

29. John W. Frece, *Sprawl and Politics: The Inside Story of Smart Growth in Maryland* (Albany: State University of New York Press, 2008).

30. Phil Wood and Charles Landry, *The Intercultural City: Planning for Diversity Advantage* (London: Earthscan, 2008): 23.

31. Executive Order No. 8-09 Policy Concerning Access of Immigrants to City Services, City of Philadelphia, Pennsylvania, November 10, 2009, accessed December 18, 2011, www.phila.gov/executive_orders/execordersnutter1.html, last accessed October 1, 2011.

32. Goździak and Bump, *New Immigrants, Changing Communities*, 17-22.

33. Doug Saunders, *Arrival City: How the Largest Migration in History is Reshaping Our World* (New York: Pantheon Books, 2010): 94-100.

34. Michael Jones-Correa, "All Immigration Is Local: Receiving Communities and Their Role in Successful Immigrant Integration," *Center for American Progress*, September 20, 2011, accessed January 25, 2012, www.americanprogress.org/issues/2011/09/rci.html.

35. DFW International Community Alliance, Dallas, Texas, accessed January 25, 2012, www.dfwinternational.org.

36. CAN DO, Inc., Hazleton, Pennsylvania, accessed January 25, 2012, www.hazletoncando.com.

37. Alan Ehrenhalt, "Suburban Influx," *Governing* 23, no. 3 (2009): 30-36.

38. Saskia Sassen, *Cities in a World Economy, 3rd Ed.* (Thousand Oaks, CA: Pine Forge Press, 2006).

39. Jim Cullen, *The American Dream: A Short History of an Idea that Shaped a Nation* (New York: Oxford University Press, 2004).

40. Hanlon, Short, and Vicino, *Cities and Suburbs*, 249.

41. John Rennie Short, *Global Metropolitan: Globalizing Cities in a Capitalist World* (New York: Routledge, 2004).

42. Thomas L. Friedman, *The World Is Flat: A Brief History of the Twenty-First Century* (New York: Farrar, Straus and Giroux, 2005).

43. Thomas J. Vicino, Bernadette Hanlon, and John Rennie Short, "A Typology of Urban Immigrant Neighborhoods," *Urban Geography* 32, no. 3 (2011): 383-405.

44. For an overview of this process, see Lucy and Phillips, *Confronting Suburban Decline*, 21-30.

45. Fareed Zakaria, *The Post-American World* (New York: W. W. Norton & Company, 2009).

Chapter Seven

Conclusion

The Fight Endures

Immigration policy should be generous; it should be fair; it should be flexible. With such a policy we can turn to the world, and to our own past, with clear hands and a clear conscience.[1]

—*President John F. Kennedy, Washington, DC, 1963*

Border-related violence and crime due to illegal immigration are critically important issues to the people of our state . . . We cannot sacrifice our safety to the murderous greed of drug cartels. We cannot stand idly by as drop houses, kidnappings and violence compromise our quality of life.[2]

—*Governor Jan Brewer, Phoenix, Arizona, April 24, 2010*

In the United States, control of immigration policy is fragmented in nature. The policy ideas are about two strong but opposing views on how people flow in and out of nations.[3] On the one hand, it is about the promotion of an open, free society for all. More than a half century ago, President Kennedy echoed this sentiment when he called for such policies. He urged policymakers to consider crafting flexible laws—homage to the nation's legacy as a country of immigrants. On the other hand, another idea is about the protection of the homeland by limiting the in-flow of people. Governor Brewer of Arizona promoted this view when she characterized illegal immigrants as violent and criminal, calling for a state immigration policy. These politicians' viewpoints are poignant examples of the disparate range of policy ideas about how to deal with immigration. One view espouses a liberal and open nation where immigrants flow with relative ease between nations. The other view supports a more restrictive idea about who is permitted to enter or remain in the country. These two views anchor a wide range of other moderate positions on immigration. Whether one holds a more open or closed vision for immigrants in society is a question of public policy. Thus, questions abound regarding the appropriate policy response and the scale of control. Is it the role of the federal government to determine these answers and responses? Or, is it the role of local and state governments? I consider these questions and the future prospects for the local control of immigration policy. What are the next steps for the communities of Carpentersville, Farmers Branch, and Hazleton? I review the findings of this study and then review some lessons learned. A research agenda is offered, and I conclude with a reflection on suburban crossroads.

CONCLUSION

In 2006, a political fight erupted in Carpentersville, Farmers Branch, and Hazleton over the proposal of a local ordinance to provide relief from illegal immigration. Social and economic tensions developed, which divided these communities and the nation. The IIRO debate established an unprecedented attempt to locally adopt and implement immigration policy. After several years of political discussions, public meetings, campaigns, and rallies, the ordinance failed in Carpentersville and was adopted in Farmers Branch and Hazleton. Legal battles quickly ensued. A national debate ignited.

The heart of the policy debate was a disagreement over the means to the same ends—how to limit illegal immigration. Leading the IIRO opposition, Village President Bill Sarto agreed with the ends. He declared, "I oppose illegal immigration."[4] However, Sarto and Trustee Ramirez-Sliwinski disagreed with the IIRO as the means on discriminatory grounds and suggested that it was a solution to the wrong problem. Yet other political actors and coalitions disagreed with the means to achieve the result of limiting illegal immigration. Leading the IIRO support, Trustees Humpfer and Sigwalt lobbied for the passage of the ordinance as the means to limit illegal immigration. They built broad support to achieve the mutually desired outcome. The key differences were the disagreements over the necessary, appropriate, and indeed, legal means to achieve the same outcome.

Carpentersville's IIRO established an unprecedented legal attempt to take *local* control of immigration policy. This case illustrates how the IIRO policy proposal failed to be adopted and implemented. Specifically, four characteristics contributed to the policy failure. Large-scale demographic change established the baseline for political support and opposition among Latinos and whites. The political will to define and confront the problem was influenced by nationalist and patriotic dialogue. The formation and mobilization of national activists and coalitions further fractured support and opposition. The process of suburban decline blurred the definitions of the problem. Consequently, the policy proposal failed.

First, the demographic realities of neighborhood racial and ethnic transition shaped the political debate. The growth of suburban diversity created political tensions among supporters and opponents of the IIRO. While these tensions are by no means surprising, new patterns of demographic diversity had political consequences in the suburbs and led to conflicts that the suburbs had yet to experience. For suburbanites in Carpentersville, this conflict was about the politics of relief. On the one hand, longtime white residents and longtime Latino residents supported the IIRO because new residents and immigrants presented a threat to the historic way of life in Carpentersville. On the other hand, new residents and immigrants opposed the IIRO because it was the wrong policy for the wrong problem. The new suburban demography was a factor that determined the fate of the IIRO.

Second, the framing of the politics of relief influenced the public will to define and confront the problem. The political process did not resolve the definition of what it means to be "illegal" nor did it settle the constitutionality of the IIRO. Furthermore, the threats to middle-class life—socioeconomic decline and crime—blurred the causal factors of the problem. Then, the debate was shaped by nationalist and patriotic dialogue about the importance of preserving the English language and American life. Politics, as a process of allocating power to decisionmakers, did not stop the policy adoption of the IIRO. Relief was not the answer to the problem, at least in the form of the IIRO.

Third, the role of policy entrepreneurs actually diluted the fight for policy adoption in Carpentersville. There were too many actors in the debate, and they all disagreed with one another. National attention and national groups and organizations took positions on multiple dimensions of the debate. A common problem definition was not reached—let alone a response on why the problems existed. Many political actors misplaced the causation for association of their town's public problems—that is, assigning blame on the immigrant population for the socioeconomic decline of their neighborhoods. Hence, elected officials failed to adopt the IIRO.

Novel forms of political communication allowed entrepreneurs to participate and influence the outcome of the policy debate. Residents and nonresidents alike participated in the political blogosphere. Village president Bill Sarto maintained a blog in addition to many advocacy groups that mobilized around the issue. The wide-reaching video distribution on YouTube of village council meetings also meant that the debate reached more residents of

Carpentersville. As a result, the village's affairs drew national attention, and political participation increased. Yet, instead of building agreement, these communication channels further split the support and opposition of the IIRO as a result of its broad appeal nationally.

Fourth, between 1970 and 2010, the socioeconomic decline of suburban Carpentersville emerged as a distinct problem. Particular measures of suburban decline indicated that patterns of decline had become more pronounced. For example, household income declined and poverty increased. Similarly, job opportunities declined and unemployment increased in a marked fashion. Infrastructure and housing aged without reinvestment. These trends threatened the suburban way of life. The cycle of neighborhood change not only reflected the process of suburban decline, but it informed the process of invasion and succession as the population diversified. During the same period of suburban decline, Carpentersville also attracted many immigrants. The white population declined as the foreign-born population grew. In context, the growth of a new Latino immigrant population occurred as the white population declined, which provided clear evidence of the spatial process of invasion and succession. This dual transformation of decline and diversity fostered a climate of tension and nativist backlash to these changes.

Ultimately, the failure to adopt the Illegal Immigration Relief Ordinance reflects tensions between problem definition and policy design. Poorly conceived designs that do not effectively address problems lead to the failure of policy implementation. The case of Carpentersville demonstrates that while the divisions in the local immigration policy debate were clearly delineated, the identification of too many disparate problems—and their disagreements on the public nature—were ill-defined by too many actors with too many diverging agendas. Different definitions of public problems require different policy designs and coordinating solutions. Public problems can be redefined and reinterpreted by a variety of actors with competing policy goals. The result is that without agreement on the public nature of a problem, the status quo is maintained and a "do-nothing" approach is adopted. Building on the Carpentersville experience, we turn to the case of Farmers Branch, Texas.

At about the same time, an intense political fight also erupted in the suburb of Farmers Branch in the Dallas-Fort Worth Metroplex. In response to a large-scale demographic transformation, coupled with socioeconomic changes, city council members proposed an ordinance to provide relief from illegal immigration. A poignant debate ensued to gain local control of immigration policy. Residents banded together and voted to take control after a yearlong debate. The voters of the City of Farmers Branch adopted their own local immigration policies.

At the center of the policy debate was a dispute over the means to the same ends: how to limit illegal immigration. The primary policy entrepreneur was

Mayor Tim O'Hare. He was strongly opposed to illegal immigration and blamed the city's problems on illegal immigrants. O'Hare solidified support among his fellow councilmen, and they collectively made the case for taking local control of immigration policy to all of their respective constituencies. This resulted in the development of broad support for the IIRO among voters in the jurisdiction. The opposition to the IIRO comprised a disparate group of local and national organizations and a few political actors such as former Mayor Bob Phelps. Supporters and opponents disagreed about legal and necessary measures to curb illegal immigration.

Farmers Branch's IIRO attracted much public attention because it was one of the nation's first attempts to broadly take *local* control of immigration policy. This case shows that an IIRO policy proposal was successfully adopted, but the implementation failed. Four characteristics contributed to the policy adoption of Ordinance 2903. Political support of the policy design was established among the city's native, white population and legal immigrants. The formation and mobilization of interest and pressure groups consolidated support for the IIRO among voters in the city, largely failing to influence local residents. The suburban decline of Farmers Branch was framed as the problem of illegal immigration. As a result, the policy proposal was adopted.

First, white residents and native-born US residents provided strong political support for the policy design of Ordinance 2903. As Farmers Branch's historic suburban population, political actors defined them as the key stakeholders in the policy debate. Furthermore, they deliberately labeled residents dichotomously: deserving and undeserving. Deserving residents obeyed the law, paid taxes, and participated in the community. Undeserving residents were labeled as criminals who did not pay taxes or participate in community life. Thus, deserving residents were entitled to relief from the illegal actions of undeserving residents. The differences between these labeled groups shaped the political debate and eventually resulted in greater tensions among supporters and opponents of the ordinance.

Second, local policymakers' political will was ardent. This allowed them to define the public nature of the problem framed in terms of the politics of relief. They effectively made the case to white, native-born residents to support Ordinance 2903 because illegal immigrants threatened the way of life and the suburban, middle-class standard of living in Farmers Branch. Illegal immigrants threatened to end this legacy. Policymakers blamed illegal immigrants for the suburban decline. For them, this situation created a public problem that needed a public solution.

Third, the formation and mobilization of interest and pressure groups consolidated support for the IIRO among voters in the city. These groups failed to influence local residents and actually empowered local policymakers to continue the fight for policy adoption in Farmers Branch. Many national interest and pressure groups became involved in the fight against the adoption of Ordinance 2903. Organizations such as the ACLU, LULAC, and MAL-DEF argued on numerous grounds that the localization of immigration policy was unconstitutional. Interest groups opposed the ordinance because they viewed 2903 as the wrong policy for the wrong problem. Local policymakers and residents became convinced of their inherent right to self-governance. They agreed on a common problem definition, designed a policy response, and navigated their political system to reach the adoption of Ordinance 2903. In the end, the national dialogue about Farmers Branch energized local policymakers' pursuit for relief.

Fourth, the suburban decline of Farmers Branch was framed as the problem of illegal immigration. Population, housing, and infrastructure declines were defined as a public problem after nearly four decades of suburban decline in Farmers Branch. The magnitude of the problem became obvious upon examination of socioeconomic trends. Real household income declined, and household poverty levels increased. Public infrastructure, commercial entities, and housing units aged without reinvestment. Suburban middle-class living was threatened. In the course of the events, numerous immigrants settled in suburban Farmers Branch, causing the proportion of white, native residents to shift dramatically as the foreign-born population grew. This caused social and economic tensions to increase; policymakers and residents viewed these changes as a problem. The dynamics of neighborhood change did not reflect the process of suburban decline, but it was rather defined as a problem created by the arrival of illegal immigrants. The problems of illegal immigration were associated with suburban decline. Yet, political actors argued that the new population caused this transformation. Residents agreed, and an atmosphere of hostility and nativist backlash followed.

The adoption of Ordinance 2903 demonstrates the results of the convergence of the problem definition stream, the policy design stream, and the politics stream. The problem of illegal immigration was defined on the political agenda. A window of opportunity opened when political actors associated the social and economic decline of their community with illegal immigrants. Ordinance 2903 was effectively designed to take control of local immigration policy. A housing provision of the ordinance would address the residency of illegal immigrants in Farmers Branch. The policy was adopted after unanimous support of the city council and a popular referendum. The case of Farmers Branch illustrates how the identification of a public problem and the causal stories on the roots of the problem lead to a politics that rewards stakeholders. A story that redefines the problem—and its public nature—can result in policy adoption. Now, building on the experiences in Carpentersville and Farmers Branch, we turn to the case of Hazleton, Pennsylvania.

Similarly in the mid-2000s, Hazleton witnessed an aggressive political fight that began as a response to a local legislative proposal to control immigration policy. Mayor Lou Barletta proposed the Illegal Immigration Relief Act to the city council in an attempt to force out the illegal immigrants and fix up the declining community. Residents and policymakers overwhelmingly supported the law and quickly adopted the measure. The city garnered national attention for its action. Legal challenges ensued, and six years later, the courts are still considering the fate of the law.

The Hazleton case is noteworthy because it emerged as a model for taking local control of immigration policy. Throughout the nation, numerous municipalities drafted similar laws. In Pennsylvania alone, 30 local laws were proposed in the year after Hazleton's fight, while hundreds more nationally were drafted. Meanwhile, Barletta remained a very popular political executive and was reelected with 90 percent of the votes cast. Two years after the fight, he was even named "Mayor of the Year."[5] Hazletonians were committed to their mayor and were not ready to give up their fight. Other municipalities were forced to repeal or stop their own fight for local control of immigration policy. In these places, the politics of relief was associated with high legal costs, constitutional issues, and community well-being that could not be resolved. Yet, Mayor Barletta passionately believed in the IIRA and welcomed the legal fight.

Hazleton's IIRA established an unprecedented legal attempt to take *local* control of immigration policy. Important legal questions confronted Hazleton. To date, the courts were "required to intervene when states and localities directly undermine the federal objectives embodied in statutes enacted by Congress." The heart of the legal challenge concerned the inherent right of a municipality to preempt the federal government. According to the courts, the City of Hazleton "attempted to usurp authority that the Constitution has placed beyond the vicissitudes of local governments" and "could not possibly be in greater conflict with Congress's intent."[6] Mayor Barletta disagreed and promised to appeal, while the ACLU's Omar Jadwat said the court's decision is "a major defeat for the misguided, divisive and expensive anti-immigrant strategy that Hazleton has tried to export to the rest of the country." Even though the city faced a conundrum as to whether to appeal, as hefty legal fees had accrued, Barletta ensured that the fight would continue.

The arrival of a new demographic structure was an important factor that determined the fate of the IIRO. Since the Second World War, the socioeconomic decline of Hazleton had become a public problem. The pattern of decline was demonstrated by numerous measures, including a decrease in household income, an increase in poverty levels, and a lack of employment opportunities. Without reinvestment, neighborhoods declined. The cycle of neighborhood change was clear; areas that once grew and prospered now faced decline. Indeed, many of Hazleton's neighborhoods witnessed a dramatic racial and ethnic transition during the 2000s. The arrival of Latinos revived the city at the margins, but this transformation of decline and diversity created tensions and a nativist backlash. Hazletonians turned to their mayor to solve this conflict.

Mayor Barletta framed the politics of relief to influence the policy process. He was able to exploit the political process to resolve the problem by defining what it means to be "illegal." The problems in his city—crime, poor public services, neighborhoods in disrepair—were the result of the recent arrival of illegal immigrants. He hoped to solve these problems with the adoption and implementation of the IIRA. The mayor and his constituents viewed illegal immigrants as a threat to their longtime middle-class life. To provide relief, Barletta's politics blurred the definitions of the problem and its causal attributes. The IIRA was to provide relief by eliminating a part of the city's problem population.

The mayor played an important role as the city's policy entrepreneur. This strengthened the fight for policy adoption in Hazleton. There were few political actors in the debate, and they agreed with one another and deferred to the mayor's leadership. National attention was focused on the debate, and national groups and organizations took positions on multiple dimensions. Creative use of political communication allowed policy entrepreneurs to participate and influence the outcome of the policy debate. Barletta portrayed a strong image nationally as he took the fight to the airwaves and Internet. The large audience empowered the city's policymakers, and ultimately, they agreed to provide relief to their residents through the IIRA.

The adoption of the Illegal Immigration Relief Act reflects the convergence of the problem, solution, and politics streams. The case of Hazleton illustrates how the fight for local control immigration policy resulted in a policy solution, but not necessarily a solution for the city's public problems. In consequence, the three circumstances that led to policy adoption of the IIRA were: (1) agreement on the public nature of a problem, (2) a policy design that addressed the defined problem, and (3) a politics of relief that consolidated decision making. However, the legal challenges suggested that while these three streams converged at the local level of government, disagreement on the legal merits of the policy showed that Hazleton's definition of its problems and policy design did not solve the problems that they intended to address.

In the end, the debate over local control of immigration policy demonstrates the rough road to an effective, efficient, feasible, and equitable policy design. Actors involved in the policymaking process failed to consider other options when they crafted solutions to public problems. This was the result of a process that was not always iterative. In fact, decisionmaking was irrational at times.[7] Generally, policymakers and voters alike only paid attention to one issue at a time.[8] In response to these circumstances, they did not consider other options when problem solving.

However, using criteria to benchmark and differentiate policy alternatives might be one way to better navigate the road from agenda setting to policy implementation. According to Wildavsky, the consideration of policy alternatives is both an analytical exercise as well as a political endeavor. Indeed, it is a prudent balancing act in which politicians and citizens find a practical middle ground to implement public policy.[9] Political tensions and limited resources are common hurdles of this balancing act. Since policymakers are faced with the constraints of open windows of opportunity, they must then work creatively to resolve these issues if policies are to be adopted and implemented. Creative work begins with policy analysis.

The analysis of various policy designs along a particular set of criteria can allow policymakers to make more informed decisions.[10] Policy designs can be analyzed along the dimensions of criteria such as effectiveness, efficiency, feasibility, and equity. Effective designs achieve the goals that the policy establishes. They are also feasible and implementable. According to local political actors, the goals of eliminating the illegal immigrant population were met—at least by anecdote. However, the designs generally failed because the implementation was not feasible. Despite policy adoption, there were too many questions about the constitutionality of the intergovernmental nature of the ordinances, which limited implementation. Efficient designs do more with less. They maximize the greatest output with the least input. Similarly, the cost of implementation is a consideration. In these cases, political actors did not consider the criterion of cost. Relief was valued at any cost. Feasible designs are politically acceptable designs for public actors and organizations. Last, equitable designs attempt to maximize the social impact of the burden. The IIRO is a case whereby various actors defined equity differently. Supporters argued that laws that treat all residents the same were equitable designs, while opponents argued that laws that place an undue harm on different populations are unequal.

Should all of these criteria matter in the policy process? Not necessarily. Perhaps policymakers might only care about a few criteria and ignore the others. It is clear that definition of criteria matter. Not only do they distinguish political support, but they also delineate the politics of who supports and opposes relief. After all, even though what makes for good public policy is subjective, the development of an analytical framework to select among policy alternatives lays out a clear understanding of the issues in accessible ways to stakeholders.

LESSONS LEARNED

The fight for local control of immigration policy persists and shows no signs of diminishing. The implications of these policy debates suggest that processes of demographic transition, economic restructuring, and suburban decline influence the definition of public problems and the policy design. The politics of relief are expressed as a reaction to these processes. Although the legal and political challenges endure, there are some valuable lessons that can be drawn from the experiences of Carpentersville, Farmers Branch, and Hazleton. However, these lessons should be accompanied with a caveat. Since new developments continue to unfold, the timely nature of this study does make it difficult to extract wider lessons for metropolitan America. But a reflection on the characteristics that influenced the policy process and outcomes is warranted if we are to understand the evolution of these debates. Let us consider the following lessons from the experiences of three communities.

The first lesson is that it is essential for policymakers, planners, and residents to understand the causes of public problems. It is not enough to craft a solution to a problem that is only associated with an issue. There might be a solution that solves the wrong problem. In these three cases, the IIRO was a solution to the wrong problem. Illegal immigrants were blamed for the socioeconomic decline of these cities. Politicians and their constituents need to understand that suburban decline, like urban decline, is real. It cannot be blamed away. Poverty has suburbanized. Crime has suburbanized. Immigrants have suburbanized. The suburbanization of these social and economic challenges is a reality. Renewal policies should address decline problems.

It is also noteworthy to distinguish between association and causality.[11] In terms of association, are the phenomena associated with each other? That is, do they occur at the same time? In terms of causality, does the phenomenon result in the occurrence of another phenomenon? In the case of the IIRO, political actors and policymakers answered these questions differently. For example, are the social and economic problems as defined by the residents of Carpentersville, Farmers Branch, and Hazleton a result of the increase of illegal immigrants? In other words, did illegal immigrants *cause* these cities to experience fiscal troubles with public services, housing stock problems, increased criminal activity, and overall infrastructure and economic decline? Or, were these problems that were simply *associated* with one another— meaning that they occurred together, at the same time? In short, we can glean from policy theory how such problems were defined through an analysis of the streams of definitions, solutions, and politics.[12]

The second lesson is that local governments should carefully consider the consequences before fighting and adopting policies like IIROs. These ordinances have long-lasting social and economic consequences. Population loss is a likely outcome. This may contribute to a decline in local revenue, or it may contribute to an increase in local revenue. This will squarely depend on who leaves: low-income residents or high-income residents. Fiscal challenges are also a likely outcome. The enforcement of IIROs can also be expensive. And, if there are legal challenges to these ordinances, a lengthy and costly judicial battle will ensue.[13] Thus, before adopting and implementing an IIRO, cities should consider whether it is the best utilization of public resources. Carpentersville, Farmers Branch, and Hazleton were faced with a variety of other issues related to socioeconomic decline that already presented a fiscal challenge. Without a doubt, residents of metropolitan America are more mobile than ever, and cities and suburbs will indeed continue to compete for residents and their resources that follow. In other words, they will vote with their feet.[14]

The third lesson is that political and policy narratives matter. Political actors appealed to the suburban nature of American identity in their cities to influence the policy debate. These policy debates demonstrate that stories were powerful tools that shaped public opinion. The framing of public problems can determine the outcome of policies. Thematic stories about how illegal immigrants committed crime, ruined schools and neighborhoods, and were unpatriotic helped to define the public nature of the problem. In turn, stories determined the policy solutions. Especially in a 24-hour information age, the news cycle never ends and new multimedia content is readily available. This enables residents to tell stories and participate in political communication through venues like blogs, YouTube, and Twitter. This further broadens the scope of the saliency of the problem. Political actors who effectively took advantage of these media outlets shaped public opinion about the issue.

The last lesson is that metropolitan America is woven together by the fabric of a multiethnic society. This is a demographic reality. The stories from these debates demonstrate that until society learns how to live together in integrated neighborhoods, there will not be tolerance and respect of human differences. Of course, this is a tough challenge—bringing people together, overcoming economic barriers, and finding a common politics. We should strive to set the goal of achieving racial and ethnic integration in our communities. Suburbs like Columbia, Maryland, a planned community by James Rouse, were born in the late 1960s to achieve racial and economic harmony.[15] Although this is unlikely given the causes of segregation and the long history of the nation's trials and errors on the road toward racial integration, it is a worthy effort.[16]

These lessons attest to the fact that other cities and suburbs can learn from these experiences. In short, they raise the question: was the fight worth it? Some said yes, and others said no. In Carpentersville, the consensus was no.

The village was bitterly divided, and the fight's aftermath left few winners. A local politician said, "The political climate was toxic. No one won."[17] In Farmers Branch, the consensus was generally yes. Mayor Tim O'Hare represented his city's majority opinion when he said, "I'd do it all over again."[18] But City Councilwoman Carol Dingman disagreed and in a fervent dissent said, "[This] fight has really changed the atmosphere of our town. We've always had a small-town feel and this issue has destroyed it. It has ruined our reputation. I've never seen such hateful rhetoric . . . I'm embarrassed to say I'm from Farmers Branch."[19] In Hazleton, the consensus was a resounding yes. For Mayor Lou Barletta, it was a worthwhile fight. His personal fight for local control continued as he began his first term in the US Congress. Whether the fight was worth it or not, these localities charted a new policy domain in American local government. Many other localities can learn what to do and what *not* to do in this fight.

FUTURE WORK

The implications of this study raise a variety of interesting issues for future research. Scholarly inquiry should first examine the demography of the US metropolis, which continues to grow more diverse. Data from the 2010 Census offer a rich opportunity to better understand how immigrants reshape society. Where do immigrants settle, and what are the characteristics of the communities that they join? What explains these phenomena? The answers will lead to the development of new theories and patterns of spatial arrangements. The examination of the social, economic, and political dimensions of metropolitan space will undoubtedly shed light on how Americans think, vote, and build social capital in cities and suburbs.

Then, there is a need to better understand the complex socio-spatial patterns in the US metropolis.[20] The political fragmentation of the metropolis continues to fuel socioeconomic inequality and the process of decline.[21] Suburban decline and its policy discontents demand more study.[22] What are the drivers of suburban decline and what explains the variation? How are suburbs—and suburban immigrants—impacted by the Great Recession?[23] Such answers will illuminate how suburban politics evolve, and then they will show how and why suburbanites respond to neoliberal policy.

Next, scholars need to further study the numerous dimensions of IIROs. What explains the likelihood of the adoption of IIROs, and what accounts for the variation? How do the politics of intergovernmental relations affect the implementation of IIROs? What happens to immigrants after IIRO policy debates? Do they stay or leave? Why? What does the future hold for federal, state, local immigration policy?

Last, the study of the politics of the policy processes is a worthy area of investigation. The political and policy implications of the process of immigrant assimilation and integration need to be better understood in the suburban context. How do the social, economic, and political contexts of suburbs determine the policy responses? Future work might also consider how the communication of political frames shapes the outcome of policy debates. Political terminology shapes how people think about issues. Terms like "illegal alien" and "undocumented resident" are politicized labels that conjure different images of immigrants.[24] How do these labels influence the policy process? Under what circumstances might we see different outcomes and why? Similarly, the impact of electronic communication on policy debates is not well understood. How do blogs, video streaming, e-mails, and text messages impact policy debates?

SUBURBAN CROSSROADS

The age of innocence in the suburbs ended a long time ago.[25] Yet, suburbs remain the cultural icon for the American Dream. The dichotomy between urban and suburban America is a powerful myth that still pervades our thinking, our living, our working, and our diversions. Americans still think in terms of "the city" and "the suburbs," despite an extensive body of work that shows that suburbs have the same characteristics as big cities.[26] Just like cities, suburbs are diverse places with diverse populations. They grow. They decline. They regenerate. This is the lifecycle of neighborhoods—urban and suburban. The social structure, economic base, and physical landscape change accordingly. These changes do not occur in a vacuum. Residents live through these changes, and at times, socioeconomic and political conflict results.

The fight for local control of immigration policy reflects these suburban realities. Immigration policy is at a crossroads; and indeed, this is evident in the nation's cities and suburbs. Policymakers are faced with numerous roads to move forward. One option is the "go-it-alone" road. Localities might continue to adopt IIROs and continue their fight to implement these policies. Immigration policy will become even more fragmented and result in disparate local policy solutions. Another option is the road to cooperation and collaboration. Localities might decide to work together through intergovernmental institutions to develop novel tools to improve the problem of illegal immigration. The final road is a do-nothing approach. Localities might simply wait for policy action from other levels of government. Whichever road these local communities follow, critical decisions will need to be made. The path on any of these roads is uncertain.

In conclusion, the fight for local control of immigration endures, and it is likely to endure for some time. This fight is about many things for many people. It is about the rule of law. It is about equal opportunity and civil rights. It is about the preservation of community, and ultimately, it is about the American Dream. While this fight was open to various interpretations of the law and public policy, concern for the public good was the thread that wove together the problem definitions, policy responses, and political debates. In these three communities, supporters and opponents of the ordinances defended their cities, residents, and local institutions. They agreed on the same end goals but disagreed on the means to achieve them. Supporters fought for the adoption and implementation of Illegal Immigration Relief Ordinances, and opponents fought them. Ultimately, it is up to the courts and legislative bodies to determine the winners and losers of this fight.

The multiethnic metropolis is a twenty-first-century reality. The battlegrounds for local control of immigration policy began in the communities of Carpentersville, Farmers Branch, and Hazleton. Other cities took notice, and the debate spread to hundreds of other municipalities. As long as Americans need to reconcile the reality of the new suburban demography, the fight will continue in city halls, state houses, and the courts.

NOTES

1. John F. Kennedy, *A Nation of Immigrants*, 77-83.

2. Randal C. Archibold, "Unexpected Governor Takes an Unwavering Course," *New York Times*, April 24, 2010.

3. See Wayne Cornelius, Takeyuki Tsuda, Philip Martin, and James Hollifield, eds. *Controlling Immigration: A Global Perspective 2nd ed.* (Stanford, CA: Stanford University Press, 2004); Caroline B. Brettell and James F. Hollifield, eds. *Migration Theory: Talking across Disciplines, 2nd ed.* (New York: Routledge, 2007); Stephen Castles and Mark J. Miller, *The Age of Migration: International Population Movements in the Modern World, 4th ed.* (New York: The Guilford Press, 2009).

4. Larrisa Chinwah, "Group Issues Carpentersville Mayor a Challenge," *Daily Herald*, October 8, 2006.

5. "Mayor of the Year," Pennsylvania State Mayors Association, accessed January 30, 2012, http://pamayors.org/PastMayorOfTheYear.html.

6. *Lozano* 496 F.Supp.2d 477, 484.

7. Bryan D. Jones, *Reconceiving Decision-Making in Democratic Politics: Attention, Choice, and Public Policy* (Chicago: University of Chicago Press, 1994). See also Frank R. Baumgartner and Bryan D. Jones, eds., *Policy Dynamics* (Chicago: University of Chicago Press, 2002).

8. Bryan D. Jones and Frank R. Baumgartner, *The Politics of Attention: How Government Prioritizes Problems* (Chicago: University of Chicago Press, 2005).

9. Aaron Wildavsky, *Speaking Truth to Power: The Art and Craft of Policy Analysis* (Boston: Little, Brown, 1979).

10. Eugene Bardach, *A Practical Guide for Policy Analysis: The Eightfold Path to More Effective Problem Solving, 4th ed.* (Washington, DC: CQ Press, 2011).

11. Michael E. Sobel, "Causal Inference in the Social Sciences," *Journal of the American Statistical Association* 95, no. 450 (2000): 647-651.

12. See generally Anne Schneider and Mara Sidney, "What Is Next for Policy Design and Social Construction Theory?" *Policy Studies Journal* 37, no. 1 (2009): 103-119; Kenneth J. Meier, "Policy Theory, Policy Theory Everywhere: Ravings of a Deranged Policy Scholar," *Policy Studies Journal* 37, no. 1 (2009): 5-11; Thomas E. James and Paul D. Jorgensen, "Policy Knowledge, Policy Formulation, and Change: Revisiting a Foundational Question," *Policy Studies Journal* 37, no. 1 (2009): 141-162.

13. Gebe Martinez, "Unconstitutional and Costly: The High Price of Local Immigration Enforcement," *Center for American Progress*, January 2011, accessed January 15, 2011, www.americanprogress.org/issues/2011/01/pdf/cost_of_enforcement.pdf.

14. Charles Tiebout, "A Pure Theory of Local Expenditures," *Journal of Political Economy* 64, no. 5 (1956): 416-424.

15. Columbia, Maryland is an unincorporated suburb of approximately 100,000 residents located in the Baltimore-Washington corridor. In 2010, the demographic composition was: 66 percent white, 20 percent black, 7 percent Asian, and 7 percent other. See generally Joseph Rocco Mitchell and David L. Stebenne, *New City Upon a Hill: A History of Columbia, Maryland* (Charleston, SC: The History Press, 2007); Joshua Olsen, *Better Places, Better Lives: A Biography of James Rouse* (Washington, DC: Urban Land Institute: 2003).

16. There is a vast literature on the racial segregation and integration in the United States. See generally Douglas Massey and Nancy Denton, *American Apartheid: Segregation and the Making of the Underclass* (Cambridge, MA: Harvard University Press, 1993); Arnold R. Hirsch, *Making the Second Ghetto: Race and Housing in Chicago 1940-1960* (Chicago: University of Chicago Press, 1998); Thomas J. Sugrue, *The Origins of the Urban Crisis: Race and Inequality in Postwar Detroit* (Princeton, NJ: Princeton University Press, 1996); Peter Dreier, Todd Swanstrom, and John H. Mollenkopf, *Place Matters: Metropolitics for the Twenty-First Century, 2nd ed.* (Lawrence, KS: University Press of Kansas, 2005); Dennis Keating, *The Suburban Racial Dilemma: Housing and Neighborhoods* (Philadelphia: Temple University Press, 1994).

17. Anonymous personal interview, May 6, 2009.

18. Branch Bulletin, City of Farmers Branch, "Tim O'Hare: The Interview," April 6, 2011.

19. Ben Shurett, "Still Skeptical About Kobach," *Sand Mountain Reporter,* April 3, 2010.

20. Paul Knox, *Metroburbia, USA* (Piscataway, NJ: Rutgers University Press, 2008); Arthur C. Nelson and Robert E. Lang, *Megapolitan America: A New Vision for Understanding America's Metropolitan Geography* (Chicago: APA Planners Press, 2011).

21. Culver, "The Politics of Suburban Distress," 1-18; Robert M. Fogelson, *The Fragmented Metropolis: Los Angeles, 1850-1930* (Berkeley: University of California Press, 1967).

22. Vicino, *Transforming Race and Class in Suburbia*, 1-18; See also Hanlon, *Once the American Dream*, 1-12.

23. Justin B. Hollander, *Sunburnt Cities: The Great Recession, Depopulation and Urban Planning in the American Sunbelt* (New York: Routledge, 2011); William H. Lucy, *Foreclosing the Dream*, 1-10; Christopher B. Leinberger, "The Next Slum," *The Atlantic Monthly* (March 2008): 70.

24. Newton, *Illegal, Alien, or Immigrant*, 163-170.

25. Charles Monroe Haar, *The End of Innocence: A Suburban Reader* (Glenview, IL: Scott, Foresman, 1972); Baldassare, *Trouble in Paradise*, 1-20.

26. Hanlon, Short, and Vicino, *Cities and Suburbs*, 247-259; Barry Schwartz, ed., *The Changing Face of the Suburbs* (Chicago: University of Chicago Press, 1976); Teaford, *The American Suburb*, 217.

Appendix A

Illegal Immigration Relief Ordinance

Appendix A provides the example of the original IIRO that was drafted and adopted into law in Hazleton, Pennsylvania. Other municipalities throughout the nation modeled their IIRO on this legislation. While the City of Hazleton revised the Ordinance several times, the original version is provided so that the intentions of policymakers can be clearly demonstrated.

ORDINANCE 2006-10
ILLEGAL IMMIGRATION RELIEF ACT ORDINANCE
BE IT ORDAINED BY THE COUNCIL OF THE CITY OF HAZLETON
AS FOLLOWS:

SECTION 1. TITLE
This chapter shall be known and may be cited as the "City of Hazleton Illegal Immigration Relief Act Ordinance."

SECTION 2. FINDINGS AND DECLARATION OF PURPOSE
The People of the City of Hazleton find and declare:
A. That illegal immigration leads to higher crime rates, contributes to overcrowded classrooms and failing schools, subjects our hospitals to fiscal hardship and legal residents to substandard quality of care, contributes to other burdens on public services, increasing their cost and diminishing their availability to lawful residents, and destroys our neighborhoods and diminishes our overall quality of life.
B. That the City of Hazleton is authorized to abate public nuisances and empowered and mandated by the People of Hazleton to abate the nuisance of

illegal immigration by diligently prohibiting the acts and policies that facilitate illegal immigration and punishing the people and businesses that aid and abet illegal aliens.

C. This ordinance seeks to secure to those lawfully present in the United States and this City, whether or not they are Citizens of the United States, the right to live in peace free of the threat of illegal alien crime, to enjoy the public services provided by this city without being burdened by the cost of providing goods, support and services to any whose presence in the United States is contrary to its laws and to be free of the debilitating effects on their economic and social well being imposed by the influx of illegal aliens to the fullest extent that these goals can be achieved consistent with the Constitution and Laws of the United States and the Commonwealth of Pennsylvania.

SECTION 3. DEFINITIONS

Whenever used in this chapter, the following terms shall have the following meanings:

"City" means the City of Hazleton.

"Contract employer" means any person who obtains the services of one or more individuals through a day labor agency.

"Illegal Alien" means any person whose initial entry into the United States was illegal and whose current status is also illegal as well as any person who, after entering legally, has failed to leave the United States upon the expiration of his or her visa.

"Legal Work Status" means that a person's employment is not in violation of any law of the United States, the Commonwealth of Pennsylvania or this Ordinance.

"Vehicle" means a vehicle as defined in Pennsylvania Vehicle Code as the same now reads or may hereafter be amended.

SECTION 4. BUSINESS PERMITS, CONTRACTS OR GRANTS

Any entity or any parent, affiliate, subsidiary or agent of any entity (other than a charity recognized as exempt from federal income taxation under Sec. 501 of the Internal Revenue Code of the United States and which has obtained and continues to have in force an exemption from federal income taxation), that employs, retains, aids or abets illegal aliens or illegal immigration into the United States, whether directly or by or through any agent, ruse, guise, device or means, no matter how indirect, and even if the agent or entity might otherwise be exempted from this section, or violates any provision of this Ordinance, shall from the date of the violation or its discovery, whichever shall be later, be denied and barred from approval of a business permit, renewal of a business permit, any city contract or grant as follows:

(1) For the first violation for a period of five years,

(2) For any subsequent violation, for a period of ten years.

A. "Aids or abets" includes, but is not limited to:

(i) hiring or attempted hiring of illegal aliens,

(ii) providing, renting or leasing real or personal property to illegal aliens,

(iii) funding or providing goods and services to illegal aliens, except as provided in Sec. 4 C.,

(iv) funding, providing goods and services to or aiding in the establishment or continuation of any day labor center or other entity providing similar services, unless the entity acts with due diligence to verify the legal work status of all persons whom it employs, provides job assistance for or in any way assists or facilitates in obtaining any employment.

B. Except as provided in C., any action or failure to act done within the boundaries of this City that aids and abets illegal aliens or facilitates their avoiding detection and apprehension anywhere in the United States, its territories or possessions violates this Ordinance.

C. This Ordinance shall not be construed to prohibit rendering emergency medical care, emergency assistance or legal assistance.

SECTION 5. RENTING TO ILLEGAL ALIENS

A. Illegal aliens are prohibited from leasing or renting property. Any property owner or renter/tenant/lessee in control of property, who knowingly allows an illegal alien to use, rent or lease their property shall be in violation of this section.

B. Any person or entity that violates this Ordinance shall be subject to a fine of not less than $1,000.00.

C. A separate violation of this Ordinance shall be deemed to have been committed on each day during or on which a violation occurs or continues.

SECTION 6. ENGLISH ONLY

A. The City of Hazleton declares that English is the official language of the City.

B. Unless explicitly mandated by the federal government, the state of Pennsylvania or the City of Hazleton, all official city business, forms, documents, signage will be written in English only.

SECTION 7. SEVERABILITY

If any part of provision of this Chapter is in conflict or inconsistent with applicable provisions of federal or state statutes, or is otherwise held to be invalid or unenforceable by any court of competent jurisdiction, such part of provision shall be suspended and superseded by such applicable laws or regulations, and the remainder of this Chapter shall not be affected thereby.

ORDAINED by Council this 13th day of July, 2006.
ORDINANCE PASSES JULY 13, 2006.

Appendix B
Methods

Appendix B briefly discusses the research strategies, questions, data collection and organization, analysis, and limitations of this study. Through the lens of an urbanist, I examined the process of metropolitan socioeconomic change and the politics of the policy process. In the tradition of scientific inquiry in the multidisciplinary field of urban affairs, I employed a mixed methods approach that allowed me to collect a range of quantitative and qualitative data and then analyze them.[1]

Based on a theoretical framework of neighborhood socioeconomic change and the policy process, I formulated three primary research questions. First, how and why do patterns of demographic change impact communities? Second, how and why does the role of suburban decline impact the social structure, the economic status, and the political power of communities? Third, what are the policy implications of local decisions and how do they affect different populations with regard to local control of immigration policy? These questions were based on increased public attention to local debates on immigration policy as well as local observations of the decline of older suburban areas.

I addressed these questions by conducting three cases studies. This was a useful method for numerous reasons. In a synthesis of case study methodology, VanWynsberghe and Khan eloquently describe the method's utility. They suggest that the prototypical case study has seven common features.[2] Case study methods provide an in-depth focus on a specific unit of analysis.[3] By providing contextual details, case studies offer a unique perspective of "an instance in action."[4] They are ideal to study complex issues in natural environments with little control over the population's behavior or societal events.[5] Case studies are bounded by temporal and spatial criteria.[6] It is also possible to learn while conducting research in the field and shift hypothesis

accordingly.[7] A triangulation of data provides and reinforces accurate findings.[8] Last, case studies allow others to extend their own experience to the
subject under investigation.[9] Indeed, case study methodology is a "transpara-
digmatic and transdisciplinary heuristic that involves the careful delineation
of the unit of analysis (i.e., event, concept, programme, or process) for which
evidence is being collected."[10] Accordingly, this study was designed as an
in-depth exploration of the relationship between socioeconomic decline and
the IIRO policy debate in the natural environment of three cities as political
events unfolded.

In this study, the cases were organized by geographic region: the Dallas-
Fort Worth Metroplex; the Chicago metropolitan area; and central Pennsylvania. The unit of analysis was delineated in three ways: by place, process, and
event. In terms of place, the unit of analysis was the census tract and census-
defined place.[11] Tracts represented neighborhoods within a community, and
places (the sum of the tracts) represented municipalities. In terms of process,
suburban decline was analyzed as a social and economic process of neighborhood change.[12] In terms of events, the political debates about the IIRO were
analyzed in multiple venues such as legislative bodies, local residents, and the
news media.[13] These multiple units provided a rich analytical depth for the
triangulation of data sources and methods.

Data were gathered from multiple sources between 2007 and 2010. Demographic data were compiled from the decennial US Census and American
Community Survey. During field visits to the three places under investigation, data were also collected from local historical societies, public and archival documents, photography, judicial rulings, key informant interviews, and
direct participant observation.

These data were analyzed using a variety of techniques. First, I employed a
spatial descriptive analysis of the census data using Geolytics' Neighborhood
Change Database. This software normalizes census tract boundaries from
1970 to 2000 so that data can be accurately compared longitudinally within
the same territorial space. Geographic information systems (GIS) software allowed me to overlay census tracts on top of census-defined places to identify
and stratify tracts that were spatially located within the place. The summation
of these tracts, and the data associated with them, facilitated the analysis of
socioeconomic change along a spectrum of socioeconomic indicators. Next,
I analyzed numerous public documents such as court rulings, master plans,
local laws, zoning, maps, and newsletters. The major newspapers of record
in each case were searched and examined for coverage of the IIRO debate
and socioeconomic decline. These data were organized by coding them according to date and theme. Then, key informant interviews were conducted. I
used a consistent protocol to secure interviews by telephone and e-mail. Key

informants were identified in local governments, local community organizations, and local newspapers. They were contacted to inquire about scheduling and conducting an interview using electronic means of communication or in person. Informants were asked about their local histories in the community, their views on immigration and the IIRO debate, their views on the social and economic transformation of the community, policy recommendations, and future thoughts. A snowball strategy grew local contacts. Last, I was engaged in participant observation during site visits. City council meetings, rallies, and elections were observed. Every neighborhood in each place was observed and photographed.

This study was limited by several factors related to scope, time, and access. The study was limited by the analysis of three cases that were located in three different regions. It was also limited to the analysis of *local* policy responses. The legal complexity and breadth of state and federal government interactions and policy responses limited the scope of the work to local policy responses. Access to key informants was limited since many interviewees requested anonymity as they worried about the implications of public statements. The timing of the interviews occurred during the peak of the intensity of the policy debate. Many were hesitant to go "on the record" to discuss their views about the IIRO debate.

NOTES

1. For other recent studies that employed similar approaches, see Justin Hollander, *Polluted and Dangerous: America's Worst Abandoned Properties and What Can Be Done About Them* (Lebanon, NH: University of Vermont Press, 2009); Vicino, *Transforming Race and Class in Suburbia*, 193-210; Colin Gordon, *Mapping Decline: St. Louis and the Fate of the American City* (Philadelphia: University of Pennsylvania Press, 2008); Juliet F. Gainsborough, *Scandalous Politics: Child Welfare Policy in the States* (Washington, DC: Georgetown University Press, 2010).

2. Rob VanWynsberghe and Samia Khan, "Redefining Case Study," *International Journal of Qualitative Methods* 6, no. 2 (2007): 83.

3. Robert Yin, *Case Study Research: Design and Methods, 4th ed.* (Thousand Oaks, CA: Sage, 2008).

4. Alexander L. George and Andrew Bennett, *Case Studies and Theory Development in the Social Sciences* (Cambridge, MA: MIT Press, 2005).

5. Ruth A. Anderson, Benjamin F. Crabtree, David J. Steele, and Reuben R. McDaniel Jr., "Case Study Research: The View from Complexity Science," *Qualitative Health Research* 15, no. 5 (2005): 669-685.

6. Sharan B. Merriam, *Case Study Research in Education: A Qualitative Approach* (San Francisco: Jossey Bass, 1988).

7. Yvonna Lincoln and Egon Guba, "The Only Generalization is: There is No Generalization," in *Case Study Method: Key Issues, Key Texts*, eds. Roger Gomm, Martyn Hammersley and Peter Foster (Thousands Oaks, CA: Sage, 2000): 27-44.

8. Robert Yin, *Case Study Research: Design and Methods, 4th ed.* (Thousand Oaks, CA: Sage, 2008).

9. Robert Donmoyer, "Generalizability and the single case study," in *Qualitative Inquiry in Education: The Continuing Debate*, eds. Elliot W. Eisner and Alan Peshkin (New York: Teachers College Press, 1990): 175-200.

10. Rob VanWynsberghe, Björn Surborg, and Elvin Wyly, "When the Games Come to Town: Neoliberalism, Mega-Events and Social Inclusion in the Vancouver 2010 Winter Olympic Games," *International Journal of Urban and Regional Research* 36, no. 2 (2012): 3.

11. See Nancey Green Leigh and Sugie Lee, "Philadelphia's Space in Between: Inner-Ring Suburbs Evolution," *Opolis: An International Journal of Suburban and Metropolitan Studies* 1, no. 1 (2004): 13-32.

12. Hanlon and J. Vicino, "The Fate of First-Tier Suburbs," 249-275.

13. Brettell and Nibbs, "Immigrant Suburban Settlement," 1-30.

Selected Bibliography

Abbott, Carl. *The New Urban America: Growth and Politics in the Sunbelt Cities, Revised Edition.* Chapel Hill, NC: University of North Carolina Press, 1987.

Abrahamson, Mark. *Urban Enclaves: Identity and Place in America.* New York: St. Martin's Press, 1996.

Adams, James Truslow. *The Epic of America.* New York: Little, Brown and Company, 1931.

Alba, Richard, and Victor Nee. "Rethinking Assimilation Theory for a New Era of Immigration." *International Migration Review* 31, no. 4 (1997): 826-74.

Alonso, William. *Location and Land Use: Toward a General Theory of Land Rent.* Cambridge, MA: Harvard University Press, 1964.

Altschuler, Glenn, and Stuart Blumin. *The GI Bill: The New Deal for Veterans.* New York: Oxford University Press, 2009.

Anderson, Kristi. *New Immigrant Communities: Finding a Place in Local Politics.* Boulder, CO: Lynne Rienner, 2010.

Anrig Jr., Greg, and Tova Andrea Wang, eds. *Immigration's New Frontiers: Experiences from the Emerging Gateway States.* New York: Century Foundation Press, 2007.

Baldassare, Mark. *Trouble in Paradise: The Suburban Transformation in America.* New York: Columbia University Press, 1986.

Bardach, Eugene. *A Practical Guide for Policy Analysis: The Eightfold Path to More Effective Problem Solving.* 4th ed. Washington, DC: CQ Press, 2011.

Barkan, Elliott R. "Return of the Nativists? California Public Opinion and Immigration in the 1980s and 1990s." *Social Science History* 27, no. 2 (2003): 229-83.

Barreto, Amílcar Antonio. *The Politics of Language in Puerto Rico.* Gainesville, FL: University Press of Florida, 2001.

Baumgartner, Frank R., and Bryan D. Jones, eds. *Policy Dynamics.* Chicago: University of Chicago Press, 2002.

Baxandall, Rosalyn, and Elizabeth Ewen. *Picture Windows: How the Suburbs Happened.* New York: Basic Books, 2001.

Bean, Frank D., and Gillian Stevens. *America's Newcomers and the Dynamics of Diversity*. New York: Russell Sage, 2003.

Beauregard, Robert. *Voices of Decline: The Postwar Fate of U.S. Cities, Second Edition Revised*. New York: Routledge, 2003.

Bluestone, Barry, and Bennett Harrison. *The Deindustrialization of America: Plant Closings, Community Abandonment, and the Dismantling of Basic Industry*. New York: Basic Books, 1984.

Bosso, Chris. *Pesticides and Politics: The Life Cycle of a Public Issue*. Pittsburgh: University of Pittsburgh Press, 1987.

———. "The Contextual Bases of Problem Definition." In *The Politics of Problem Definition*, edited by David A. Rochefort and Roger W. Cobb, 181-202. Lawrence, KS: University Press of Kansas, 1994.

Bollens, Scott. "State Growth Management." *Journal of the American Planning Association* 58, no. 4 (1992): 454-78.

Bourdieu, Pierre. *Distinction: A Social Critique of the Judgement of Taste*. Cambridge, MA: Harvard University Press, 1984.

Bowen, William M., Ronnie A. Dunn, and David O. Kasdan. "What is Urban Studies? Context, Internal Structure, and Content." *Journal of Urban Affairs* 32, no. 2 (2010): 199-227.

Bradbury, Katharine L., Anthony Downs, and Kenneth A. Small. *Urban Decline and the Future of American Cities*. Washington, DC: Brookings Institution Press, 1982.

Brettell, Caroline B., and James F. Hollifield, eds. *Migration Theory: Talking across Disciplines*. 2nd ed. New York: Routledge, 2007.

Brettell, Caroline B., and Faith G. Nibbs. "Immigrant Suburban Settlement and the 'Threat' to Middle Class Status and Identity: The Case of Farmers Branch, Texas." *International Migration* 49, no. 1 (2011): 1-30.

Burgess, Ernest Watson. "The Growth of the City: An Introduction to a Research Project." In *The City*, edited by Robert E. Park, Ernest Watson Burgess, and Roderick Duncan McKenzie, 47-62. Chicago: University of Chicago Press, 1925.

Burnham, Daniel, and Edward Bennett. *Plan of Chicago*. Chicago: Chicago Plan Commission, 1909.

Callaghan, Karen J., and Frauke Schnell, eds. *Framing American Politics*. Pittsburgh: University of Pittsburgh Press, 2005.

Carpini, Michael X. Delli. "News from Somewhere: Journalistic Frames and the Debate over Public Journalism." In *Framing American Politics*, edited by Karen J. Callaghan and Frauke Schnell, 21-53. Pittsburgh: University of Pittsburgh Press, 2005.

Castles, Stephen, and Mark J. Miller. *The Age of Migration: International Population Movements in the Modern World*. 4th ed. New York: The Guilford Press, 2009.

Chandler, Charles R., and Tsai Yung-mei. "Social Factors Influencing Immigration Attitudes: An Analysis of Data from the General Social Survey." *The Social Science Journal* 38, no. 2 (2001): 177-188.

Clark, William A.V. *Immigrants and the American Dream: Remaking the Middle Class*. New York: The Guilford Press, 2003.

Cobb, Roger, and Charles Elder. *Participation in American Politics: The Dynamics of Agenda-Building.* 2nd ed. Baltimore: The Johns Hopkins University Press, 1983.
———. "The Politics of Agenda-Building: An Alternative Perspective for Modern Democratic Theory." *Journal of Politics* 33, no. 4 (1971): 892-915.
Conlan, Timothy. *From New Federalism to Devolution: Twenty-Five Years of Intergovernmental Reform.* Rev. ed. Washington, DC: Brookings Institution Press, 1998.
Cornelius, Wayne A. "Controlling 'Unwanted' Immigration: Lessons from the United States, 1993-2004." *Journal of Ethnic and Migration Studies* 31, no. 4 (2005): 775-94.
Cornelius, Wayne, Takeyuki Tsuda, Philip Martin, and James Hollifield, eds. *Controlling Immigration: A Global Perspective.* 2nd ed. Stanford, CA: Stanford University Press, 2004.
Corwin, Edward Samuel, Harold William Chase, and Craig R. Ducat. *Edward Corwin's The Constitution and What It Means Today.* 14th ed. Princeton, NJ: Princeton University Press, 1978.
Cullen, Jim. *The American Dream: A Short History of an Idea that Shaped a Nation.* New York: Oxford University Press, 2004.
Culver, Lowell W. "The Politics of Suburban Distress." *Journal of Urban Affairs* 4, no. 1 (1982): 1-18.
Davis, Richard. *Typing Politics: The Role of Blogs in American Politics.* New York: Oxford University Press, 2009.
Danielsen, Karen, Robert Lang, and William Fulton. "Retracting Suburbia: Smart Growth and the Future of Housing." *Housing Policy Debate* 10, no. 3 (1999): 513-40.
Danielson, Michael S. "All Immigrations Politics is Local: The Day Labor Ordinance in Vista, California." In *Taking Local Control*, edited by Monica Varsanyi, 239-254. Stanford, CA: Stanford University Press, 2010.
Delaney, David, and Helga Leitner. "The Political Construction of Scale." *Political Geography* 16, no. 2 (1997): 93-97.
Dery, David. *Problem Definition in Policy Analysis.* Lawrence, KS: University Press of Kansas, 1984.
Downs, Anthony. *Opening Up the Suburbs: An Urban Strategy for America.* New Haven, CT: Yale University Press, 1973.
———. "Up and Down with Ecology: The Issue-Attention Cycle." *The Public Interest* 28 (1972): 38-50.
Dreier, Peter, John Mollenkopf, and Todd Swanstrom. *Place Matters: Metropolitics for the Twenty-first Century.* 2nd ed. Lawrence, KS: University Press of Kansas, 2004.
Duany, Andres, Jeff Speck, and Mike Lydon. *The Smart Growth Manual.* New York: McGraw-Hill Professional, 2009.
Durr, Kenneth D. *Behind the Backlash: White Working-Class Politics in Baltimore, 1940-1980.* Chapel Hill, NC: The University of North Carolina Press, 2003.
Easton, David. *The Political System: An Inquiry into the State of Political Science.* New York: Knopf, 1953.

———. *A Framework for Political Analysis.* Englewood Cliffs, NJ: Prentice-Hall, 1965.

Ellis, Mark. "Unsettling Immigrant Geographies: US Immigration and the Politics of Scale." *Tijdschrift voor Economische en Sociale Geografie* 97, no. 1 (2006): 49-58.

Elkins, Stanley, and Eric McKitrick. *The Age of Federalism: The Early American Republic, 1788-1800.* New York: Oxford University Press, 1995.

Esbenshade, Jill, and Barbara Obzurt. "Local Immigration Regulation: A Problematic Trend in Public Policy." *Harvard Journal of Hispanic Policy* 20 (2008): 33-47.

Fainstein, Susan. *The Just City.* Ithaca, NY: Cornell University Press, 2011.

Fetzer, Joel S. "Economic Self-Interest or Cultural Marginality? Anti-Immigration Sentiment and Nativist Political Movements in France, Germany, and the USA." *Journal of Ethnic and Migration Studies* 26, no. 1 (2000): 5-23.

Fishman, Robert A. *Bourgeois Utopias: The Rise and Fall of Suburbia.* New York: Basic Books, 1987.

Fogelson, Robert M. *Downtown: Its Rise and Fall, 1880-1950.* New Haven, CT: Yale University Press, 2001.

Formisano, Ronald P. *Boston Against Busing: Race, Class, and Ethnicity in the 1960s and 1970s.* 2nd ed. Chapel Hill, NC: The University of North Carolina Press, 2004.

Forsyth, Ann. *Reforming Suburbia: The Planned Communities of Irvine, Columbia, and The Woodlands.* Berkeley and Los Angeles: University of California Press, 2005.

Frece, John W. *Sprawl and Politics: The Inside Story of Smart Growth in Maryland.* Albany, NY: State University of New York Press, 2008.

Freund, David M. *Colored Property: State Policy and White Racial Politics in Suburban America.* Chicago: University of Chicago Press, 2007.

Frey, William H. "Melting Pot Cities and Suburbs: Racial and Ethnic Change in Metro America in the 2000s." Washington, DC: The Brookings Institution, May, 2011.

Friedman, Thomas L. *The World Is Flat: A Brief History of the Twenty-First Century.* New York: Farrar, Straus and Giroux, 2005.

Funk, Richard W. *Around Hazleton.* Charleston, SC: Arcadia Publishing, 2005.

Furuseth, Owen J., and Heather A. Smith. "Localized Immigration Policy: The View from Charlotte, North Carolina, A New Immigrant Gateway." In *Taking Local Control*, edited by Monica Varsanyi, 173-192. Stanford, CA: Stanford University Press, 2010.

Gans, Herbert J. *The Levittowners: Ways of Life and Politics in a New Suburban Community.* New York: Pantheon Books, 1967.

Garner, John S., ed. *The Company Town: Architecture and Society in the Early Industrial Age.* New York: Oxford University Press, 1992.

Gerstle, Gary, and John Mollenkopf, eds. *E Pluribus Unum? Contemporary and Historical Perspectives on Immigrant Political Incorporation.* New York: Russell Sage Foundation, 2001.

Gerston, Larry N. *American Federalism: A Concise Introduction.* Armonk, NY: M.E. Sharpe, 2007.

Goździak, Elżbieta M., and Susan Forbes Martin, eds. *Beyond the Gateway: Immigrants in a Changing America.* Lanham, MD: Lexington Books, 2005.

Goździak, Elżbieta M., and Micah N. Bump. *New Immigrants, Changing Communities: Best Practices for a Better America.* Lanham, MD: Lexington Books, 2009.

Grigsby, William G., Morton Baratz, George Galster, and Duncan Maclennan. *The Dynamics of Neighborhood Change and Decline.* London: Pergamon Press, 1987.

Gusfield, Joseph R. *The Culture of Public Problems: Drinking-Driving and the Symbolic Order.* Chicago: University of Chicago Press, 1981.

Gutfreund, Owen D. *Twentieth-Century Sprawl: Highways and the Reshaping of the American Landscape.* New York: Oxford University Press, 2005.

Haar, Charles Monroe. *The End of Innocence: A Suburban Reader.* Glenview, IL: Scott, Foresman, 1972.

Hanlon, Bernadette. *Once the American Dream: Inner-Ring Suburbs of the Metropolitan United States.* Philadelphia: Temple University Press, 2009.

———. "The Decline of Older, Inner Suburbs in Metropolitan America." *Housing Policy Debate* 19, no. 3 (2008): 423-55.

Hanlon, Bernadette, and Thomas J. Vicino. "The Fate of Inner Suburbs: Evidence from Metropolitan Baltimore." *Urban Geography* 28, no. 3 (2007): 254-63.

Hanlon, Bernadette, Thomas J. Vicino, and John Rennie Short. "The New Metropolitan Reality in the US: Rethinking the Traditional Model." *Urban Studies* 43, no. 12 (2006): 2129-43.

———. *Cities and Suburbs: New Metropolitan Realities in the US.* New York: Routledge, 2010.

Harris, Chauncy, and Edward Ullman. "The Nature of Cities." *Annals of the American Academy of Political and Social Science* 242, no. 1 (1945): 7-17.

Hauser, Philip Morris, and Leo Francis Schnore, eds. *The Study of Urbanization.* New York: John Wiley and Sons, 1965.

Hayden, Dolores. *Building Suburbia: Green Fields and Urban Growth, 1820-2000.* New York: Vintage, 2004.

Hirsch, Arnold R. *Making the Second Ghetto: Race and Housing in Chicago 1940-1960.* Chicago: University of Chicago Press, 1998.

Hirschman, Charles, and Douglas S. Massey. "Places and Peoples: The New American Mosaic." In *New Faces in New Places: The Changing Geography of American Immigration,* edited by Douglas S. Massey, 1-19. New York: Russell Sage Foundation, 2010.

Hollander, Justin B. *Sunburnt Cities: The Great Recession, Depopulation and Urban Planning in the American Sunbelt.* New York: Routledge, 2011.

Hoyt, Homer. "The Structure and Growth of Residential Neighborhoods in American Cities." Washington, DC: Federal Housing Administration, 1939.

Hudnut, William H. *Halfway to Everywhere: A Portrait of America's First-Tier Suburbs.* Washington, DC: Urban Land Institute, 2004.

Iceland, John. *Where We Live Now: Immigration and Race in the United States.* Berkeley and Los Angeles: University of California Press, 2009.

Irazábal, Clara, ed. *Ordinary Places, Extraordinary Events: Citizenship, Democracy and Public Space in Latin America.* New York: Routledge, 2008.

Iyengar, Shanto. *Is Anyone Responsible? How Television Frames Political Issues.* Chicago: University of Chicago Press, 1991.

Jackson, Kenneth T. *Crabgrass Frontier: The Suburbanization of the United States.* New York: Oxford University Press, 1987.

Jacobs, Jane. *The Death and Life of Great American Cities.* New York: Random House, 1961.

James, Thomas E., and Paul D. Jorgensen. "Policy Knowledge, Policy Formulation, and Change: Revisiting a Foundational Question." *Policy Studies Journal* 37, no. 1 (2009): 141-62.

Johnson-Cartee, Karen S. *News Narratives and News Framing: Constructing Political Reality.* Lanham, MD: Rowman & Littlefield, 2005.

Jones, Bryan D. *Reconceiving Decision-Making in Democratic Politics: Attention, Choice, and Public Policy.* Chicago: University of Chicago Press, 1994.

Jones, Bryan D. and Frank R. Baumgartner. *The Politics of Attention: How Government Prioritizes Problems.* Chicago: University of Chicago Press, 2005.

Jones-Correa, Michael. "All Immigration Is Local: Receiving Communities and Their Role in Successful Immigrant Integration." Center for American Progress, September 20, 2011.

Judd, Dennis. "Everything is Always Going to Hell: Urban Scholars as End-Times Prophets." *Urban Affairs Review* 41, no. 2 (2005): 119-31.

Judd, Dennis, and Paul Kantor. *Enduring Tensions in Urban Politics.* New York: Macmillan, 1992.

Katz, Michael B., Mathew J. Creighton, Daniel Amsterdam, and Merlin Chowkwanyun. "Immigration and the New Metropolitan Geography." *Journal of Urban Affairs* 32, no. 5 (2010): 523-47.

Kelly, Barbara. *Expanding the American Dream: Building and Rebuilding Levittown.* Albany, NY: State University of New York Press, 1993.

Kennedy, Garrett. "Illegal Is Not Simply Illegal: The Broad Ramifications of a Pennsylvania Town's Attempt at Immigration Control, and The Inherent Problems of Racial Discrimination." *University of Pennsylvania Journal of Business and Employment Law* 10, no. 4 (2008): 1029-58.

Kingdon, John. *Agendas, Alternatives, and Public Policies.* 2nd ed. New York: Addison Wesley, 1995.

Klebaner, Benjamin J. "State and Local Immigration Regulation in the United States Before 1882." *International Review of Social History* 3, no. 2 (1958): 267-95.

Kruse, Kevin M., and Thomas J. Sugrue, eds. *The New Suburban History.* Chicago, IL: University of Chicago Press, 2006.

Lassiter, Matthew D. *The Silent Majority: Suburban Politics in the Sunbelt South.* Princeton, NJ: Princeton University Press, 2007.

Levy, John M. *Essential Microeconomics for Public Policy Analysis.* Westport, CT: Praeger Publishers, 1994.

Lewis, Paul G., and S. Karthick Ramakrishnan. "Police Practices in Immigrant-Destination Cities: Political Control or Bureaucratic Professionalism?" *Urban Affairs Review* 42, no. 6 (2007): 874-900.

Li, Wei. *Ethnoburb: The New Ethnic Community in Urban America.* Honolulu, HI: University of Hawaii Press, 2009.

Longstreth, Richard. *The American Department Store Transformed, 1920-1960*. New Haven, CT: Yale University Press, 2010.

Lowi, Theodore J. *The End of the Republican Era*. Norman, OK: University of Oklahoma Press, 1995.

Lucy, William H., and David A. Peterson. *Foreclosing the Dream: How America's Housing Crisis Is Reshaping Our Cities and Suburbs*. Chicago: APA Planners Press, 2010.

Lucy, William H., and David L. Phillips. *Confronting Suburban Decline: Strategic Planning for Metropolitan Renewal*. Washington, DC: Island Press, 2000.

Masotti, Louis H., and Jeffrey K. Hadden, eds. *The Urbanization of the Suburbs: Urban Affairs Annual Review*. Vol. 7. Beverly Hills and London: Sage Publications, 1973.

———. *Suburbia in Transition*. New York: New Viewpoints, 1974.

Massey, Douglas, and Nancy Denton. *American Apartheid: Segregation and the Making of the Underclass*. Cambridge, MA: Harvard University Press, 1993.

McGirr, Lisa. *Suburban Warriors: The Origins of the New American Right*. Princeton, NJ: Princeton University Press, 2001.

Meier, Kenneth J. "Policy Theory, Policy Theory Everywhere: Ravings of a Deranged Policy Scholar." *Policy Studies Journal* 37, no. 1 (2009): 5-11.

Mill, John Stuart. *On Liberty*. London: Longman, Roberts & Green, 1869.

Mitchell, Don. *The Right to the City: Social Justice and the Fight for Public Space*. New York: Guilford Press, 2003.

Mitchell, Joseph Rocco, and David L. Stebenne. *New City Upon a Hill: A History of Columbia, Maryland*. Charleston, SC: The History Press, 2007.

Nagel, Robert F. *The Implosion of American Federalism*. New York: Oxford University Press, 2002.

Newton, Lina. *Illegal, Alien, or Immigrant: The Politics of Immigration Reform*. New York: NYU Press, 2008.

———. "Policy Innovation or Vertical Integration? A View of Immigration Federalism from the States." *Law & Policy* 34, no. 2 (2012): 113-137.

Ogle, Georgia Myers. *Elm Fork Settlement: Farmers Branch and Carrollton*. Commemorative Ed. Austin, TX: Eakin Press, 1996.

Olsen, Joshua. *Better Places, Better Lives: A Biography of James Rouse*. Washington, DC: Urban Land Institute: 2003.

Orfield, Myron. *Metropolitics: A Regional Agenda for Community and Stability*. Washington, DC: Brookings Institution Press, 1997.

Pantoja, Adrian. "Against the Tide? Core American Values and Attitudes Toward US Immigration Policy in the Mid-1990s." *Journal of Ethnic and Migration Studies* 32, no. 3 (2006): 515-531.

Passel, Jeffrey S., and D'Vera Cohn. "Trends in Unauthorized Immigration: Undocumented Inflow Now Trails Legal Inflow." Washington, DC: Pew Hispanic Center, October 2008.

Perlmutter, David D. *Blogwars*. New York: Oxford University Press, 2008.

Plachno, Larry. *Sunset Lines: The Story of the Chicago Aurora & Elgin Railroad: 2-History*. Polo, IL: Transportation Trails, 1989.

Portes, Alejandro, and Ruben G. Rumbaut. *Legacies: The Story of the Immigrant Second Generation.* New York: Russell Sage, 2001.

———. *Immigrant America: A Portrait.* 3rd ed. Berkeley and Los Angeles: University of California Press, 2006.

Price, Marie, and Lisa Benton-Short, eds. *Migrants to the Metropolis: The Rise of Immigrant Gateway Cities.* Syracuse, NY: Syracuse University Press, 2008.

Puentes, Robert and David Warren. "One Fifth of America: A Comprehensive Guide to America's First Suburbs." The Brookings Institution, Washington, DC. February, 2006.

Purcell, Mark. "Citizenship and the Right to the Global City: Reimagining the Capitalist World Order." *International Journal of Urban and Regional Research* 27, no. 3 (2003): 564-590.

Ramakrishnan, S. Karthick, and Tom Wong. "Partisanship, Not Spanish: Explaining Municipal Ordinances Affecting Undocumented Workers." In *Taking Local Control,* edited by Monica Varsanyi, 73-96. Stanford, CA: Stanford University Press, 2010.

———. *Liquid City: Megalopolis and the Contemporary Northeast.* Washington, DC: Resources for the Future Press, 2007.

Rochefort, David A., and Roger W. Cobb, eds. *The Politics of Problem Definition: Shaping the Policy Agenda.* Lawrence, KS: University Press of Kansas, 1994.

Rose, Mark H. *Interstate: Express Highway Politics, 1939-1989.* Rev. ed. Knoxville, TN: University of Tennessee, 1990.

Samuelson, Paul A. "The Pure Theory of Public Expenditure." *Review of Economics and Statistics* 36, no. 4 (1954): 387-389.

Sapotichne, Joshua, Bryan D. Jones, and Michelle Wolfe. "Is Urban Politics a Black Hole? Analyzing the Boundary Between Political Science and Urban Politics." *Urban Affairs Review* 43, no. 1 (2007): 76-106.

Sassen, Saskia. *Cities in a World Economy.* 3rd ed. Thousand Oaks, CA: Pine Forge Press, 2006.

Saunders, Doug. *Arrival City: How the Largest Migration in History in Reshaping Our World.* New York: Pantheon Books, 2010.

Schattschneider, Elmer Eric. *The Semisovereign People: A Realist's View of Democracy in America.* Hinsdale, IL: Dryden Press, 1960.

———. "Intensity, Visibility, Direction and Scope." *American Political Science Review* 51, no. 4 (1957): 933-942.

Schneider, Anne, and Mara Sidney. "What Is Next for Policy Design and Social Construction Theory?" *Policy Studies Journal* 37, no. 1 (2009): 103-119.

Schneider, Anne, and Helen Ingram. "The Social Construction of Target Populations: Implications for Politics and Policy." *American Political Science Review* 87, no. 2 (1993): 334-347.

Seif, Hinda. "'Tired of Illegals:' Immigrant Driver's Licenses, Constituent Letters, and Shifting Restrictionist Discourse in California." In *Taking Local Control,* edited by Monica Varsanyi, 275-294. Stanford, CA: Stanford University Press, 2010.

Self, Robert O. *American Babylon: Race and the Struggle for Postwar Oakland.* Princeton, NJ: Princeton University Press, 2004.

Short, John Rennie. *Global Metropolitan: Globalizing Cities in a Capitalist World.* New York: Routledge, 2004.

Seidman, Edward, and Julian Rappaport. *Redefining Social Problems.* New York: Plenum Press, 1986.

Sharp, Elaine B. "Paradoxes of National Antidrug Policymaking." In *The Politics of Problem Definition*, edited by David A. Rochefort and Roger W. Cobb, 98-116. Lawrence, KS: University Press of Kansas, 1994.

Short, John Rennie, Bernadette Hanlon, and Thomas J. Vicino. "The Decline of Inner Suburbs: The New Suburban Gothic in the United States." *Geography Compass* 1, no. 3 (2007): 641-656.

Silverstein, Paul A. "Immigrant Racialization and the New Savage Slot: Race, Migration, and Immigration in the New Europe." *Annual Review of Anthropology* 34, (2005): 363-384.

Singer, Audrey, et al., eds. *Twenty-First Century Gateways: Immigrant Incorporation in Suburban America.* Washington, DC: Brookings Institution Press, 2008.

Siry, Joseph M. *Carson Pirie Scott: Louis Sullivan and the Chicago Department Store.* Chicago: University of Chicago Press, 1988.

Skop, Emily and Wei Li. "Asians in America's Suburbs: Patterns and Consequences of Settlement." *Geographical Review* 95, no. 2 (2005): 167-188.

Skop, Emily Hayes. "Saffron Suburbs: Indian Immigrant Community Formation in Phoenix." PhD Diss., Arizona State University, 2002.

Smith, Carl. *The Plan of Chicago: Daniel Burnham and the Remaking of the American City.* Chicago: University of Chicago Press, 2006.

Sobel, Michael E. "Causal Inference in the Social Sciences." *Journal of the American Statistical Association* 95, no. 450 (2000): 647-651.

Squires, Gregory D., ed. *Urban Sprawl: Causes, Consequences, and Policy Responses.* Washington, DC: Urban Institute Press, 2002.

Stanback, Thomas M. Jr. *The New Suburbanization: Challenge to the Central City.* Boulder, CO: Westview Press, 1991.

Stone, Clarence N. *Regime Politics: Governing Atlanta, 1946-1988.* Lawrence, KS: University Press of Kansas, 1989.

Stone, Deborah A. "Causal Stories and the Formation of Policy Agendas." *Political Science Quarterly* 104, no. 2 (1989): 281-300.

———. *Policy Paradox: The Art of Political Decision Making.* New York: W.W. Norton, 2001.

———. "Causal Stories and the Formation of Policy Agendas." *Political Science Quarterly* 104, no. 2 (1989): 281-300.

Sugrue, Thomas J. *The Origins of the Urban Crisis: Race and Inequality in Postwar Detroit.* Princeton, NJ: Princeton University Press, 1996.

Teaford, Jon C. *The Metropolitan Revolution: The Rise of Post-Urban America.* New York: Columbia University Press, 2006.

———. *The Rough Road to Renaissance: Urban Revitalization in America, 1940-1985.* Baltimore, MD: Johns Hopkins University Press, 1990.

Tichenor, Daniel J. *Dividing Lines: The Politics of Immigration Control in America.* Princeton, NJ: Princeton University Press, 2002.

Tiebout, Charles. "A Pure Theory of Local Expenditures." *Journal of Political Economy* 64, no. 5 (1956): 416-424.

Ueda, Reed. *Postwar Immigrant America: A Social History*. New York: St. Martin's Press, 1994.

Varsanyi, Monica, ed. *Taking Local Control: Immigration Policy Activism in U.S. Cities and States*. Stanford, CA: Stanford University Press, 2010.

———. "City Ordinances as 'Immigration Policing By Proxy:' Local Governments and the Regulation of Undocumented Day Laborers." In *Taking Local Control*, edited by Monica Varsanyi, 135-156. Stanford, CA: Stanford University Press, 2010.

———. "Immigration Policy Activism in U.S. States and Cities: Interdisciplinary Perspectives." In *Taking Local Control*, edited by Monica Varsanyi, 1-30. Stanford, CA: Stanford University Press, 2010.

———. "Neoliberalism and Nativism: Local Anti-immigrant Policy Activism and an Emerging Politics of Scale." *International Journal of Urban and Regional Research* 35, no. 2 (2010): 295-311.

———. "Rescaling the 'Alien,' Rescaling Personhood: Neoliberalism, Immigration, and the State." *Annals of the Association of American Geographers* 98, no. 4 (2008): 877-896.

Vicino, Thomas J. "The Quest to Confront Suburban Decline: Political Realities and Lessons." *Urban Affairs Review* 43, no. 4 (2008): 553-581.

———. *Transforming Race and Class in Suburbia*. New York: Palgrave Macmillan, 2008.

Vicino, Thomas J., Bernadette Hanlon, and John Rennie Short. "A Typology of Urban Immigrant Neighborhoods." *Urban Geography* 32, no. 3 (2011): 383-405.

Walker, Kyle, and Helga Leitner. "The Variegated Landscape of Local Immigration Policies in the United States." *Urban Geography* 32, no. 2 (2011): 156-178.

Warner, Sam Bass. *Streetcar Suburbs: The Process of Growth in Boston, 1870-1900*. 2nd ed. Cambridge, MA: Harvard University Press, 1978.

Warner, Sam Bass, and Andrew H. Whittemore. *American Urban Form*. Cambridge, MA: The MIT Press, 2012.

Weiher, Gregory. *The Fractured Metropolis: Political Fragmentation and Metropolitan Segregation*. Albany, NY: State University of New York Press, 1991.

Weimer, David Leo, and Aidan R. Vining. *Policy Analysis: Concepts and Practice*. 5th ed. New York: Longman, 2010.

Weinstein, Bernard L., and Robert E. Firestine. *Regional Growth and Decline in the United States: The Rise of the Sunbelt and the Decline of the Northeast*. New York: Praeger Publishers, 1978.

Wesolowsky, Tony. "A Jewel In the Crown of Old King Coal Eckley Miners' Village." *Pennsylvania Heritage Magazine* 22, no. 1 (1996): 30.

Wildavsky, Aaron. *Speaking Truth to Power: The Art and Craft of Policy Analysis*. Boston: Little, Brown, 1979.

Wilson, Jill H., Audrey Singer, and Brooke DeRenzis. "Growing Pains: Local Response to Recent Immigrant Settlement in Suburban Washington, DC." In *Taking Local Control*, edited by Monica Varsanyi, 193-216. Stanford, CA: Stanford University Press, 2010.

Wood, Phil, and Charles Landry. *The Intercultural City: Planning for Diversity Advantage*. London: Earthscan, 2008.

Zakari, Fareed. *The Post-American World*. New York: W. W. Norton & Company, 2009.

Zolberg, Aristide D. *A Nation by Design: Immigration Policy in the Fashioning of America*. Cambridge, MA: Harvard University Press, 2006.

Index

About the Author

Thomas J. Vicino is assistant professor of political science and a member of the core faculty in the School of Public Policy and Urban Affairs at Northeastern University in Boston. He is the chair of the Master of Public Administration Program. At the undergraduate level, he teaches in the urban studies minor and baccalaureate major in political science, and at the graduate level, he teaches courses in public policy. He specializes in the political economy of cities and suburbs, focusing on issues of metropolitan development, housing, and demographic analysis. He is the author of the book *Transforming Race and Class in Suburbia* (2008) and co-author of the bestselling book *Cities and Suburbs: New Metropolitan Realities in the US* (2010). He has also published numerous research articles in the urban affairs field. He has served on the Executive Council of the Urban Politics Section of the *American Political Science Association*, and he is a member of the *Urban Affairs Association* and *Association of Collegiate Schools of Planning*.